TRADE MATTERS

Englisch für Groß- und Außenhandelskaufleute

von
Michael Benford
Ken Thomson

in Zusammenarbeit mit
der Verlagsredaktion

Cornelsen

Verfasser:	Michael Benford, Bochum Ken Thomson, Berlin
Berater:	Joanne Glen, Bad Nauheim Marco Henkel, Geislingen Caroline Okerika, Loxstedt Christian Schmidt, Nördlingen
Projektleitung:	Jim Austin
Verlagsredaktion:	Merlene Griffin
Redaktionelle Mitarbeit:	Oliver Busch (Wortlisten), Felix Bellermann, Alice Gleeson, Stefanie Heimann
Layout und technische Umsetzung:	Arnold & Domnick, Leipzig
Bildredaktion:	Gertha Maly, Alice Gleeson
Umschlaggestaltung:	Sergio Vitale, VitaleDesign, Berlin
Titelfoto:	Getty Images RM / Thierry Dosogne

Erhältlich sind auch:	**Handreichungen für den Unterricht mit CD-ROM und Audio-CD ISBN 978-3-06-520516-0**
Online-Ergänzungen unter:	**www.cornelsen.de/matters**

1. Auflage, 2. Druck 2014

Alle Drucke dieser Auflage sind inhaltlich unverändert
und können im Unterricht nebeneinander verwendet werden.

Druck: Stürtz GmbH, Würzburg

ISBN 978-3-06-520514-6

PEFC
PEFC/04-31-1404

PEFC zertifiziert
Dieses Produkt stammt aus nachhaltig bewirtschafteten Wäldern und kontrollierten Quellen.

www.pefc.de

VORWORT

Trade Matters – 3rd Edition ist die komplett aktualisierte Neubearbeitung des bewährten Lehrwerks für Groß- und Außenhandelskaufleute und wurde für die Ausbildung in Berufsschulen sowie die innerbetriebliche Aus- und Weiterbildung konzipiert. Das Lehrwerk basiert auf den Lehrplänen der Bundesländer für Berufsschulen.

Es ist auf Lernende zugeschnitten, deren Englischkenntnisse den Anforderungen eines mittleren Bildungsabschlusses bzw. eines durchschnittlichen gymnasialen Grundkursabschlusses entsprechen und setzt Englischkenntnisse, die der Stufe B1 des Europäischen Referenzrahmens (*Common European Framework of Reference*) entsprechen, voraus. Darüber hinaus gibt es in den Rubriken *Extra material* auch anspruchsvolleren Lernstoff für fortgeschrittene Schüler/innen (B2). Neu an der *3rd Edition* ist auch die durchgängige Vorbereitung auf die KMK-Zertifikatsprüfung in Englisch (Stufe II). Dies geschieht anhand prüfungsbezogener und mit einem KMK-Symbol gekennzeichneter Aufgaben im Schülerbuch, einer KMK-Seite pro Unit sowie einem KMK *mock exam* im Anhang.

Trade Matters – 3rd Edition besteht aus zehn Units, in denen handlungsorientiert aktuelle Themen aus unterschiedlichen Bereichen des beruflichen Alltags aufgegriffen werden und von denen jede eine in sich abgeschlossene Handlung enthält. Es ist möglich, einzelne Units auszulassen, jedoch wird empfohlen, wann immer Zeit und Lehrpläne es ermöglichen, die gegebene Reihenfolge einzuhalten, um einen kontinuierlichen Aufbau des Fachvokabulars zu gewährleisten. Landeskundliche Informationen über englischsprachige Länder werden ebenfalls vermittelt.

In berufsbezogenen, praxisnahen Situationen werden die Lernenden mit allen wesentlichen Aspekten des Englischen vertraut gemacht, die ihnen in ihrem beruflichen Alltag begegnen können. Ob es um Kontakte zu Geschäftspartnern, um den Umgang mit Handelsdokumenten, das Schreiben von E-Mails, um Buchungen, Rechnungen, Preisverhandlungen oder Präsentationen geht, **Trade Matters – 3rd Edition** bietet in jedem Fall das passende sprachliche Rüstzeug. Um die Realitätsnähe der einzelnen Handlungsabläufe zu gewährleisten, wurden den meisten Units authentische Fälle aus deutschen Firmen *(case-study approach)* zu Grunde gelegt.

Die Sprachkompetenz der Schülerinnen und Schüler wird anhand zahlreicher Leseverständnis-, Hörverständnis- und Sprechübungen, die von gelenkten Dialogen bis zu freien Diskussionen reichen, geschult. Das nötige Fachvokabular und wichtige Redewendungen, die in *Language boxes* sowie in erweiterter Form im Anhang aufgeführt sind, werden in Rollenspielen und Partnerübungen gefestigt. Anhand motivierender Aufgaben werden Hemmungen, sich in der Fremdsprache auszudrücken, abgebaut. Neben der Aufarbeitung des Fachvokabulars und der spezifischen Redemittel werden auch Grundlagen der Grammatik zur Wiederholung angeboten. Sie werden in deutscher Sprache mit Hilfe von Beispielen erklärt und im handlungsbezogenen Kontext geübt.

Im Anhang wird eine komplette KMK-Zertifikatsprüfung angeboten. Weiterhin werden *Partner files*, zwei Wörterlisten – alphabetisch sowie nach Units gegliedert – ein Deutsch-Englisches Glossar, eine Aufstellung von nützlichen Redewendungen und die Incoterms® 2010 aufgeführt.

Der Verlag, die Autoren und die Berater/innen wünschen Ihnen viel Erfolg und Freude bei der Arbeit mit **Trade Matters – 3rd Edition**.

2	Dialog bzw. Hörtext auf der Audio-CD
KMK	Übungen zur Vorbereitung auf die KMK-Zertifikatsprüfung
PAGE **135**	Verweis auf nützliche Materialien im Anhang
WEBCODE **TRMU0101**	Die Webcodes weisen auf Zusatzmaterial zur selbstständigen Weiterarbeit hin und können unter www.cornelsen.de/matters abgerufen werden.

UNIT 1

Getting to know Fresssh GmbH

- Introducing yourself and others
- Welcoming visitors to a company
- Showing a visitor around

1 Warm-up

Ask your classmates as many questions as possible to find out about them and their companies.

1 What is your name and what company do you work for?

I'm/My name is … and I work for …

2 Where is your company based?

My company is based/located in … 50 km from …/between … and …/near …

3 What does your company do?

We import/export/sell/specialize in …

4 What type of customers does it have?

We have mainly commercial/industrial/private …

5 How many people work for your company?

We have … administrative staff, … warehouse staff and …

2 A visitor arrives at Fresssh GmbH

02

Fresssh GmbH is a wholesaler of energy and health drinks based in Hamburg. The company imports the products it sells from various European countries before exporting them to customers in the UK and North America. Today a visitor comes to the company.

A Listen to or read the dialogue. Then say who is visiting the company and why.

Receptionist Guten Morgen. Willkommen bei Fresssh.
Brian Oh, I'm sorry. Can we speak English?
Receptionist Yes, of course. Welcome to Fresssh. How can I help you?
Brian My name's Brian Holmes and I'm from Crawford Food Wholesale Group in Chicago. I have an appointment with Detlef Sommer at 9 a.m. Could you please let him know I've arrived?
Receptionist Yes, of course … Hallo. Ist Herr Sommer gerade zu sprechen? Mr Holmes ist gerade bei mir angekommen. OK. Ja, gut.
So, Mr Holmes, unfortunately, Herr Sommer has been delayed. However, one of his assistants is coming down to look after you.
Brian OK. Thank you.

A few minutes later Peter Schütze arrives at reception.

Receptionist Ah, Peter. This is Brian Holmes. Mr Holmes, this is Peter Schütze from Herr Sommer's department.
Brian Hello, Peter. I'm very pleased to meet you.
Peter Hello, Mr Holmes. Pleased to meet you too.
Brian Please, call me Brian.
Peter OK, Brian.
Receptionist I'll just leave you in Peter's hands now.
Brian Thank you for your help.
Receptionist You're welcome. Enjoy your visit.

Brian and Peter make their way to the staff café.

Peter So, Brian. I'm sorry that Herr Sommer is not at work yet. I'm afraid there's been an accident on the motorway. He's sitting in a long traffic jam.
Brian Oh, dear. Do you think it'll take him long to get here?
Peter I think he should probably be here in around half an hour. Can I offer you tea or coffee while you wait?
Brian Please. I really need a coffee.
Peter OK. If you'd just like to come this way … Here we are. Now, would you like milk and sugar in your coffee?
Brian Milk, please, but no sugar.
Peter OK, here you are.
Brian Thank you, Peter. So, what exactly do you do around here?
Peter I'm just finishing the final year of my apprenticeship in wholesale and export.
Brian And you're Detlef Sommer's assistant?
Peter Well, not officially, but I finish my apprenticeship next month. After that, I'll be taken on here full-time, and then I'll officially be one of Herr Sommer's assistants.
Brian Well, that's just great! Well done! You must be looking forward to …

B **Listen to or read the dialogue again and say which statements are true or false. Correct the false statements.**

1 Brian can't speak any German.
2 Brian says he would like to make an appointment with Detlef Sommer.
3 Herr Sommer is not in the office yet; he's on his way to work.
4 Peter Schütze will have the meeting with Brian in Herr Sommer's place.
5 Brian and Peter have met before.
6 Peter has already finished his apprenticeship.

3 Key words

A **Match the expressions from the dialogue (1–6) to their definitions (a–f).**

1	appointment	a	transporting goods from one country to another
2	department	b	a business which sells products to shops and not directly to end customers
3	customer	c	a two to three year traineeship in a specific kind of job
4	apprenticeship	d	a section of a company responsible for a specific function, such as sales
5	wholesaler	e	a previously arranged time to meet with someone
6	export	f	someone who buys a company's products or services

B **Find phrases in the dialogue which have a similar meaning to the phrases below.**

1 How can I be of assistance to you?
2 Can I introduce you to Brian Holmes?
3 It's a pleasure to meet you.
4 Can I get you some refreshments?
5 Coffee would be great, thanks.
6 What do you take in your coffee?

C **Now translate the phrases from exercise B into German.**

TIP

Intercultural awareness

Ideas about what is polite and socially acceptable can vary quite widely between cultures. So, before you meet and do business with people from other countries, it is a good idea to check out what the major cultural differences might be.

The fastest way to do this is to look it up on the internet where there are increasing numbers of websites on the subject of intercultural awareness, or to observe meetings between colleagues and clients from other companies.

LANGUAGE

Greeting people

Offering help
How can I be of assistance to you?
What can I do for you?

Introducing yourself
Hello. I'm … / My name is …
I work in the … department.

Introducing people who do not know each other
This is …
Can I introduce you to …?
I'd like you to meet …
May I / Let me introduce you to …
Have you met …?

Greeting someone you don't know
I'm very pleased to meet you.
It's good / a pleasure to meet you.
How do you do? (Answer: How do you do?)

Offering your first name
Please, call me Brian.
It's Peter, by the way.

Offering and accepting refreshments
Can I offer you tea or coffee / something to drink?
I'd love a coffee / glass of water, please.
What would you like / do you take in your tea/coffee? – Milk, please, but no sugar.

4 Role-play: welcoming a visitor

PAGE 136

A visitor from the USA, Bill / Fearne Cotton arrives at your company. Read the tip box on page 8 and then carry out the following dialogue in English with your partner.

Empfang	Bill/Fearne Cotton
Begrüßen Sie den Besucher / die Besucherin.	
	Stellen Sie sich mit Ihrem Namen und Ihrem Betrieb vor.
Fragen Sie den Besucher / die Besucherin, was Sie für ihn/sie tun können.	
	Sagen Sie, dass Sie einen Termin mit Frau X um 10.00 Uhr haben.
Sagen Sie ihm/ihr, dass Sie Frau X Bescheid geben, dass er/sie angekommen ist. Teilen Sie mit, wann Frau X kommen wird. Bieten Sie Erfrischungen an.	
	Sagen Sie der Person am Empfang welches Heißgetränk Sie gerne hätten.
Milch und Zucker?	
	Sagen Sie, wie Sie Ihr Getränk am liebsten trinken.
Frau X kommt zum Empfang. Stellen Sie ihr den Besucher / die Besucherin vor.	
	Teilen Sie Frau X mit, dass Sie sich freuen, sie zu treffen. Bedanken Sie sich bei der Person am Empfang.
Reagieren Sie entsprechend.	

5 A company profile

While waiting for Detlef Sommer to arrive, Brian looks at the Fresssh company profile again. Read it and then do the tasks below.

...(a)

Fresssh, the wholesale importer and exporter of energy and health drinks from around Europe, is based near Hamburg. We have a large warehouse at our Hamburg premises, which is used to service customer orders from the UK and North America. A smaller warehouse in Dresden fulfils orders from customers in our new markets in Central and Eastern Europe.

...(b)

The company, which was originally founded in 1972 as a soft drinks wholesaler for the German domestic market, moved into the export business in 1984. Since then, our overseas customer base among retailers has grown continually so that, today, the company generates around 80% of its turnover in export markets.

...(c)

Fresssh employs a staff of 45, 15 of whom work in administration at our headquarters in Hamburg. The remaining 30 employees work in the warehouse facilities in Hamburg and Dresden. We sell around 2.4 million litres of energy and health drinks per annum. We source the soft drinks we sell from quality beverage manufacturers around Europe.

...(d)

We are always on the lookout for fresh, new drinks, which we are happy to supply our customers with. We'd be delighted to tell you more about the product range we supply. Click here or on the 'Products' tab above to find out more about our exciting range of energy and health drinks.

A **Decide which sections of the text (a–d) the three headings below should be matched to. Then write a heading for the section of the text which is left.**

1 Important statistics
2 Company history
3 Where we are

B **Find the synonyms of the following words and phrases in the text.**

1 shipper of foreign goods
2 situated near
3 site
4 distribution centre
5 established
6 home
7 stores
8 revenue
9 main office
10 selection

6 Mediation

KMK

Sie arbeiten bei der Fresssh GmbH als Auszubildende/r. Ihre Abteilung plant für das Firmenjubiläum einen Messeprospekt zu veröffentlichen.

Verwenden Sie den vorliegenden Text als Informationsquelle und stellen Sie in Stichworten auf Deutsch wichtige geschichtliche Meilensteine aus der Vergangenheit sowie die Aufstellung in Europa zusammen.

7 About your company

Read Fresssh's company profile again. Then write a similar profile for your own company.

8 A tour of the company

03

A Listen as Detlef gives Brian a tour of the company, starting at the staff café. Then match the words in the box with the numbers on the floor plan of the company.

distribution area • finance department • marketing department • sales department • senior management • warehouse

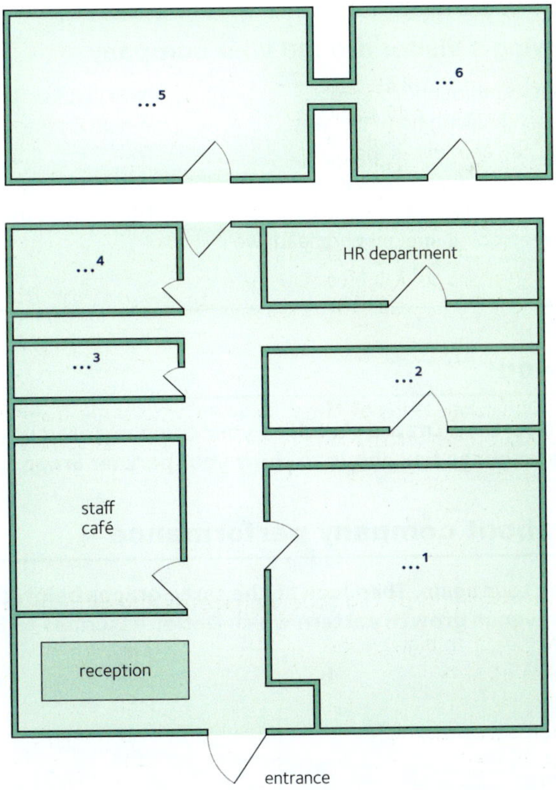

KMK **B** **Entscheiden Sie, ob die Aussagen (1–4) richtig oder falsch sind. Begründen Sie Ihre Antwort. Danach beantworten Sie die Verständnisfragen (5–8) in kurzen Stichworten auf Deutsch.**

1. Brian hat sich die Produktpalette angeschaut, während er auf Detlef gewartet hat.
2. Detlef bietet Brian an, ihn zum Lager zu bringen, um sich dort die Firmenprodukte anzusehen.
3. Bevor sie ins Lager gehen, besuchen sie die Verkaufsabteilung.
4. Irena Niemann ist die Sekretärin von Hartmut Lange.
5. Wie groß war der Wachstumseinschnitt, den die Firma letztes Jahr erlitten hatte?
6. Warum möchte Detlef Sommer sobald wie möglich Produkte von Brians Firma importieren?
7. Wie groß ist das Lager?
8. Wie viel Prozent der Exporte gehen nach Großbritannien und Nordamerika?

C **Listen again and complete the sentences from the dialogue.**

1. If you … with me, we'll get going.
2. … the corridor here is the sales department.
3. We'll just turn left now and … .
4. … is the marketing department.
5. Also … marketing, is the human resources department.
6. On the left here … marketing is the finance department.
7. … that is the senior management suite.
8. … the door for you.

LANGUAGE

Showing a visitor around your company

I'll take you through/along to …
Let's just go along here/this way.
As you can see, this is the …
At the end of/Just across the corridor/hall is the …
If we keep going straight on/ahead, we'll come to …

We'll just turn left/right and go this way.
In here on the right/left is the …
The … is in front of/behind/opposite/beside the staff café.
The … department is between … and …

9 Over to you

Work with a partner. Draw a sketch of your company or your department's floor plan and use the language box above to show your partner around.

10 Talking about company performance

PAGE 140

03

Listen to the tour again. Then look at the three graphs below (a–c) and say which one shows the revenue growth pattern which Detlef describes to Brian.

a

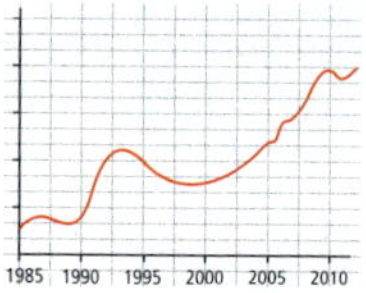

b

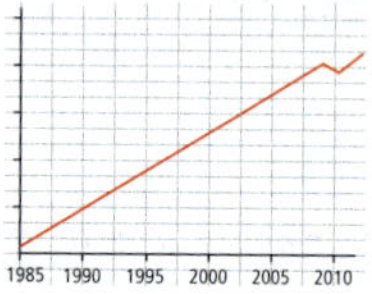

c

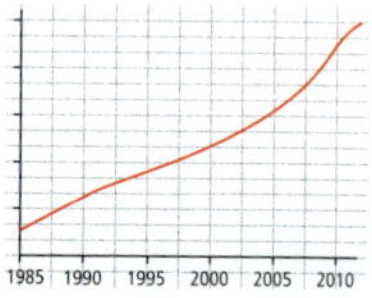

11 Company structure

WEBCODE **TRMU0101**

A Use the words in the box to complete the sentences about work relationships at Fresssh GmbH. There will be one option left over.

alongside • in charge of • heads up • looks after • reports to • responsible for • responsibility for

1. Silke Papzien reports directly to Hartmut Lange and is … one staff member.
2. Thomas König is … two members of staff and reports to Irena Niemann.
3. Franka Marquardt … Thomas König.
4. Mehmet Faki has … a team of three members of staff.
5. Stefan Döring … two managers in the company.
6. Monika Kropp works … her colleague Franka Marquardt.

B Now read the sentences in exercise A again and look at the organization chart below. Then decide who does which job.

Example:
Helga Müller is responsible for four members of staff. *She is the Shipping Manager.*

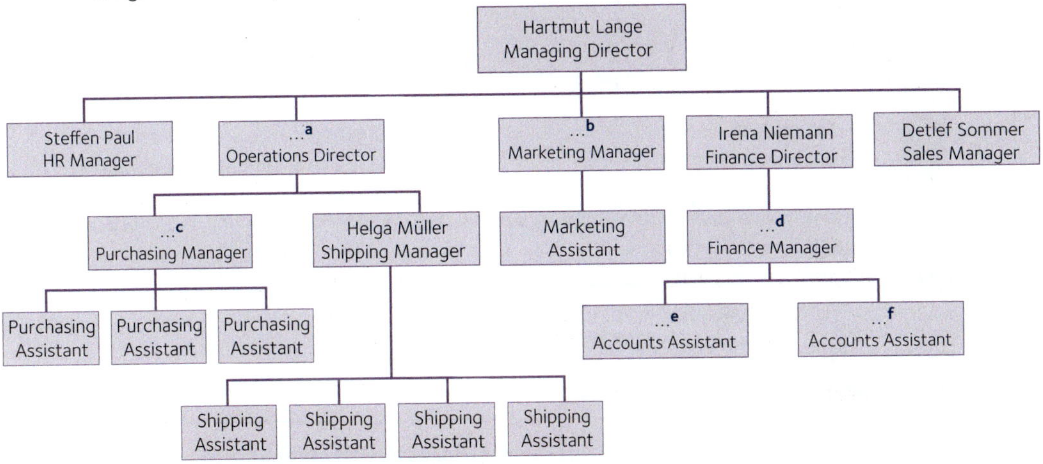

C Find a department for each of the descriptions below using the organization chart above and the plan on page 11.

1 We're responsible for recruiting and training new employees. We also handle the payment of salaries.

2 Our department deals with taxation, investment and cash management. Customers get their invoices from us.

3 We take care of our company's public relations. All the necessary paperwork for sales is done here. The after-sales service team looks after customers' queries.

4 We make sure the products are packaged properly so that they arrive with the customer undamaged.

D Find as many ways as possible to say "I'm responsible for" in exercises A and C.

12 Over to you

Draw an organization chart of your own company. Then work with a partner and ask each other questions about jobs and responsibilities in your companies.

GRAMMAR

Simple present and present progressive

1 We **export** soft drinks to the UK and North America.
2 The company **ships** its products via the port of Hamburg.
3 **Does** it always **take** him this long to get here? No, it **doesn't**.
4 I **don't** really **know** when Herr Sommer will get here.
5 Detlef **is showing** Brian around Fresssh's premises today.
6 **Are** you **working** in the Hamburg office at the moment?

- Das **simple present** wird für regelmäßige, wiederholte Handlungen und Zustände verwendet (1, 2). Es steht oft in Verbindung mit Signalwörtern wie *regularly, usually, always* usw. (3).
- Es wird aus der Grundform des Verbs gebildet (1). In der 3. Person Singular *(he/she/it)* wird *-(e)s* an das Verb angehängt (2).
- Außer bei dem Verb *be* und bei Modalverben (*can* usw.) werden Fragen und Verneinungen mit dem Hilfsverb *do* (Verneinung *don't*) bzw. in der 3. Person Singular mit *does* (Verneinung *doesn't*) gebildet (3, 4).

- Das **present progressive** wird für eine nur vorübergehend andauernde Handlung verwendet, die im Augenblick des Sprechens geschieht. Es steht oft in Verbindung mit Signalwörtern wie *at the moment, currently, now* usw. (5, 6).
- Es wird aus einer Form von *be (is/am/are)* und der *ing*-Form des Vollverbs gebildet (5, 6).

13 Practice

Use the simple present or the present progressive to complete the sentences.

1 A warehouse in Dresden … orders to customers in Central and Eastern Europe. (fulfil)
2 At the moment the company … developing its customer base in CEE. (concentrate on)
3 Fresssh … 45 members of staff. (employ)
4 The company … its products from beverage manufacturers in the USA. (not get)
5 Fresssh … more revenue in the UK due to the recession in the USA. (currently generate)
6 This year, the company's sales … as quickly as two years ago. (not grow)
7 Peter … in the marketing department at Fresssh. (not work)
8 … his three-year apprenticeship at the moment? (Peter / complete)

14 Rezeption: Hörverstehen

04

Viele deutsche Firmen exportieren nach Nordamerika. Hören Sie dem Direktor einer solchen Firma zu, wie er seine Strategie erklärt, die Exporte in die USA zu erhöhen.

Machen Sie sich Notizen und beantworten Sie die folgenden Fragen.
Lesen Sie sich die Aufgaben vorher gut durch.
Sie hören den Dialog zwei Mal.

1. Inwieweit war Avotec von der Rezession in den USA betroffen?
2. Mit welchen Herausforderungen ist die Firma nun konfrontiert und wie sollen sie überwunden werden?
3. Was wurde in den letzten Jahren umstrukturiert?
4. Was hat die Firma von Herrn Krall während der Rezession gemacht und warum?
5. Was wird in den nächsten Wochen in den USA passieren?
6. Wie erklärt Herr Krall die momentane Situation der deutschen Exporteure und was müssen sie machen, um ihre Verkaufszahlen beizubehalten?

15 Interaktion

Erstellen Sie in Partnerarbeit einen Dialog aus den folgenden Rollenkarten.

Situation
James/Jenny Carter von Crawford Food Wholesale Group in Chicago (USA) ist auf der Hannover Messe und sucht englische Verkaufsliteratur von verschiedenen deutschen Firmen. Die Person, die gerade Standdienst macht, nutzt die Gelegenheit, ihre Firma kurz zu präsentieren.

Mitarbeiter/in Ihrer Firma

Sie stellen sich vor. Sie beschreiben:
- die Produkte Ihres Unternehmens (kurze Beschreibungen)
- die Dienstleistungen
- die Lieferzeiten
- den/die Standort/e

Sie geben dem/der Besucher/in:
- Verkaufsliteratur
- Ihre Karte

James/Jenny Carter

Sie stellen sich vor. Sie stellen Fragen über:
- die Qualität der Produkte
- die Dienstleistungen
- Problemlösung/Troubleshooting (z. B. Wartezeit)
- Gewährleistung

Sie geben dem/der Mitarbeiter/in Ihre Visitenkarte.
Sie bitten um ein Angebot für … (Produkt).

16 Produktion

Ihr Unternehmen möchte Kundennähe fördern und verschickt ab sofort einen monatlichen Newsletter an alle Kunden im In- und Ausland.

Verfassen Sie für die englischsprachige Ausgabe vier Mitarbeiterporträts von jeweils 60–70 Wörtern. Schreiben Sie in der ersten Person.

It may seem pretty obvious that making a good first impression is important. It can, however, be easy to forget how important a role body language plays in this. That's where Nicky Govan comes in. She provides body language training for business people who need a bit of practice.

Nicky told us, "You'd be amazed how many successful business people need to practise their body language skills. Most people, in fact, could definitely benefit from some training in this area from time to time."

"You'd be amazed how many successful business people need to practise their body language skills."

So, how can you make the best impression when meeting somebody for the first time? "The first and most important thing is, for goodness' sake, stand up! This allows you to engage the person on an equal level – eye to eye. By remaining seated, you send the message that you don't think the other person was important enough to get up for."

And what about the all-important handshake? "Yes, it's true that the first handshake is very important. It should be firm, but certainly not hand-crushing. At the same time, it should also not be too soft."

As you're shaking hands, Nicky explains, it's important to smile and make eye contact. "Smiling shows that you are happy to be meeting somebody. Looking them in the eye demonstrates that you are open and interested in them."

So, you've shaken hands and the first introductions have been made. What's next? "It's important at this stage to continue to use friendly and open body language. Don't cross your arms in front of you, but keep them at your side in a relaxed way. Use your hands to illustrate points when you're speaking, but be sure not to wave them about frantically in front of you. This can make you appear nervous and can be off-putting for the person you're speaking to."

Meeting people for the first time can be nerve wracking, but by following Nicky's tips about body language, you'll be sure to make a good impression.

BUSINESS

Source: adapted from: http://www.businessknowhow.com/growth/meet.htm

17 Understanding the text

A **Read the article and then write a headline which summarizes what it is about.**

B **Make a word spider to show what the text says about using body language to make a good impression.**

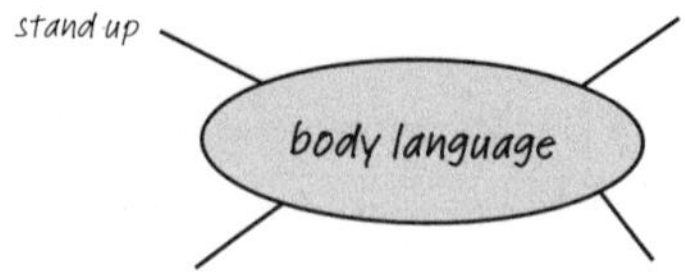

18 Further discussion

A **Work with a partner and discuss how you react to new people when you meet them for the first time. What mistakes have you made in the past?**

B **In groups, brainstorm other tips for making a good impression which could be added to the list in the text. Discuss your results with the class.**

A phone call to Skater Style GmbH

- Making telephone calls
- Understanding messages
- Being polite

1 Warm-up

A **What difficulties do you have when making or answering telephone calls in English? Tell your partner/group.**

B **Match the advice below about telephoning in English (1–3) to the illustrations (a–c).**

C **Which is the best piece of advice for making telephone calls in English? Why?**

D **What other advice can you offer based on your experiences of telephoning in English?**

2 The most important thing to remember when you're telephoning in English is to prepare yourself for a call. Write down the phrases you think you'll use and have these in front of you when you're making the call.

1 My advice about telephoning in English is to ask the person to repeat themselves if they say something you don't understand; it's really not that bad!

a

b

3 If a telephone call is too difficult, you can always say that the line is bad and that you'll call back. Then you can take a deep breath and start again.

c

! *a piece of* advice or *some* advice but NOT *an* advice

2 The first phone call

05 **A Listen as Tom Evans from Hoodies Ltd in the UK calls Skater Style GmbH in Germany and say what he is calling about.**

Tina Skater Style GmbH. Tina Schröder. Guten Morgen.
Tom Oh, hello. Do you speak English? I'm afraid my German's not that good.
Tina Yes, of course. Tina Schröder speaking. How can I help you?
Tom Thank you, Tina. My name's Tom Evans. I'd like to speak to someone in the sales department, please.
Tina Could you tell me what it's about, please?
Tom Sure. I work for Hoodies Ltd. We're a clothing chain which sells sports and street wear. We're interested in stocking your skater clothing.
Tina Ah, OK. I'll put you through to Bernd Müller, our Sales Director. Can you hold the line for a moment, please?
Tom Yes, no problem.

Tina Hello again, Tom. I'm afraid that Herr Müller is in a meeting at the moment. Can I take a message? Or can I get him to call you back?
Tom Yes, please. He could call me back.
Tina That's fine. Could you give me your number, please?
Tom Yes, sure. Dial 0044 for the UK. Then 1342 73982. My extension is 38. So, if …
Tina Sorry, I didn't catch the last bit. Could you say it again, please?
Tom Yes. 38. If you dial that at the end of our number, you'll get right through to me.
Tina Right. I'll just read that back to you. 0044 1342 73982, extension 38.
Tom That's right.
Tina Fine, Tom. I'll let Herr Müller know that you called as soon as he comes out of his meeting. Is there anything else I can do for you now?
Tom No, thanks, that was everything. Thanks for your help. Bye now.
Tina You're welcome. Goodbye.

About an hour later, Bernd Müller tries to reach Tom Evans on the phone.

Secretary Good afternoon, Hoodies Ltd. How can I help you?
Bernd Hello. My name's Bernd Müller. I'm from Skater Style in Germany. I'd expected to reach Tom Evans.
Secretary Ah, did you call his extension?
Bernd Yes, I did.
Secretary Oh, let me just check. I'm sorry, his line is engaged; that's why you've reached me.
Bernd I see. Well, I'm returning his call from this morning. He's expecting me to call back. It's rather urgent, I believe.
Secretary OK. I'll just put you on hold and see if I can get him for you.
Bernd No problem.

Tom Hello, is that Bernd Müller?
Bernd Yes, hello.
Tom Hi, this is Tom Evans. Thanks for returning my call.
Bernd That's no problem. But … I'm sorry, Mr Evans. Hold on a moment, please. I'm calling on my mobile from our production line and it's a little loud. Just let me step in here … That's better; I should be able to hear you now. So, what can I do for you?

B **Write in your own words why …**

1. Tom wants to speak English.
2. Bernd can't take Tom's call.
3. Tom leaves his number for Bernd.
4. Bernd gets put through to Tom's secretary.
5. Bernd asks Tom to wait when he finally gets through to him.

C **Your boss would like to know what the two telephone calls were about. Summarize them for him/her.**

TIP

Addressing people on the phone

It is common for English-speaking people to use first names on the phone even if they do not know each other. If someone does this, it appears open and friendly if you do the same.

However, it is a good idea to wait until someone invites you to use their first name. While many people prefer to use first names with business contacts, some English-speakers use a more formal approach saying *Mr* ['mɪstə(r)], *Mrs* ['mɪsɪz] or *Ms* [mɪz].

If you do not know whether or not a woman is married, you should use *Ms.* She will probably tell you if she prefers to be addressed as *Mrs.* For years the expression *Miss* [mɪs] was seen as being old-fashioned, but it is slowly becoming acceptable again.

3 Important telephone phrases

A **Read the telephone conversation again and write down the English equivalents of the following phrases.**

1. Könnten Sie mir sagen, worum es geht?
2. Ich stelle Sie zu Bernd Müller, unserem Verkaufsdirektor durch.
3. Könnten Sie kurz dran bleiben?
4. Soll ich ihm sagen, dass er Sie zurückrufen soll?
5. Könnten Sie mir Ihre Nummer geben?
6. Bei ihm ist besetzt.
7. Er wartet auf meinen Rückruf.
8. Vielen Dank für den Rückruf.

B **Now match the phrases below with the phrases from the conversation which have the same or a similar meaning.**

1. Thank you for getting back to me.
2. Can I ask what it's in connection with?
3. He's probably waiting for my call.
4. I'll connect you with …
5. Can I ask him to return your call?
6. What number can he reach you on?
7. I'll just put you on hold, if that's OK.
8. His extension is busy.

TIP

Saying telephone numbers

Say each digit separately, except for double digits.
e.g. 01233 4567899 = *oh (AE zero) one two double-three, four five six, seven eight double-nine.*

You usually say all of the numbers in a country code separately.
e.g. 0044 = *oh oh four four* (or) *zero zero four four*

country code = *Vorwahl*
extension = *Durchwahl*
mobile phone (AE cell phone) = *Handy*
landline = *Festnetz*

4 Making a telephone call

KMK

Act out this telephone conversation with a partner. The language box on page 21 will help you.

Skater Style Mitarbeiter/in

Melden Sie sich am Telefon mit Vor- und Nachnamen und mit Firmennamen.

British customer

Introduce yourself and ask if you can speak to someone in the sales department.

Fragen Sie, warum der Kunde / die Kundin anruft.

Say that you are interested in buying some of the company's clothing for your shop.

Sagen Sie, dass Sie den Anrufer / die Anruferin mit Arista Marquardt verbinden, die im Verkauf arbeitet und dass Sie ihn/sie in die Warteschleife schalten. Dann sagen Sie, dass bei Frau Marquardt besetzt ist und fragen Sie, ob er/sie eine Nachricht hinterlassen möchte.

Ask if you can leave your telephone number so that Frau Marquardt can call you back.

Reagieren Sie entsprechend und fragen Sie nach der Telefonnummer des Anrufers / der Anruferin.

Give your number: 0044 1548 7174566

Sie haben nicht verstanden. Bitten Sie den Anrufer / die Anruferin, die Nummer zu wiederholen.

Repeat your number to the employee.

Wiederholen Sie die Nummer noch einmal laut.

Thank the person you are speaking to for their help and say goodbye.

Verabschieden Sie sich.

LANGUAGE

Expressions for telephoning

Making a call
My name is .... I'd like to speak to someone in the marketing/sales/finance department, please.
Can I speak to ..., please?
Could you put me through to the ... department, please?

Saying what the call is about
I'm interested in ...
I'd like to speak to somebody about ...
The reason I'm calling is ...

Answering the phone
Good morning/afternoon/evening (,Fynton Industries Ltd). How can I help you?
Hello, ... speaking.

Asking the caller for more information
Could you tell me what it's about, please?
Can/May I ask why you're calling?

Transferring the call
I'll put you through to ...
I'll connect you with ...
Can you hold the line for a moment, please?

Explaining / Apologizing
I'm afraid that ... is in a meeting at the moment.
I'm sorry, but ... isn't in the office/available at the moment.
I'm afraid his/her line is engaged.
Sorry, his/her extension is busy right now.
Can I get him/her to call you back?
Can I take a message?
Would you like to leave a message?
Could you give me your number, please?
What number can he/she reach you on?

Asking the caller to repeat something
Sorry, I didn't catch/understand that.
Could you say it/that again, please?
Could you spell that for me, please?
Could you read that back to me, please?

Ending a call
Is there anything else I can do for you?
Thanks for your help.
Thank you for calling.
Bye now.
Goodbye.

5 Tom and Bernd telephone again

06

A During the conversation between Tom and Bernd, the line goes dead. Listen as Bernd calls again from his office. Which of the statements best summarizes their conversation?

1. Bernd tries to get Tom to buy some of the new line of sweatshirts, but Tom doesn't seem very interested.
2. Tom expresses his interest in a new line of sweatshirts and Bernd offers to send him the details by email.
3. Tom says he's not interested in the sweatshirts which are already on Skater Style's website and that he would rather see some new designs.

B Listen again. What order are these expressions used in?

- **a** Could I have your email address, please?
- **b** Could you speak a little more slowly, please?
- **c** The line just went dead.
- **d** Let's talk again soon.

C Bernd notes down Tom's email address, but he doesn't note it down correctly. Find and correct his mistakes in your exercise book.

Tomivans@hoodeis_ldt.co.uk

LANGUAGE

Saying internet and email addresses

www.skaterstyle.de	*w-w-w-(dot)-skaterstyle-(all one word)-(dot)-d-e*
www.hoodies-ltd.co.uk/sales	*w-w-w-(dot)-hoodies-(hyphen)-l-t-d-(dot)-co-(dot)-u-k-(forward slash)-sales*
b_mueller@skaterstyle.de	*b-(underscore)-mueller-(with 'ue')-(at)-skaterstyle-(all one word)-(dot)-d-e*

6 Practising saying email addresses

A How do you say each of these symbols? Match them to the words in the box.

1 @ **2** / **3** . **4** - **5** _

forward slash • hyphen • at • underscore • dot

B With a partner, practise saying these email addresses. Say them clearly and spell the names to your partner to make it easy for your partner to understand.

1. yvonne.gilford@rosworth-products.com
2. jillcraig@bosworth_solutions.biz
3. vanessa_williams@tulsonsteelpipes.co.uk
4. terri-quantrill@xlogistics.co.uk

C Now practise spelling your own private and work email addresses to your partner.

7 Understanding answerphone messages

07

A The next day, Tom Evans' secretary listens to an answerphone message from Bernd Müller. Look at her notes and find the three mistakes she made.

Tom,
Bernd Müller from Skater Style left a message for you. He has sent you the pdf by email. Can you give him a call on his mobile (0049 1703 684948) so that he can give you his email address?
Janet

KMK 08

B **Hören Sie sich die anderen beiden Nachrichten auf Toms Mailbox. Notieren Sie die erforderlichen Angaben im Formular für Anrufbenachrichtigungen.**

Name:	…
E-Mail-Adresse:	…
Grund des Anrufes:	…
Telefonnummer:	…

8 Leave a message after the tone …

WEBCODE **TRMU0201**

Read the instructions below and then record your own answerphone message.

It's several weeks later and Hoodies Ltd are about to receive their first order from Skater Style. Bernd Müller writes you an email asking you to call Tom Evans to confirm the details of the order. Tom isn't in his office when you call, so you have to leave a message on his answerphone …

Betreff: **Bestellbestätigung für Hoodies Ltd**

Von: b_mueller@skaterstyle.de Signatur: Ohne

Könnten Sie bitte kurz bei Tom Evans in England anrufen, um die Einzelheiten zu seiner Bestellung zu bestätigen?

Die Bestellung beinhaltet 45 Sweatshirts der Serie „StreetSurf" (Nr. 54983) und 25 Sweatshirts der Serie „KoolKult" (Nr. 38928). Die Artikel werden, wie mit Tom besprochen, am 18. März FOB geliefert. Obwohl schwer zu sagen ist, wann genau die Sendung ankommt, schätzen wir, dass der mit der Lieferung beladene Lkw gegen 15 Uhr im Lager von Hoodies Ltd sein wird.

Vielen Dank
Bernd Müller

TIP

Politeness

English speakers frequently use 'extra' words to give a polite and helpful impression. If your answers are short, the person you are speaking to may feel that you are too direct and a bit rude.

Tips to help you sound more polite:

1. Always use "please" when you want the caller to do something for you such as repeat what they have just said, and "thank you" when they have done it.
2. Use expressions such as "Could you …?", "Would you mind …?", and "Would it be possible for you to …?" to 'soften' what you are asking.
3. Try to avoid giving answers with just "yes" and "no". For example: "Did you get my email?" – "Yes, thanks, I did."

9 Politeness on the phone

A **Complete the quiz about how to politely ask a caller to do something. Then check your answers at the bottom.**

Business English FAQs

It's normal to have to ask people to slow down or repeat something when telephoning in English. But what's the most polite way of doing it? Complete our quiz to find out how polite you are.

1 The person you are calling is speaking unclearly. What do you say?
a Sorry. Would you mind speaking a little more clearly, please?
b Sorry. Can you speak more clearly?

2 The caller is speaking too fast. What do you say?
a Sorry, speak more slowly.
b Could you speak more slowly, please?

3 The person on the other end of the line is speaking quietly. What do you say?
a Sorry, would you mind speaking up, please?
b Please speak up.

4 You want the caller to repeat themselves. What do you say?
a Would it be possible to repeat that, please?
b Say that again.

5 You want the person you are talking to to spell something. What do you say?
a Please spell that.
b Would you spell that for me, please?

Answers: 1a, 2b, 3a, 4a, 5b

B **Now look at the more polite sentences again and make a note of the 'extra' words which make them more polite.**

10 Putting politeness into action

Rephrase the sentences below to make them more polite.

1. Ask him to return my call.
2. What's the reason for your call?
3. Send me an email.
4. Did you call me? – No.
5. Wait a moment.
6. Did you get the email I sent? – Yes.
7. Give me your email address.
8. What time will he be back in the office?

11 Role-play

Read your partner file at the back of the book and the information on the Skater Style website below. Then work with a partner and act out the role-play.

Student A: turn to partner file 8 on page 119. / **Student B:** turn to partner file 1 on page 117.

GRAMMAR

Future tenses – the *going to*-future and the *will*-future

1. I**'ll be** in the office all afternoon.
2. I have checked and you**'ll receive** the delivery next Monday.
3. **Will** she **be** in the office this afternoon?
4. We **will deliver** the consignment by 4 p.m. on Friday.
5. I**'ll take a look** and see if he's in his office.
6. Kate**'s going to be** in a meeting until after 5 p.m.

- Das **will-future** wird aus *will* und der Grundform des Verbs gebildet (1–5).
- Das *will-future* wird oft für zukünftige Situationen oder Ereignisse, die mit Sicherheit eintreten werden (1, 2, 4), für Vermutungen und für spontane Entscheidungen verwendet.
- In der gesprochenen Sprache kommt die betonte Form *will* selten vor. Meistens (vor allem mit Pronomen) wird die Kurzform *'ll* benutzt (1, 2). In Fragen ohne Fragewort ist nur die betonte Form möglich (3). In der Schriftsprache ist die betonte Form üblich: die unbetonte Form wirkt dort informell (4).

- Das **going to-future** wird aus *going to* und der Grundform des Verbs gebildet (6).
- Es wird benutzt, um über Pläne oder Absichten zu Sprechen. In der gesprochenen Sprache drückt man damit auch aus, dass etwas mit Sicherheit eintreffen wird (6).

12 Practice

Use the verbs in brackets in the appropriate future form to complete the sentences.

1. OK, I … you back first thing in the morning and let you know. (call)
2. The consignment … on time because of the early-morning traffic jams. (not arrive)
3. I … him that you called and ask him to call you back as soon as he's free. (tell)
4. What time … speak to me tomorrow? (you / be able to)
5. I … you once the order has arrived and … you know if I want to order more. (call, let)
6. I … in a meeting until lunchtime, but I … at 2 p.m. (be, call back)
7. I'm not sure if he's in; I … check. (have to)
8. Please tell her that I … later this afternoon. (call back)

13 Mediation

Übertragen Sie den folgenden Auszug sinngemäß in die deutsche Sprache.

Telephone greetings that customers – and employees – will love

by Mary Sandro

Many companies make their telephone greetings so long and complicated that employees hate saying them, and customers hate listening to them. But there is power in being simple. For best results, telephone greetings should be friendly, short and sound honest.

Pleasant

A friendly greeting is essential to a successful call because it creates the right emotional tone. In general, listeners tend to mirror or 'catch' the emotional states of speakers. This is a rule of communication that is true whether one is speaking to a group of 1000, a small meeting of ten, or a single customer on the telephone. In other words, people respond in the way they are spoken to. If we answer the phone in an unfriendly way, chances are the caller will be unfriendly. If we answer the phone in a friendly way, chances are the caller will be friendly, and we all know which caller is easier to work with.

One of the easiest ways to guarantee that you sound friendly and positive when answering the phone is to use the right body language. I recommend sitting on the edge of your chair, taking a deep breath and then smiling.

Sincerity

Telephone greetings have to be natural if they are to sound sincere or, in other words, honest. The key elements of a telephone greeting should be: company and department, your name, and then an offer to help.

That means that company marketing slogans or phrases such as "We're so glad you called" or "It's a lovely day here at company XYZ and even better since you called" are out. Sentiments like this just don't sound sincere and honest. And customers won't thank you for taking up their time with them.

Brevity

Keep your telephone greeting short. I've heard greetings that are so long, I feared the person answering the phone was going to run out of air just trying to say them. Excessively long greetings are unprofessional for many reasons: they don't sound pleasant or sincere because technically they are impossible to execute; employees hate them and those feelings come through; and callers hate them because they waste their time. Fortunately, if you follow the guidelines mentioned above, brevity is assured.

Source: adapted from http://www.proedgeskills.com/Customer_Service_Articles/telephone_greetings_that_custome.htm

My first mobile phone was almost the size of a brick. It also weighed about as much as a brick and, as well as making telephone calls with it, I could use the phone to hold open my office door as it recharged on the floor. It spent a lot of time there because its battery provided power for just a few hours at a time.

My new smartphone sits neatly in my hand and has more computing power under its large screen than NASA used to send the first man to the moon. I can read and send emails with it, take part in web conferences, access my company's databases, send and receive videos of product demonstrations, work on documents and, yes, make phone calls.

These small but incredible devices have a big future in business. I would even argue that they will become the business communication tool in the coming years. It's easy to see why they will make PCs obsolete: business in the globalized world is increasingly about being mobile and, in this context, smartphones leave PCs standing – on the desk.

Some people might argue that laptops, notepads and tablets are the ideal mobile IT solutions for business people. But, the point is, they're still not mobile enough. I gave up on my tablet because of the pain I got in my shoulder from carrying it around. Now everything I need fits into my jacket pocket. You might think I'm a fan of smartphones. You'd be right. In fact, the only disadvantage I can see is that they're so easy to lose. And that could be really frustrating if you've got important – and private – company data on your phone.

But this would be a small loss to companies compared to the big cost savings they would make by switching to smartphones. We might currently think of smartphones as being quite expensive, but the reality is that it would be cheaper to equip a workforce with smartphones than with a traditional IT infrastructure. So if the coolness and impressive functionality of smartphones aren't enough to convince companies to switch to them, the cost savings they promise certainly will.

14 Understanding the text

A Read the article and choose the headline which summarizes it best.

1. Why smartphones can't replace laptops and tablets
2. Why phones will outsmart PCs to become *the* business communication tool
3. Smartphones only have a future in business if they become cheaper

B Make a list of the advantages for companies of smartphones mentioned in the article.

15 Over to you

A The article mentions one disadvantage of smartphones; how many more can you think of? Discuss your ideas with a partner.

B Think of the type of jobs that people do in your company. In which of these jobs does it make most sense to use a smartphone and for which tasks?

UNIT 3

Equipment for a festival

- Writing enquiries
- Making an appointment
- Dealing with offers and orders

1 Warm-up

a

b

c

d

A **You wish to send an enquiry to a supplier of goods or services. Where can you find the address of a suitable company? Look at the photos (a–d) for help.**

B **What information do you ask for in an enquiry?**

2 Making an enquiry

PAGE **127**

Top Act Event Management GmbH has won a contract to organize a five-day multi-cultural festival near Lake Kemnader in Bochum. They will need to build a temporary village to house the organizers, artists and competitors, so Nina Wittstock, the Purchasing Director, writes to a supplier of modular buildings who has been recommended to her by a business partner.

A **Read Nina's enquiry on the page opposite and find phrases for the following headings.**

1 source of address
2 description of companies
3 reason for enquiry
4 requirements
5 references

Tel: +49 211 93288154
Fax: +49 211 93288150
www.top-act-event.de
nina.wittstock@top-act-event.de

TOP Act EVENT

Top Act Event Management GmbH [1]
Graf-Adolf-Str. 240
40210 Düsseldorf
Germany

NW/TT [2]
09 December 20.. [3]

Modular Buildings Ltd [4]
99 Canterbury Road
FOLKESTONE
CT18 8HT
GREAT BRITAIN

Attn. Mr Donald Campbell, Export Sales Director [5]

Dear Mr Campbell [6]

Enquiry about modular buildings [7]

Your company has been recommended to us by Ms Sarah Parkinson of Catering Solutions in Newcastle, who tells us that you supply high-quality modular buildings at competitive prices. [8]

We are a leading event management company with major customers all over Europe and beyond.

In August 20.. there will be a five-day cultural festival held at Lake Kemnader in Bochum, Germany. For this we will need to build a temporary village near the lake to house the organizers, artists and competitors. Please let us have details of your entire range of products and your current export price list, including all discounts. Details of your terms of delivery and payment would also be appreciated. Delivery would need to be made by 31 May 20.. at the latest.

For your information, a plan of the site with details of all the buildings needed is enclosed.

Should you require references, please refer to our website for a list of satisfied clients.

We look forward to hearing from you soon.

Yours sincerely [9]
Top Act Event Management GmbH

Nina Wittstock [10]

Nina Wittstock [11]
Purchasing Director

Enc [12]

B Find the English equivalents of these expressions in the letter.

1 zu Händen
2 Produktpalette
3 Rabatte
4 Zahlungsbedingungen
5 Lieferung
6 im Anhang

C Match the words in the box with the parts of the business letter (1–12).

attention line • body of the letter • complimentary close • date • enclosure • inside address • letterhead • reference initials • salutation • signatory's name • signature • subject line

3 Writing an enquiry

PAGE 127 & 138 KMK

Sie sind Azubi bei der Top Act Event Management GmbH. Ihre Firma holt im Moment Angebote zur Vermietung *(rental)* von Bühnenbeleuchtung für das Festival ein, u. a. von der irischen Firma Stage Equipment Ltd (35 Brunswick Place, Dublin 2, Irland).

Die Einkaufsleiterin Ihrer Firma, Frau Nina Wittstock, bittet Sie, ein Schreiben an Stage Equipment Ltd zu verfassen. Sie wird den Brief selbst unterschreiben. Benutzen Sie die Anfrage auf Seite 29 (oder 127) und die Phrasen im Anhang auf Seite 138 als Hilfe. Schließen Sie folgende Informationen in Ihren Brief ein.

- Ansprechpartnerin: Ms Majella O'Casey, Exportleiterin
- Anrede und Bezug auf Homepage der irischen Firma
- kurze Beschreibung Ihrer Firma
- Anlass der Anfrage: 5-tägiges Event mit drei beleuchteten Bühnen
- Bitte um Verkaufsmaterial über gesamte Produktpalette, einschl. aller Rabatte
- Liefer- und Zahlungsbedingungen?
- Bitte um Lieferung spätestens bis 31. Juli 20..
- höfliche Schlussformel

4 Taking a message

09

Ein Mitarbeiter von Modular Buildings Ltd liest Nina Wittstocks Brief und ruft sie an.

KMK

A **Da Frau Wittstock außer Haus ist, nimmt ihre Sekretärin Dominika das Gespräch entgegen. Hören Sie das Telefonat und machen Sie sich Notizen, die Dominika an Frau Wittstock weitergeben soll.**

Anrufer (Name, Firma, Stadt, Land):	...
Kontaktdaten:	...
Datum:	...
Grund und Ergebnis des Anrufes:	...

B **Listen again and complete the language box below with words from the dialogue.**

LANGUAGE

Making an appointment

Getting started
I'd like to make an ...[1].
Let me just check her ...[2].
Just let me see when she's ...[3].

Suggesting a time
When would ...[4] you?
How ... [5] Monday at 9 a.m.?

Suggesting an alternative
Monday's a ...[6] day for me.
I'm afraid not. She's ...[7] up all day until 4.30.
What about Wednesday? Preferably in the morning.
Would 9.30 be ...[8]?

Agreeing
Yes, that's ...[9] with me.

5 Arranging an appointment

Next week Nina Wittstock is flying to London for two days of business meetings. She would like to see an ex colleague Marlon Gibson of Showbiz Promotions Ltd again, so she phones him on his mobile.

Use the partner files at the back of the book to agree on a day and time for a two-hour meeting in London. The language box on page 30 will help you.

Student A: turn to partner file 2 on page 117.
Student B: turn to partner file 10 on page 120.

6 Donald sends a quotation

Donald Campbell from Modular Buildings Ltd in Folkestone sends an offer to Nina Wittstock after visiting her in Germany.

Read the quotation and answer the following questions in your own words.

1 What advantages of using modular buildings does Donald mention?
2 What are the terms of delivery?
3 How long will delivery take?
4 What are the terms of payment for new customers?
5 How does Donald express his wish for a reply from Nina?

To: nina.wittstock@top-act-event.de
Copy:
Subject: Offer for modular buildings
From: d.campbell@btopenworld.com

Dear Nina

Many thanks for finding the time to meet me last Wednesday. As you know, our company manufactures a wide range of high-quality products with many satisfied customers throughout Europe, and judging by the information you gave me about the five-day festival, I believe we have exactly what you are looking for. I would also like to point out that our modular buildings can be dismantled and stored when not needed, and used for many years. They also have a high re-sale value.

As regards the units discussed, we are pleased to submit the following quotation:

- *Flexi* modular office unit, 8 m x 3 m, article no. FMOU-001, at €4,500 per unit
- *Saniclean* male/female/disabled toilet/shower unit, 5 m x 3 m, article no. MSTSU-004 at €2,500 per unit
- *Sleeptight* modular 6-bed dormitory, 4 m x 10 m, article no. ST6D-006, at €6,000 per unit

Please refer to the attachments for further details.

Our prices are quoted CPT Bochum festival site. Delivery can be made within 30 days after receipt of order. Our usual terms of payment for new customers are cash with order.

We hope our offer is to your liking and look forward to receiving your order.

Best wishes

Donald Campbell
Export Sales Director
Modular Buildings Ltd

7 Over to you

PAGE 127 & 138 KMK

You work in the sales department of Marathon Sportartikel GmbH (Gerberau 28, 79098 Freiburg). Your company produces a wide range of sportswear and has many satisfied customers Europe-wide. You receive an enquiry about basketball shirts from the Swedish firm Terra Firma Sports (Pajalagatan 2, 162 65 Vällingby, Sweden).

Use the phrases on page 138 to write an offer (with today's date) to the Swedish firm. Take the following into account:

- Contact person: Ms Gundela Lindblom in the purchasing department
- Thanks for enquiry (add detail)
- Description of your company
- Current catalogue and price list enclosed
- All prices CIP Stockholm-Arlanda airport
- Wholesaler discount of 20%
- Terms of payment on first order: cash with order
- Delivery within 30 days of order
- Polite finish

TIP

Incoterms® 2010

In international trade, the eleven Incoterms® 2010 Rules (**in**ternational **co**mmercial **terms**) are used in contracts of sale to define the rights and obligations of the buyer and seller as regards risk, transport, insurance, packing, customs duty and documentation. They are terms of delivery.

8 Evaluating Donald's offer

PAGE 128 WEBCODE TRMU0301

Study the Incoterms® 2010 Rules CPT and DAP and then do the tasks on page 33.

CPT – CARRIAGE PAID TO (... named place of destination): Multimodal transport
The seller pays for the main carriage of the goods. The seller delivers the goods in the customary packing, cleared for export to the carrier which he nominates. The seller bears the risk until the goods have been delivered into the custody of the first carrier. The seller pays the transport costs for the goods, excluding transport insurance, up to the named destination.
The buyer is responsible for insuring the goods for the main carriage and pays all import duties and taxes.

DAP – DELIVERED AT PLACE (... named place of destination): Multimodal transport
The seller pays for the carriage of the goods in the customary packing, cleared for export to the named place of destination by the carrier which he nominates. He bears the risk until the goods have been delivered to the named place of destination. The buyer is responsible for unloading the goods at the place of destination and pays all import duties and taxes.

A **Answer the following questions about the Incoterms® 2010 Rules CPT and DAP.**

1. Who pays for the main carriage?
2. Who packs the goods?
3. Who chooses the freight forwarder?
4. When does the risk pass from the seller to the buyer?
5. Who pays for damage to the goods during the main carriage?
6. Who pays for (un)loading the goods?

B **Explain what expenses Top Act Event Management will have to cover if they accept delivery CPT Bochum festival site.**

9 Nina negotiates better terms

PAGE 130

10

Listen as Nina Wittstock phones Donald Campbell to discuss the terms in his offer. Then do the tasks on the next page.

Donald Good morning, Modular Buildings Ltd, Donald Campbell speaking. What can I do for you?

Nina Good morning Donald! It's Nina Wittstock from Top Event Management in Germany.

Donald Hello, Nina! Nice to talk to you again. How are you?

Nina Fine, thanks. And you?

Donald Mustn't grumble. It's a bit windy here in Folkestone, though. Did you get my offer?

Nina Yes, thanks. I got it yesterday, and since then I've talked to my team and the finance department and we've got a few queries.

Donald No problem. What would you like to know?

Nina Well, we've looked at the terms of delivery – CPT Bochum festival site – and we'd like to talk about insurance for the main carriage from Folkestone to Bochum.

Donald No problem, Nina. We can get you insurance for that. We could make it CIP not CPT.

Nina Carriage and insurance paid to the destination – the festival site in this case, right?

Donald That's right. The load would be insured from when the freight forwarder collects it until they deliver it to you at the festival. If anything goes wrong, you contact the insurance company and get compensation.

Nina I see. Why didn't you put that in your offer, Donald?

Donald We left it out because our main customers have always used their own insurers, so we quote them without insurance. I'll have to talk to our insurers, but I'm sure it won't cost you more than about 1 or 2% more. They've insured a lot of very big loads for our customers up to now and their rates are very competitive.

Nina All right, it's a deal. Now what about payment?

Donald Well, as I said in the offer, it's CWO – cash with order.

Nina But in this case that would mean paying about a month before the goods arrive, because your delivery period is 30 days. Surely you can offer us better terms, Donald! It's such a big order!

Donald OK, we can give you D/P, so you don't pay so early.

Nina And that would mean …?

Donald Well, documents against payment means we would ship the goods and send the documents to your bank. You go there, pay for them and use them to take delivery of the goods when they arrive at the festival site.

Nina Well now, that sounds a lot better!

A Find words in the dialogue to match the definitions (1–8) below.

1 prices
2 place to which something is sent
3 time it takes for goods to reach the buyer
4 company which transports goods
5 questions
6 money paid if goods are lost or damaged
7 transport
8 goods

B Listen to or read the dialogue again and do the following tasks.

1 Explain why Nina Wittstock phones Donald Campbell.
2 Describe what Top Act Event Management GmbH would have to do if there were damage to the load during the main carriage from Folkestone to Bochum.
3 Give Nina Wittstock's reasons for choosing D/P.

GRAMMAR

Present perfect and simple past

1 I**'ve talked** to my team since then.
2 We**'ve** always **dealt with** insurance ourselves.
3 We**'ve seen** the terms of delivery.
4 They **transported** the goods.
5 I **got** it yesterday.
6 **Did** you **get** my offer?
7 Why **didn't** you **put** that in your offer?

- Das **present perfect** wird verwendet, wenn der durch den Satz angegebene Zeitraum bis in die Gegenwart andauert (*unfinished time*) (1–3), z. B. mit Zeitadverbien wie *ever, since then, up to now, yet* (1, 2), oder wenn keine Zeit angegeben wird (3). Es bezieht sich auf Ereignisse oder Handlungen, deren Ergebnisse in der Gegenwart sichtbar, spürbar oder von Bedeutung sind (3).
- Das *present perfect* wird mit dem Hilfsverb *have/has* + Partizip Perfekt (3. Form) des Verbs gebildet (1–3).

- Das **simple past** wird verwendet, um abgeschlossene Handlungen und Ereignisse in der Vergangenheit auszudrücken (*finished time*) (4–7). Bestimmte Zeitadverbien stehen oft in Verbindung mit dem *simple past*, z. B. *last week, two years ago, yesterday* (5).
- Das *simple past* wird mit der 2. Form von unregelmäßgen Verben gebildet (5). Siehe Liste der unregelmäßigen Verben auf Seite 191. Bei regelmäßigen Verben wird das *simple past* durch das Anhängen von *-ed* an den Infinitiv gebildet (4). Fragen und Verneinungen werden mit *did/didn't* + Grundform gebildet (6, 7).

!

- I've been here ~~since~~ **for** three weeks.
- I started working here ~~for~~ two weeks **ago**.

10 Practice

A **Decide whether these expressions of time are about *finished time* (simple past) or *unfinished time* (present perfect). None of them are about the future.**

today • last month • in 2000 • on my birthday • this week • on Friday • ever • 2 years ago • since 2011 • at Christmas • never • yesterday • in February • just • in the spring • yet • at 7 o'clock • this morning

B **Complete these sentences using the present perfect or the simple past.**

1 We … all the goods yet. (not deliver)
2 We … everything last week. (deliver)
3 We … many contracts this month. (not have)
4 We last … a new customer six weeks ago. (get)
5 … him yet? (you/meet)
6 Our new lorry … three times already. (break down)
7 It … last week. (not break down)
8 It … this week. (break down)
9 I … a car crash outside the office. (just see)
10 None of our drivers … since 2011. (crash)

11 Nina places an order

Top Act Event Management GmbH place the following order with Modular Buildings Ltd.

A **Look at the CPT prices first offered in Donald Campbell's email on page 31 and then calculate the increase in price for CIP delivery.**

B **Calculate the percentage increase for CIP delivery as compared to CPT.**

C **With a partner, discuss what the next steps are once an order is placed.**

Dear Mr Campbell

Order for modular buildings

Many thanks for your offer dated 15 January 20..

We now wish to place an order for the following units:

Quantity	Description	Article No.	Unit Price (€)	Total (€)
4	*Flexi* modular office unit	FMOU-001	4,567.50	18,270.00
4	*Saniclean* toilet/shower unit	MSTSU-004	2,537.50	10,150.00
	Total price		**28,420.00**	

Delivery: CIP Bochum festival site (Incoterms® 2010), by 31 May 20..
Payment: by documentary credit in your favour, payable at a UK bank

We look forward to receiving your confirmation of order.

12 Rezeption: Leseverstehen

Sie absolvieren ein Auslandspraktikum bei einer kleinen Firma für Desktop-Publishing in Preston, Nordengland und stellen fest, dass die Mitarbeiter kaum Zeit haben, Rechnungen an ihre Kunden auszustellen. Folglich kommt es oft zu Zahlungsengpässen. Sie finden folgenden Artikel in einer englischen Fachzeitschrift.

Invoice factoring

Many businesses do not get paid right away for their products or services. This negatively impacts cash flow and can make it hard for them to deal with new orders. Invoice factoring helps businesses that do not get paid for 30, 60, 90 or more days by advancing up to 90% of the invoice total as soon as the goods have been delivered.

So how does it work? Company A delivers goods or services to Company B. Company A invoices Company B and sells this invoice at a discount to Company C – a factoring company. The discount is the factoring company's profit. Company C provides Company A with immediate cash in an amount equal to 80 or 90% of the face value of the invoice. Company B then pays Company C when the invoice is due. Company C transfers the rest of the invoice amount to Company A and deducts its professional fees and interest charges.

The fees charged depend on the creditworthiness of the client's customers. To qualify for factoring, the small business must be engaged in B2B commerce, not B2C.

So what's the downside? Many people believe that as soon as Company A has sold an invoice to the factoring company (Company C), that's the end of the matter for Company A. This is wrong, because if Company B cannot pay, e. g. due to bankruptcy, Company A must pay the full amount of the invoice to Company C – the factoring company.

If your small business is in need of immediate cash, factoring may be your best option.

Entscheiden Sie, ob die Aussagen (1–3) richtig oder falsch sind und begründen Sie Ihre Antwort. Beantworten Sie anschließend die Verständnisfragen (4–11) auf Deutsch.

1 Ein Factoring-Unternehmen stellt dem Verkäufer Geldmittel für eine Transaktion zur Verfügung, bevor er hierfür die Rechnung ausgestellt hat.
2 Der Verkäufer erhält nicht den vollen Rechnungsbetrag.
3 Nachdem der Verkäufer seine Forderungen verkauft hat, geht das Risiko der Nichtzahlung auf den Factor über.
4 Welches Problem wird durch Factoring gelöst?
5 Was geschieht mit einer Rechnung?
6 Wie schnell erhält der Verkäufer sein Geld?
7 Wieviel vom Rechnungsbetrag erhält der Verkäufer zunächst?
8 Warum erhält der Verkäufer nicht den vollen Rechnungsbetrag?
9 Von welchen Faktoren hängt die Höhe der Gebühren ab, die vom Factoring-Unternehmen berechnet werden?
10 Unter welchen Umständen ist ein Factoring-Unternehmen nicht bereit, Forderungen zu kaufen?
11 Was sind die Nachteile des Factoring?

Chinese CCC Certificate

When electrical goods are exported to China, it is necessary to obtain a CCC Certificate *(China Compulsory Certificate)*. This is a safety mark shown on products sold in China.

<table>
<tr><th colspan="3">Confirmation of products which are out of scope of Compulsory Product Certification
(Free of CCC)</th></tr>
<tr><td colspan="2">Applicant:
Ritter Starkstromtechnik GmbH & Co. KG</td><td>Address:
Essener Str. 10a, D-57234 Wilnsdorf</td></tr>
<tr><td colspan="2">Name of Manufacturer:
Ritter Starkstromtechnik GmbH & Co. KG</td><td>Address:
Essener Str. 10a, D-57234 Wilnsdorf</td></tr>
<tr><td>Name of Product:
Disconnector/ Isolator</td><td>Model:
SCC-M, SCC-D, SCC-GL</td><td>HS / HS code:
853655000</td></tr>
<tr><td colspan="3">Standard of Product:
EN 50123-3</td></tr>
<tr><td colspan="2">Description of Product:
a. Working principle:
The switch is a special design for the use in high current application in electrolysis processes. The switch is for the production process to make a cell or a group of cells "voltage free". This will be done by making a short circuit in the supply voltage. After switching on, the current flows through the short circuit switch and the cell is without current/voltage.</td><td>Please insert a picture of the product here or on the next page:
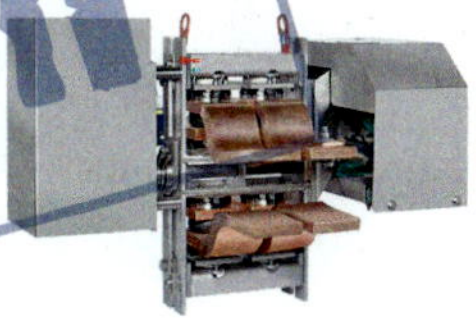</td></tr>
<tr><td colspan="2">b. Technical data:
Operation voltage type SCC-M/-D 20 V DC
Rated current from 6 kA up to 60 kA
Indoor application
Protection class: IP 00
Weight: SCC-M 45 kg to 170 kg
Dimensions: See data sheet</td><td>Type: SCC-M</td></tr>
<tr><td colspan="3">c. Site of use:
The switch is in use in all metal electrolysis (copper, zinc, ...).
In order to serve you better, please tell your Series No. of Conformation for Free of CCC to Mr. Larry Xu of Cisema Beijing Office at phone 0086-10-82563005 or email to larry@cisema.de if there are any problems when your products enter China. We will always assist you with customs clearance.</td></tr>
</table>

Specimen

13 Understanding the document

Study the certificate shown and do the following tasks.

1. Decide whether it is a CCC certificate or not and give your reasons.
2. Name the product for which the certificate has been issued.
3. State where the product will be used.
4. Give the weight of the product.
5. Explain what you must do if there are any difficulties when this product enters China.

14 Over to you

Make a list of the shipping documents most commonly used at your company.

UNIT 4

Arranging travel to a trade fair

- Making travel arrangements
- Booking a flight
- Reserving hotel rooms

1 Warm-up

A **Make a checklist like the one below of the things you have to remember to do when planning a trip. Use the photographs to help you and add your own ideas.**

Travel arrangements: checklist

1 Book train tickets

B **Compare your checklist with the person sitting next to you.**

C **Read the list below. Then decide what the four most important items are that you should take with you on a trip abroad. Explain why to your partner.**

1 credit card
2 passport
3 map of the city you're going to
4 money
5 mobile phone
6 ticket for your flight / boarding card

2 Arranging travel to a trade fair

11

Auto Teile Anderson GmbH is a wholesaler that sells car parts and is based in Ratingen, near Düsseldorf. The company language is English.

A Christoph Eckstein calls his colleague Heather Longman to ask her to make some travel arrangements for him. Listen to or read their conversation and say where Christoph is going to and why.

Heather Morning. Heather Longman here. How can I help?
Christoph Morning, Heather. It's Christoph Eckstein from business development here.
Heather Oh hi, Christoph. What can I do for you?
Christoph A colleague and I are attending the Eco-Cars trade fair in Aberdeen in Scotland. Could you take care of our travel and hotel reservations, please?
Heather No problem. What are the dates of your trip?
Christoph Well, the event is on 18 and 19 May. We'd like to travel really early on 18 May.
Heather OK. When will you be returning?
Christoph Jörg would like to fly back straight after the trade fair at about 7 p.m. I'm going to stay until 20 May as I have to attend a meeting just outside Glasgow. I'd like a rental car for that. Could you take care of that booking for me too, please?
Heather Sure. Now, what about 20 May? What time would you like to depart?
Christoph I'd like to catch a flight early in the evening if possible, just after the meeting.
Heather OK. And what about your accommodation in Aberdeen?
Christoph My what?
Heather Accommodation – you know, your hotel.
Christoph Oh, I see.
Heather Is there anything special I need to know about your hotel?
Christoph No, not really anything special. But, most importantly, we'd like a hotel as close as possible to the Exhibition and Conference Centre. And I should tell you that Jörg is a smoker, so he'll need a room that he can smoke in. That's also pretty important.
Heather OK. I'll keep that in mind.
Christoph Oh, and it's not essential, but a gym and sauna would be good.
Heather Fine. And you'll need another night in the hotel in Aberdeen on 19 May, right?
Christoph That's right.
Heather Do you want to pick up your rental car early the next morning?
Christoph Yes, that would be great. What would I do without you to keep me organized?
Heather That's what I'm here for! I'll take care of all the reservations and let you know the details.

ECO Cars

B Choose the correct sentence ending to make true statements about the conversation.

1 Christoph wants Heather to …
a … take care of travel and accommodation arrangements for a trip to a trade fair.
b … book places at a trade fair for him and his colleague.
c … change his travel arrangements for a trip to a trade fair.

2 Christoph and Jörg will be travelling together on 18 May, but …
a … Jörg will be returning alone on 19 May.
b … Christoph will be staying in Aberdeen until 21 May.

3 Christoph will need a car to drive …
a … to the Exhibition and Conference Centre.
b … to a meeting near Glasgow.
c … from the Exhibition and Conference Centre to Glasgow airport.

4 The most important thing Heather will have to remember when choosing a hotel is that …
a … it has a gym and a sauna.
b … it has rooms for smokers.
c … it's not far from the Exhibition and Conference Centre.

5 Heather does not need to book accommodation in Glasgow because …
a … Christoph will be flying back straight after his meeting.
b … a hotel reservation has already been made for him there.
c … he has already reserved a hotel room in Glasgow himself.

C **Read the conversation again and find the English translations of these German sentences.**

1. Kann ich Ihnen helfen?
2. Können Sie sich um unsere Reiseorganisation und die Hotelreservierungen kümmern?
3. Wann fliegen Sie los?
4. Wann fliegen Sie zurück?
5. Zu welcher Uhrzeit möchten Sie (ab)fliegen?
6. Wenn möglich möchte ich am frühen Abend (zurück)fliegen.
7. Gibt es noch Informationen, die ich zu Ihrem Hotel wissen sollte?
8. Möchten Sie Ihr Mietauto früh am nächsten Morgen abholen?

LANGUAGE

Making travel arrangements

Asking for help making travel reservations
Could you take care of our travel and hotel reservations/the car rental booking for me, please?
Could you book me a flight/hotel room/rental car for …, please?

Asking for details about travel arrangements
What are the dates of your trip?
When will you be returning?
What time would you like to depart?
Is there anything special I need to know?

Giving details about when you want to travel
We'd like to travel early on …
I'm going to stay until …
I'd like to catch a flight early/late in the morning/afternoon/evening if possible.

3 Confirming the bookings

PAGE **140**

You are Heather Longman. Write an email to Christoph Eckstein to confirm the bookings.

4 Role-play: making travel reservations

Work with a partner and act out the role-play.

Student A: turn to partner file 3 on page 117.
Student B: read the partner file below.

Student B

You plan to travel to a conference in Valencia, Spain. Call your colleague to ask him/her to make travel arrangements. Be polite and make small talk with your colleague.

- Tell your colleague who is calling (own name)
- Ask your colleague to arrange your travel
- Departing: 14 October (early in the morning)
- Returning: 15 October (evening)
- Thank your colleague for their help

TIP

Times and dates

The 24-hour clock is used less frequently in English than in German, but it is often used in Britain when making travel bookings.
e.g. Departure time: 07.00 = *(oh) seven hundred (hours)*
Arrival time: 15.00 = *fifteen hundred hours*

Note, though, that while travel times are usually *written* using the 24-hour clock, when *talking* about these, people generally do not use this system and instead say:
My flight departs at seven a.m. and arrives at three p.m.

To avoid confusion, it is also worth knowing that people from the US and the UK use a different system to talk about dates. People from America would read the date *07/04/20..* as *4 July*, while people from the United Kingdom would read it as *7 April*.

5 Writing the date

A Write out these dates in European form, then read them to a partner.

Example: 17.9.2022 *17 September 2022*

1	7.2.2016	**4**	1.5.1998
2	8.12.2014	**5**	11.7.1916
3	4.10.2017	**6**	29.11.2020

B Write out these dates from an American colleague in European form.

Example: 4.2.2011 *2 April 2011*

1	8.30.2013	**4**	3.26.1977
2	4.18.2019	**5**	6.1.1911
3	9.11.2025	**6**	1.3.2046

6 Making flight reservations online

Heather makes flight reservations for Christoph's return journey online.

A Look at the website and find four mistakes in her booking. Then correct the mistakes in your exercise book.

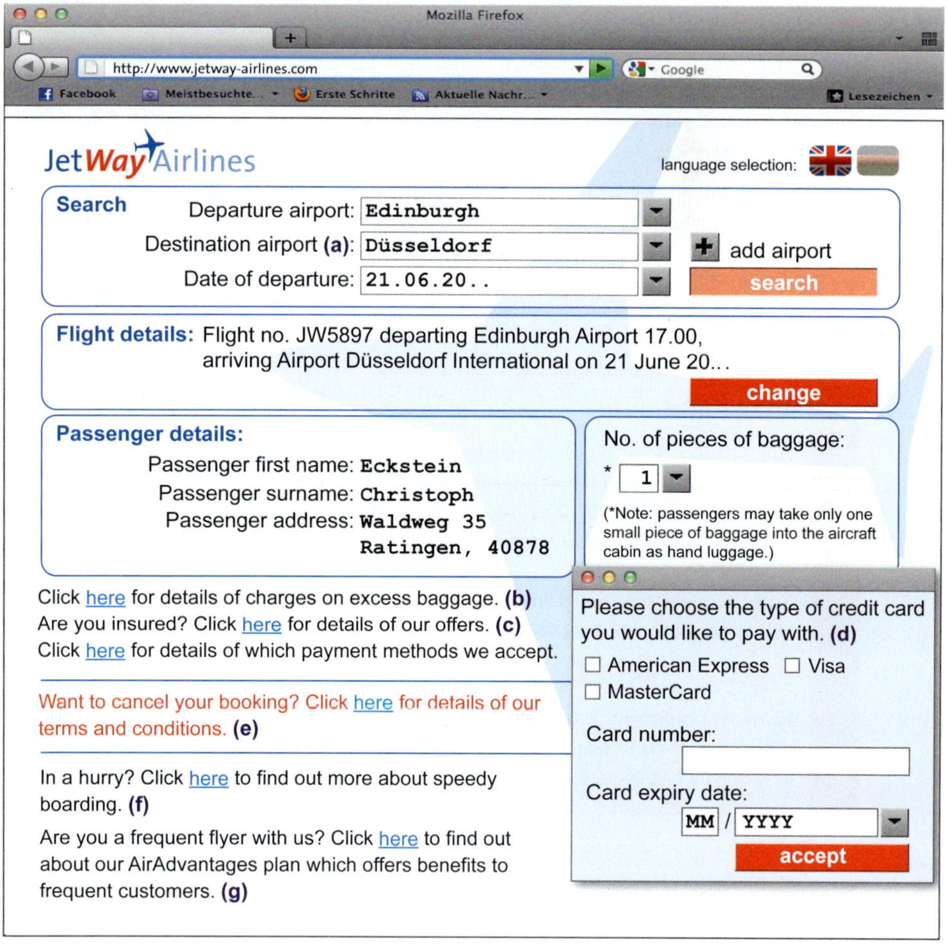

B Say where you would find the following on the screen (a–g).

1. details of the airline's customer loyalty scheme
2. information about travel insurance
3. information about how much you have to pay if your luggage weighs more than is allowed
4. the name of the airport you want to fly to
5. details of what the airline can offer you if you are not able to travel on the flight you have booked
6. details of what arrangements can be made so that you don't have to arrive early at the airport to check in for your flight
7. the area in which you enter the details of how you are going to pay

7 Finding the right hotel

Heather finds two hotels which are close to the Exhibition and Conference Centre. Look at the flyers for the hotels and do the tasks on page 44.

THE ROYAL DON CONFERENCE HOTEL

"Where it's a pleasure to do business"

Welcome to the Royal Don Conference Hotel, situated within easy walking distance of the Aberdeen Exhibition and Conference Centre.

The Royal Don offers first-class, modern accommodation and business facilities. Its accommodation comprises three suites, 14 single rooms and 22 double rooms, each of them fully-equipped with satellite TV and en-suite bathrooms.

The Royal Don also offers three conference rooms, each of which can accommodate up to 60 participants, as well as eight meeting rooms. Our conference and meeting rooms are equipped with the latest presentation technology such as digital projectors and cordless microphones. These facilities are complemented by our business centre which offers fax, printing and photocopying services, as well as wireless internet access.

It's not all business!

The hotel also offers a full range of leisure facilities to help you unwind after you've completed your business. These include:

Dining at the Royal Don

Guests at the hotel are spoilt for choice when it comes to dining. Visit our three eateries which can offer you anything from a snack to a 5-course meal.

Guests who prefer the peace and quiet of their rooms can enjoy the full room service which we are pleased to offer.

For the comfort of all its guests, the Royal Don Conference Hotel operates a strict no-smoking policy on its premises.

The Hillfoots Hotel ****

The best choice if you're in business!

If you're visiting Aberdeen on business, you couldn't do better than to stay with us. The Hillfoots Hotel is situated just three miles away from the Aberdeen Exhibition Centre.

Our facilities include a fully-equipped sports centre and restaurants where you can relax after a hard day at the conference.

But it's our business facilities which we are really well-known for! Our business centre offers full printing and copying services as well as a confidential secretarial service. Our meeting rooms offer full videoconferencing facilities in addition to the most up-to-date presentation technology, including interactive whiteboards and digital projectors.

Full room service available.

Several bedrooms are available for guests who wish to smoke.

A Say which of the hotels offers the following facilities.

1 sauna
2 wireless internet access
3 shuttle bus service

B Read the flyers again and decide if the statements about the hotels and their facilities are true or false. Correct the false statements.

1 The Royal Don Conference Hotel is situated closer to the exhibition centre than the Hillfoots Hotel.
2 Some of the Royal Don Conference Hotel's rooms do not have bathroom facilities.
3 Wireless internet access is only offered by the Hillfoots Hotel.
4 Smoking is not allowed in either of the hotels.
5 It is possible for guests of either hotel to have their meals in their rooms.

C Which aspect of each hotel might mean that it is unsuitable for Christoph and Jörg?

KMK **D Übertragen Sie den Inhalt der Flyer in die deutsche Sprache. Beschränken Sie sich dabei speziell auf die Punkte, die für Jörg und Christoph interessant sind.**

8 Reserving the hotel rooms

12 **A Listen as Heather calls the Royal Don Conference Hotel to make the reservations. Then say which order the following points are mentioned in.**

1 luggage
2 check-in times
3 price of the rooms
4 dates of hotel stay
5 method of payment
6 colleagues' names

B Put the following sentences from the dialogue between Heather and the receptionist in a logical order. Then listen again to check your answers.

Heather begins the conversation:
Two colleagues of mine are attending a trade fair in Aberdeen in May. I'd like to reserve two rooms with you.

a **Heather:** What do single rooms cost?
b **Heather:** They'll be paying with MasterCard.
c **Receptionist:** When will your colleagues be arriving?
d **Heather:** OK, then we'll go for single rooms, please.
e **Receptionist:** We certainly have rooms free. Would your colleagues like to have single or double rooms?
f **Receptionist:** No problem. We accept MasterCard.
g **Heather:** They're arriving on 18 May.
h **Receptionist:** Single rooms cost £112 per night. Double rooms are £179.
i **Receptionist:** Now, can I ask how the rooms will be paid for?

9 Role-play: reserving a hotel room

KMK

Work with a partner and act out the role-play.

Student A: read the partner file below.
Student B: turn to partner file 5 on page 118.

Student A

You want to reserve a hotel room for a colleague and his wife who are travelling to Bristol in the UK for a meeting. Call the Avon View Hotel to make a reservation using your own name and the details below.

- Dates of stay: 3 nights from 22–25 September
- Accommodation required: double room (twin room also OK; single rooms not an option)
- Budget: max. £180 per double room, per night
- Payment method: Visa
- Sports facilities? Your colleague enjoys playing squash and swimming.

10 Rental car reservation

Heather receives an email confirming her reservation of Christoph's rental car.

A Complete the email with the words from the box.

additional • charged • collect • confirm • exceed • mileage allowance • rental period • returned • tank of fuel • vehicle

To: Heather Longman
Copy:
Subject: Confirmation of your reservation
From: CarPort Service Team **Signature:**

Dear Ms Longman

We are delighted to ...[1] your reservation of a Ford Focus for 20 May 20...

The total cost for the one-day ...[2] will be £63*. This includes a daily ...[3] of 100 miles. Should you ...[4] this over the period of your rental, you will be billed with an ...[5] charge of 17 pence per mile.

Additionally, your car will have a full ...[6] when you ...[7] it. Should the fuel tank not be full upon the vehicle's return, you will be ...[8] the cost of refilling the tank.

Your ...[9] will be ready for you to collect at our premises at the Aberdeen Exhibition and Conference Centre from 7 a.m. on 20 May. The vehicle can be ...[10] to CarPort's premises at Aberdeen Airport on 20 May before 10 p.m.

We look forward to being of further service to you. If you require any further information, we will be happy to provide it.

Best regards

Your CarPort Service Team

*All prices quoted in this email include VAT.

B **Read the email again and find information to match the following headings.**

1 Period of hire
2 Type of car
3 Hire fee per day
4 Additional fee per mile
5 Other costs incurred
6 Where to return the car to
7 What is included in the price
8 How the employee offers more help

GRAMMAR

Talking about the future (2)

1 He**'s staying** at the Royal Don Conference Hotel next week.
2 We**'re meeting** at 8 a.m. sharp to go to the trade fair.
3 There**'s** a big conference and exhibition in May.
4 Your flight **departs** at 13.00.
5 The conference **starts** at 9 a.m. tomorrow morning.

- Das **present progressive** und das **simple present** können beide für zukünftige Ereignisse verwendet werden, für die ein Plan, eine Verabredung oder ein Programm vorliegt (1–5).
- Dies gilt insbesondere, wenn eine Zeitangabe Missverständnisse mit der Gegenwart ausschließt (3, 4).
- Beim Vollverb *be* ist in diesem Zusammenhang nur das *simple present* möglich (3).
- Bei anderen Verben wird das *simple present* verwendet, wenn die zukünftigen Ereignisse als feststehend betrachtet werden, z.B. wenn es sich um Fahrpläne oder Stundenpläne handelt (4, 5).

11 Practice

WEBCODE **TRMU0401**

A **Use the simple present or the present progressive to express these sentences in English.**

1 Jörgs Präsentation beginnt um Punkt 11 Uhr.
2 Er fliegt heute um 15:30 Uhr zurück.
3 Christoph und Jörg sind nächste Woche wegen einer Konferenz in Aberdeen.
4 Ich treffe mich nächsten Montag mit neuen Kunden in Bristol.
5 Die Ausstellung endet am 24. März.
6 Ihr Taxi holt Sie um 16:15 Uhr ab.
7 Es kommen noch fünf weitere Gäste.
8 Ich sehe sie morgen früh.

B **Use the simple present or the present progressive to complete the sentences.**

1 Flight no. NG 4386 … at 21.45. (arrive)
2 The International Water Quality Conference … on 13 June this year. (finish)
3 Mike Boyd from Enercor Ltd … the opening presentation on "The importance of clean energy for your business" at 9.15 this morning. (give)
4 Lunch … from 1 p.m. until 2 p.m. this afternoon. (be)

KMK exam practice

12 Interaktion

Work with a partner and act out the role-play.

Situation
An employee from Auto Teile Anderson GmbH calls up Sean/Shauna McManus from the Scottish Board of Fairs and Exhibitions to book a booth and a conference room at next year's Eco-Cars Trade Fair in Aberdeen, Scotland.

Employee from Auto Teile

Your boss has given you the following information and has asked you to phone Sean/Shauna McManus to book a booth at the fair next year. Be polite and introduce yourself.

- One small booth with walls and spotlights – approx. 15 m^2 (no bigger than 20 m^2)
- Company ID sign included? size? (will pay up to £150 extra)
- Dates: 15–17 May 20..
- Equipment required in booth:
  - 1 table and 6 chairs
  - 1 counter and 1 stool
  - Carpet
  - 10 shelves (straight)
  - Wi-Fi and telephone connection
  - Other equipment available? (Choose two or three options suitable for your type of company.)
- Conference room:
  - Up to 20 people (no bigger)
  - For 3 days if possible: 15–17 May
  - Equipment: digital projector / interactive whiteboard / wireless internet access
- Price?
- Payment methods available?: prefer Visa but also have MasterCard

Sean/Shauna McManus

A client calls and wants to book a booth at the fair next year. Be polite and introduce yourself. Answer their questions and give them the following information.

- Smallest booth 18 m^2
- Included in price of booth rental:
  - Company ID sign (7'x44") (send logo as jpeg or pdf file)
  - 2x380V and 3x240V sockets
  - 1 table and up to 4 chairs
  - 1 counter and up to 3 stools
  - Carpet
  - Up to 40 shelves per booth – straight and inclined
  - Wi-Fi
- Other booth-related expenses:
  - Telephone connection: £100 (excl. calls)
  - Booth cleaning: £50–100
- Conference room:
  - Smallest room for 30 people (no smaller)
  - Only available on 16 May
  - Equipment: digital projector / wireless internet access – interactive whiteboards not available
- Price: small booth £295 per m^2 + VAT; conference room: £200 per day
- Payment method: only accept MasterCard or payment in advance

ECO-CARS Trade Fair

3rd International Trade Fair for Alternative-Energy Vehicles
Aberdeen Exhibition and Conference Centre

The Eco-Cars Trade Fair is rapidly becoming one of the UK's largest platforms on which to showcase the best in alternative-energy vehicles. First run in 2009, the show proved a success among visitors and exhibitors mainly from the UK. In 2010 it grew by a considerable 30% and pulled in visitors from across Europe and beyond. 852 exhibitors from 16 countries presented their new and enhanced products at the last event, 267 of which came from outside the UK, making the Eco-Cars Trade Fair the perfect platform for establishing international connections.

Target group:

» Over 35% of the last Eco-Cars **visitors** were trade representatives. For **visitors**, admission to the exhibition is **free of charge** to all with a professional interest in alternative-energy vehicles. Please see the **visitor profile** for more information.

» For **exhibitors**, Eco-Cars is highly relevant to retailers and wholesalers alike – to companies actively involved in manufacturing or exporting parts for hybrid and other alternative-energy vehicles. These companies come from both sides of the "buying/selling fence". For companies eager to become involved in this industry for the first time, take a look at the **exhibitor profile** section. Our exhibitor list for 2012 is growing! View it **here**. If you're looking for distributors in other countries, simply place a "reps wanted" sign in your booth, and you will be approached by companies wishing to represent your firm throughout the world.

Space prices:

Remember that Eco-Cars' prices are all-inclusive, with no extra costs for show guide entry, exhibitor badges or admission to the exhibition. Even parking is free!

» **Space only** (ideal for custom-made stands – minimum 18 m^2 applies): £245 + VAT per m^2

» **Space + shell** per m^2. This package is perfect for those who want to just turn up on the day and have everything organized for them. This standardized booth costs £295 + VAT per m^2 and includes* the following features:

» 2.5m high walls
» 2x120w spotlights
» 3x240V socket
» 1 table and 2 chairs
» 1 information counter and stool
» Fascia panel with exhibitor name on name board
» Ceiling grid and overhead lighting
» Carpet

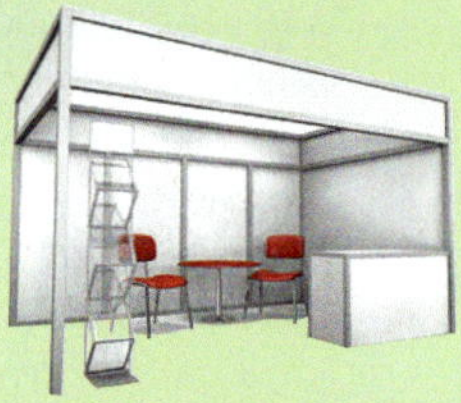

Since the exhibitor ID panel is included in the cost, all you have to do to customize your look is to choose the colours of the walls and carpets, pick out some furniture, and add some a/v equipment such as plasma screens.

*Wi-Fi internet access and a telephone connection cost extra. Click **here** for our price list.

13 Trade fair terminology

Match the highlighted words in the text with their German equivalents.

1	anlockte	**3**	Eintritt	**5**	Aussteller	**7**	Vertreter
2	Stand	**4**	Außenhändler	**6**	präsentieren	**8**	Einzelhändler

14 Discussing the text

Answer the following questions about the text

1. What does the term 'target group' mean? Define the target group of your company.
2. Would your company choose the option 'space only' or 'space + shell'? Why?
3. Would the booth with the features above suit your company at a trade fair? Explain why to your partner.

An international meeting

UNIT 5

- Preparing for a conference
- Writing emails
- Small talk

1 Warm-up

A What different types of meeting can you see here? Label the pictures (a–d) with the words from the box.

conference call • face-to-face meeting • online conference • video conference

a

b

c

d

B What types of meeting would be suitable for each of the following situations?

1 conferences in countries with extreme weather conditions
2 firing an employee
3 a job interview
4 discussions between North Sea oil workers and Head Office on land
5 technical presentations
6 weekly international team meetings

C In pairs, draw a mind map of all the factors that need to be considered before setting up each of the four types of meeting. Discuss your results with your class. Then rank the factors in order of importance for the different types of meeting.

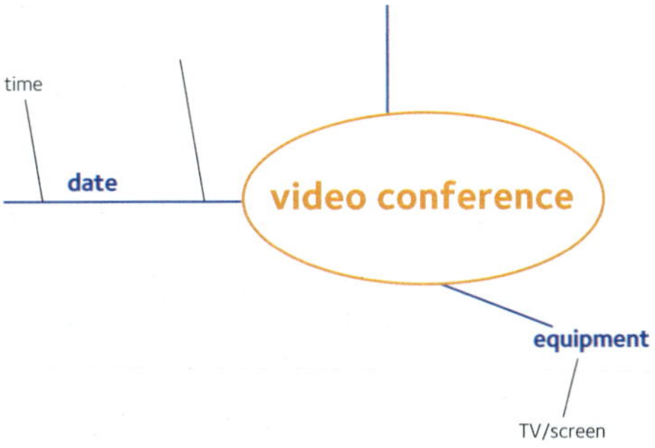

TIP

How to make a mind map

First, put your main idea in a circle in the middle of your mind map. Use a strong colour like red. Your main idea can be a word, a picture or both. Next, draw thick lines (branches) coming out from the circle, and label them with important ideas. Use a different colour for the branches. For example, if the word in the circle is **video conference**, the branches radiating out could be **blue** and labelled ***date, equipment***, etc. Next add thinner lines to each thick branch, e.g. to the line labelled ***equipment*** you could add the words *TV* and *screen*. Do this until you have filled your mind map with ideas.

2 Preparing for a conference

Sarah Bonrath is the Export Sales Director of Brewery-2-Brewery GmbH in Gelsenkirchen. Her company produces and exports brewing equipment all over the world. She organizes a video conference with colleagues from other companies in the UK, India and Singapore. Before the video conference, Sarah writes an email to all the participants.

Read her email and do the tasks on the next page.

Kopie: Waldemar Neumann
Betreff: **Draft agenda for video conference at 9 a.m. CET on 26 June 20..**
Von: sarah.bonrath@b2b.info   Signatur: Ohne

Dear all

I hope you are all well.

You will no doubt remember that our last conference was postponed because some of the participants were unable to attend. After consulting Mr Neumann, and phoning some of you, I have scheduled our video conference for 9 a.m. CET on 26 June.
The draft agenda currently includes the following topics:

1 Presentation: Indian sales figures (Rajiv Mittal, Mumbai, India)
2 Current order situation
3 Installing and operating equipment
4 Deliveries
5 Any other business (AOB)

Please let me have any suggestions as regards changes or additions, so that I can circulate the final agenda in advance. As always, the minutes of the meeting will be emailed to you one day after the conference.

Larissa Afanasiev will unfortunately not be able to take part in the meeting as she has to attend an important conference in Moscow that day.

Best regards

Sarah

Sarah Bonrath
Export Sales Director
Brewery-2-Brewery GmbH, Gelsenkirchen, HRB 7099, Amtsgericht Gelsenkirchen
Geschäftsführer: Waldemar Neumann

A Explain in your own words why Sarah Bonrath has written her email.

B Match the definitions (1–8) with the highlighted words in Sarah's email.

1. extra points discussed at the end of a meeting
2. the first version of a document
3. a list of points to be discussed at a meeting
4. a record of all the things said or decided at a meeting
5. to go to (a meeting)
6. changed to a later date
7. arranged
8. people who take part in / attend (a meeting)

3 Finalizing the agenda

Within the next few days, each of the participants replies to Sarah's email with their suggested changes to the agenda.

Read the emails (a–c) and Sarah's email in exercise 2. Then list the points for the final agenda for the conference.

a

Subject: **Re: Draft agenda for video conference**

From: Fan Wen Fang **Signature:** None

Dear Ms Bonrath

Thank you for your draft agenda.

Please add the very important issue of customer complaints, above all as regards punctual delivery, to the agenda. Some customers have also asked about second-hand equipment, and I think this could bring in a lot of business, so please include this as well.

Best regards
Fan Wen Fang
Singapore Trading Pte Ltd

b

From: Donald Masters **Signature:** None

Dear Sarah

The agenda's fine apart from one thing. We need to discuss after-sales service because some of the microbreweries over here need repairs.

Best
Donald Masters
UK Wholesale Trading

c

From: Rajiv Mittal **Signature:** None

Dear Ms Bonrath

I am in agreement with the agenda you suggest, but would kindly ask you to include the topic of travel expenses when visiting customers under Any Other Business.

Yours sincerely
Rajiv Mittal
India Trading Services Pvt Ltd

4 Writing a reply

PAGE 140 KMK

Schreiben Sie eine zweite E-Mail von Sarah Bonrath an die Vertreter. Die folgenden Punkte sollten darin enthalten sein:

- passende Anrede (siehe die *Tip Box* unten)
- Dank für Vorschläge
- Entschuldigung für Herrn Neumanns Fehlen bei der Sitzung, der an diesem Tag an einer wichtigen Tagung in London teilnehmen muss
- voraussichtliche Dauer der Sitzung: 2 Stunden
- Liste der Tagesordnungspunkte
- Bitte um rechtzeitige Benachrichtigung bei Verhinderung
- aufgrund von Zeitmangel: nicht behandelte Themen werden auf die nächste Sitzung verschoben
- höfliche Schlussformel

TIP

How to write an email

- Make sure the subject box shows what the email is about.
- Use first names if you know the recipient well, and sign off with "Best wishes" or "Best regards". Otherwise, use "Dear Mr/ Ms" (+ name) and sign off with "Yours sincerely".
- Start your email with a capital letter.
- Begin with a polite reference to a previous phone call, meeting, letter or email. If this is your first contact, introduce yourself.
- Split your email into paragraphs separated by a free line.
- Refer to any attachments to the email.
- Finish with a polite phrase.

To: "Rob Jones" <rob.jones@linkall.com>
Copy: "Bill Hampton, President" <bill.hampton@cherry-sol.com>
Subject: **"Get the world online" conference in Düsseldorf, Germany**
From: Nina Graham   Attachments: brochure.pdf

Dear Rob

Many thanks for speaking at the World Aids Day meeting in South Africa last month. I also hope you had a good trip back home to Ireland and am delighted that you will be coming to Düsseldorf to be a guest speaker at Cherry Solutions Incorporated's annual convention in May.

The theme this year is "Get the world online", and I know how passionately you support internet access for poor countries and the "One laptop per child" charity. Our brochure on this year's programme is attached for your information.

Please let us know when you would be available and what your fee would be. All travel and hotel expenses will, of course, be paid for by Cherry Solutions Incorporated.

I very much look forward to welcoming you in Düsseldorf in May!

Best wishes

Nina
Chief Executive Officer
Cherry Solutions Inc.

- Include your position and the name of your company under your name.

LANGUAGE

Expressions for emailing

Starting an email
How are things?
I hope you're well / you had a good trip to …
I am writing to ask for information on … / book a room for … / confirm that …

Answering or forwarding an email
I was delighted to receive your email …
Many thanks for your email about … / inviting me to …
I've just got your email / an email from … / a phone call from …

Getting to the point
I'd / We'd / They'd like to know if/what …
I'm pleased/delighted to accept your invitation/offer.
My plane/train arrives at …

Making requests
Please let me have some information on …
Could you tell me if/what …?
Could someone pick me/us up at the airport?
Would you send us …?

Giving information
Please refer to the attachment for the timetable for the visit.
Click on the link for more details / directions to the hotel / conference centre / firm.

Closing sentence
Many thanks for your assistance/help.
Looking forward to …
I/We look forward to meeting you / your friends.
Please let me know what your plans are.

WEBCODE **TRMU0501**

5 The video conference

13

Sarah Bonrath has a video conference with Donald Masters (UK), Rajiv Mittal (India) and Wen Fang (Singapore).

Listen to the dialogue and do the tasks on page 54.

Sarah Good morning, everybody and welcome to today's video conference. I'm Sarah Bonrath, Export Sales Director at B2B here in Germany. Since we don't all know each other, the first point, before we get to today's agenda, is introductions. Would you like to go first, Wen Fang?

Wen Fang Sure. I'm Wen Fang from Singapore Trading. I came on board six months ago, so I'm the new girl.

Sarah Thanks for that, Wen Fang. Donald?

Donald Hi. I'm Donald Masters from UK Wholesale Trading in London. I've been acting as an agent for B2B for about three years.

Sarah Thanks, Donald. Rajiv?

Rajiv Good morning. My name is Rajiv Mittal. My company is called India Trading Services Private Limited and I have had the pleasure of acting on behalf of B2B for ten years now.

Sarah Many thanks, Rajiv. Our next topic is Rajiv's presentation, so would you go ahead please, Rajiv?

Rajiv Certainly, Sarah. Thanks. My presentation is called "The upward trend of Indian sales figures" …
… To conclude, I would say that microbreweries have been extremely well received here in India.

Sarah Many thanks, Rajiv. Would anyone like to comment or ask any questions?

Donald I'd just like to say that Rajiv's done a great job!

Sarah Yes, I agree. Well done, Rajiv! OK. Let's move on to the next topic, which is our current order situation. We already know about India, so can Donald and Wen Fang now give us a brief update? Donald?

Donald As you can see from this graph, my sales are up 10% on last year.

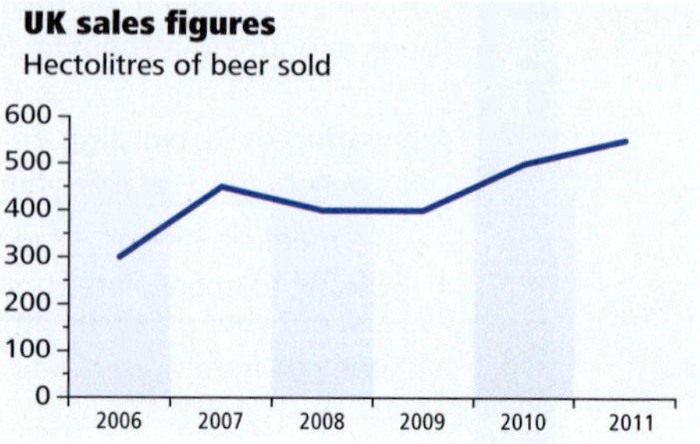

Sarah Wen Fang?

Wen Fang It's too early to tell, but they're rising.

Sarah Good. Let's move on to the next point on our agenda, shall we, which is second-hand equipment. I'm pleased to say that we have some here in Germany. We'll be posting a list on our website next month.

Wen Fang Thank you, Sarah. My customers will be very pleased.

Sarah Good. The next point is deliveries. How are things going here? Are there any issues?

Wen Fang Could I just say that my customers expect deliveries to be punctual and not two or three days late?

Sarah Is that what you meant by complaints in your email, Wen Fang?

Wen Fang Yes, that's right.

Donald Can I come in on that, Sarah?

Sarah Go ahead, Donald.

Donald I thoroughly agree with Wen Fang. We can't have late delivery. It's bad for business.

Sarah OK. I'll pass that on to our logistics department. Any other complaints? No? All right, so delivery has been covered … and complaints have been covered, too, which is point number 6 on the agenda. We've decided to postpone point number 7, which was going to be installing and operating equipment, so our next point today is after-sales service.

Rajiv Wouldn't it be better to spend just a few moments on installing and operating equipment, Sarah?

Sarah I see your point, Rajiv, but we can't really do much without the report from our service department. As soon as it's been written, I'll put it on the agenda. Can we move on to after-sales service? Is that all right? Good, would you go ahead please, Donald?

Donald Yes certainly, Sarah …

Sarah … Right. Let's wrap up the meeting with AOB shall we? I just have one final point here – travel expenses when visiting customers. I've checked with the finance department and they'll get back to you, Rajiv. Is that all right?

Rajiv That's fine, Sarah.

Sarah Well, that would seem to be it. You'll be getting the minutes by email tomorrow. Many thanks for joining us today and goodbye to everybody.

A Put the points on the agenda (1–9) in the correct order. Which point cannot be discussed?

1 after-sales service
2 AOB
3 complaints
4 current order situation
5 deliveries
6 installing and operating equipment
7 introductions
8 Rajiv's presentation ("The upward trend of Indian sales figures")
9 second-hand equipment

B **Listen again and answer the following questions about the dialogue.**

1. Which agent has been working for B2B the longest?
2. What is the sales situation in the UK?
3. Who wants to buy second-hand equipment?
4. Why does Sarah decide to postpone talking about installing and operating equipment?

C **Find expressions in the dialogue to match the following headings. Then add ideas of your own.**

starting the meeting • introducing yourself • asking someone to speak • asking for reactions • asking to speak/interrupting • agreeing • disagreeing • finishing the meeting

LANGUAGE

Describing trends

Upward movement		Horizontal movement		Downward movement	
to rise/grow to go up to increase	from … to … by …%	to keep stable to remain constant to even out	at …	to fall/drop to go down to decrease	from … to … by …%

Adverbs to indicate a degree of change

small change	medium change	large change
negligibly, slightly	significantly, considerably	sharply, dramatically

Indian sales figures over past 12 months
Hectolitres of beer sold (608)

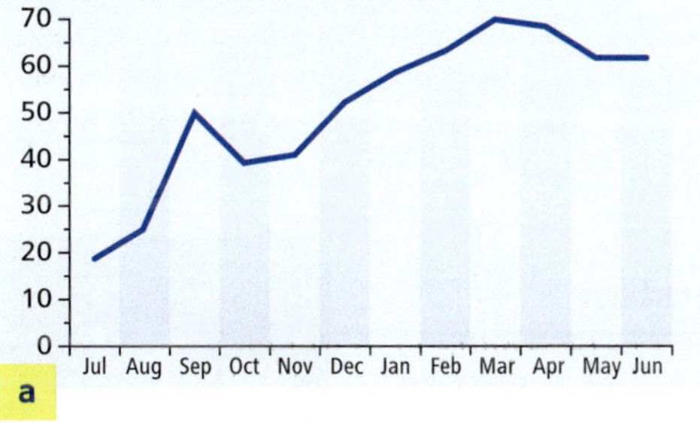

Indian sales figures previous year
Hectolitres of beer sold (338)

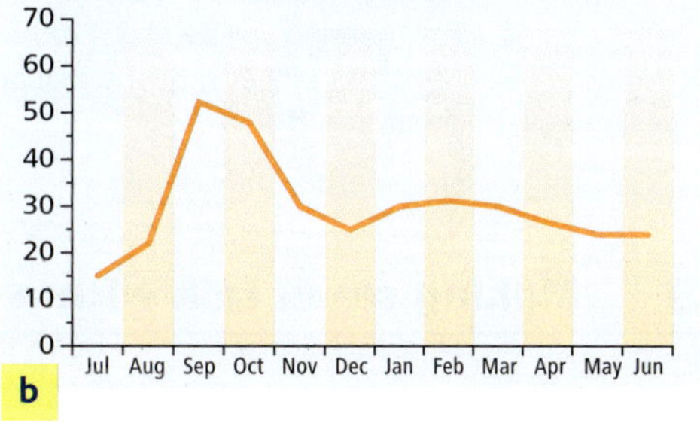

6 Describing sales figures

Look at line graph a and complete the text with the words from the box. Then describe line graph b in your own words.

at • between • decrease slightly • drop negligibly • from • grow considerably • increase slightly • remain constant • rise sharply • to

As you can see from this chart, in July last year, the sales figures stood …[1] 18 hectolitres. Between July and August, they …[2] and then …[3] by September. After that, between September and October, they …[4] from 50 …[5] 39 hectolitres. …[6] October and March, however, the sales figures …[7]. Then they …[8] from March to April, and again …[9] April to May. Between May and June, however, they …[10] at 62 hectolitres.

GRAMMAR

Question formation

1 **Has** he **gone** for lunch yet?
2 **Are** you **married**?
3 **Can** I **give** you any more information?
4 Who **installs** the equipment?
5 You knew. – **Did** you **know**?
6 Why **was** the meeting not **organized** earlier?

- Fragen werden im Englischen grundsätzlich mit einem Hilfsverb gebildet.
- Fragen mit den Hilfsverben *have/has/had*, *will* und *would* (1), mit einer Form von *be* (2), mit Modalverben (3) (Ausnahmen: Modalverben mit *to*, z. B. *want to*) und Fragen mit einem Fragewort, das Subjekt oder Teil des Subjekts ist (4) werden **ohne** das Hilfsverb *do* gebildet.
- Sollte kein Hilfsverb vorhanden sein, benutzt man eine form von *do* (*do/does/did*) (5).
- Fragen mit Fragewörtern beginnen mit *when, where, how, why, who, which* usw. (4, 6).

7 Practice

Write questions to match the following answers.

Example: Mr Winter works in the exports department. *Where does Mr Winter work?*

1 Mrs Jones is waiting at reception.
2 The director has brought the report.
3 No, we don't. We only have five sales representatives.
4 The meeting will be at 3 p.m.
5 The press officer met the managing director in the lift.
6 He phoned his secretary because his train was late.
7 No. Our brochures are only in English.
8 The managing director owns three houses.
9 He spent €500 on a business trip last weekend.
10 She flies to New York three times a year.

8 Making small talk with a visitor

14

Marco Kowalski is a trainee at Brewery-2-Brewery. Today his company has sent him to Düsseldorf Airport to collect Jane Seymour, the training officer from the Watermill Brewery in Cumbria, UK.

A **Read the tip box on page 57. Then listen and write down the things Marco *shouldn't* have said or asked.**

B **Listen again and make a list of the topics and questions mentioned which are suitable for small talk.**

C **Use the table in the tip box on page 57 to structure a small-talk conversation with a partner. Choose two or three small-talk topics from the box below.**

cars • celebrities • computers • culture • entertainment • fashion • food and drink • hobbies • music • sport • the weather • TV programmes

TIP

Making small talk

Native speakers of English always begin a meeting with a few minutes of small talk. It is considered impolite to leave it out. For this reason, it is important to understand how small talk works. Small talk is not about information; it is about creating a good atmosphere, so it is important to give more than just a short answer to a small-talk question, and, above all, to show interest in the other person by asking questions too. Always make sure you ask your partner the same question he or she has just asked you.
Try to avoid topics such as politics, religion, health and salaries, as they are usually not suitable topics for small talk.

Holidays

Person A

1 Question
- Did you have a nice holiday last year?

4 Answer
- Yes, thanks. We went to Italy.

6 Comment
- Yes, I love the heat.

Person B

2 Answer
- Yes, we did. We went to Spain.

3 Same question to Person A
- Did *you* have a nice holiday last year?

5 Comment
- I see we both like hot countries.

9 Role-play: discussing plans for a visit

KMK

Next year four trainees from the UK will be coming to Germany to shadow some employees at your company. Jane/Jack Seymour, their training officer, comes to discuss the details of the visit.

Use the agenda and the partner files at the back of the book to act out a meeting about the details.

English trainees' visit 20..
Meeting with Jane/Jack Seymour
Thursday, 27 September 20.., 9.30 a.m.

Agenda

1 Introductions
2 Date of visit
3 Accommodation for trainees
4 Return visit
5 AOB

Student A: turn to partner file 7 on page 119.
Student B: turn to partner file 9 on page 119.
Student C: turn to partner file 4 on page 118.

Student D

You are a trainee at your company (own name).
- Take the minutes of the meeting (see page 57)
- Inform the others of how you plan to send the minutes and when they will receive them

10 Taking the minutes

15

The English trainees from the Watermill Brewery in Cumbria, UK have just spent a week at Brewery-2-Brewery GmbH in Gelsenkirchen. Today is the last day of their stay, and they are at a meeting with German trainees to review their experiences and plan their next visit.

Matthias Beling writes the minutes of the meeting with the English trainees but makes five mistakes. Listen to the recording. Then find and correct his mistakes in your exercise book.

Brewery-2-Brewery, Gelsenkirchen, Germany
Meeting with English trainees from the Watermill Brewery in Cumbria, UK - Minutes

21 September 20..

Attendees:
Andrea Kegelmann, Training Officer at Brewery-2-Brewery,
Emma Jones (English trainee), Tony Harding (English trainee),
Sevda Yildiz (German trainee), Matthias Beling (German trainee)

Item 1
Review of the week
Tony Harding said the English trainees had very much enjoyed the week, especially the visit to the football match.

Emma Jones agreed and added that she now understands much better how people work in Germany and is glad she speaks German.

Matthias Beling and Sevda Yildiz said their English had improved because they spoke English to the English trainees all week.

Tony Harding said he was unable to start work at 6 a.m.

Item 2
Visit to the UK next year
Emma Jones asked if the German trainees would like to take part in a marathon in Cumbria next year to collect money for children with learning disabilities. She will be taking part in the marathon with Tony Harding. Matthias Beling and Sevda Yildiz both wish to run in the marathon.

Emma Jones said Jane Seymour would like to know whether the German trainees would prefer homestay or guest house accommodation. They decided that the German trainees would stay at a guest house with Wi-Fi.

Sevda Yildiz suggested that a similar charitable event for the local community should be organized in Germany.
This topic will be included on the agenda at next month's board meeting.

Everyone agreed the visit had been a great success.

AOB
None

11 Interaktion

Work with a partner and act out the role-play.

Situation

Mr/Mrs Kumar, a sales representative from New Delhi in India, has come to Germany to meet members of the export sales department of a brewery in Essen, which exports beer all over the world. The main reason for his/her trip is to give the employees a presentation on the Indian sales figures (see graphs below) for the last two years. When he/she arrives at the company, one of the members of the export sales department greets him/her and takes them to their office for a chat before the meeting.

Eigener Name

You work in the export sales department of the brewery in Essen. You meet Mr/Mrs Kumar at reception when he/she arrives and take him/her to your office for a chat. Use the following points to structure your conversation:

- Small talk
- Topic of presentation?
- Any time for sightseeing?
- Recommend local sights
- Offer to get information (internet)
- Describe German food
- Suggest some restaurants
- Invent extra details
- End conversation politely

Mr/Mrs Kumar

You are Mr/Mrs Kumar from India. One of the members of the export sales department picks you up at reception and takes you to their office for a chat. Use the following points to structure your conversation.

- Small talk
- Topic of presentation: description of sales figures (graphs)
- Free Saturday (flight on Sunday)
- Local sights?
- Opening hours of … (museum, gallery)?
- Directions to … (hotel, company, etc.)?
- Ticket for … (event)?
- Typical German food?
- Restaurants locally?
- Invent extra details
- End conversation politely

Indian sales figures over past 12 months

Hectolitres of beer sold (608)

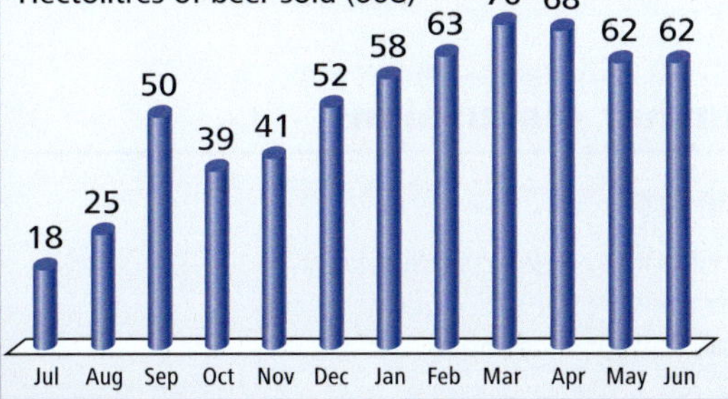

Indian sales figures previous year

Hectolitres of beer sold (338)

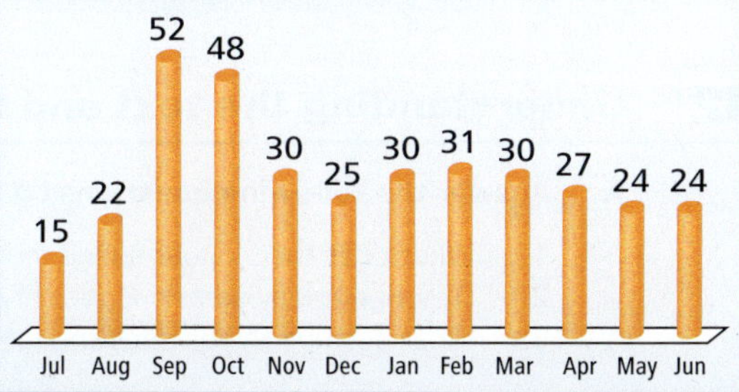

Facebook | Meistbesuchte… | Erste Schritte | Aktuelle Nachr… | Lesezeichen

I hate meetings and they stink

Extract from Dannielle Blumenthal's blog

I have had this happen to me SO many times.

I'm sitting in a meeting, and something is going on. Not something like an actual thing, but a tense, negative, or unproductive social dynamic between two people or within the group. I must be like the Terminator of sociology, because I can actually sense these situations, like in the movie where the heat-seeking goggles glowed red when there were humans around.

Bad vibes like this are why I usually hate meetings. Particularly because people are generally averse to working out conflict openly, so I have to watch it and not talk while it's actually going on. Just sit there and have to wait it out till it's over and I can be real again.

Here are some examples:

1. **asserting, without explanation, that an idea will definitely not work**
2. **completely ignoring a suggestion and going on to the next person**
3. **making the "Are you crazy?" face**
4. **rolling eyeballs behind someone's back**
5. **responding to idea with blank stare / silence**
6. **ganging up on someone (meeting their suggestion with two "No's")**
7. **laughing at someone's ideas**
8. **standing up and leaving the meeting without explanation**
9. **going into "deep chair slouch"**
10. **closing eyes**

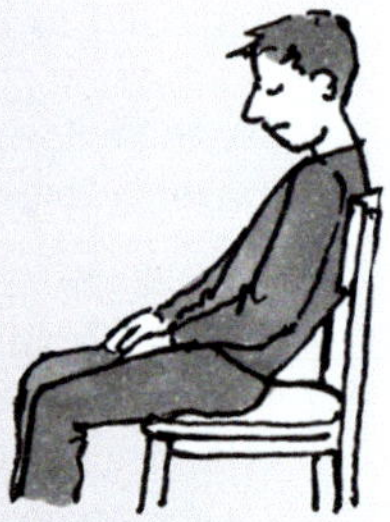

True, sometimes I find myself entertained by the goings-on. Sometimes I hear things that are funny, or the group gets along and there are decent jokes. There is always some gossip that's not too bad. Meetings can be educational as well, seriously. But more often than not, as soon as they get into full swing, I feel like I am nine years old again and watching a big family dinner degenerate.

Please don't start writing comments about how YOUR place of work has fantastic meetings and how you feel bad for me, OK? It's not about any particular agency; I've been around for more than a dozen years, both in government and outside it, and they all generally stink. As soon as you call it a 'meeting' and whip out the leather portfolios and play business card roulette, group dynamics start going into motion and the pain begins.

Source: abridged from: http://www.govloop.com/profiles/blogs/i-hate-meetings-and-they-stink

12 Understanding the text and further discussion

A Answer the following questions on the text.

1. What does the blogger spend most of her time doing at meetings?
2. Describe briefly what happens at the meetings the blogger describes.
3. What positive things does she mention about meetings?

B In groups, choose two of the following points and discuss them.

1. What rules of behaviour should be followed at meetings?
2. How can you make a meeting less boring?
3. Describe some meetings you have attended and explain why they were good or bad.

Kendal Cycles market their latest product

- Discussing marketing strategies
- The four Ps
- Presenting a logo for a new product

1 Warm-up

Work with a partner and use the words in the box to talk about the various marketing activities in the photographs.

advertising • analyse the potential market • booth • carry out research • exhibition • media • plan an advertising campaign • poster campaign • potential customers • represent a company • street • trade fair

a

b

c

d

2 Kendal Cycles launches a new bicycle

Kendal Cycles, based in the north of England, manufactures bicycles. The company would like to move into the European market and is planning to launch a new model of bicycle.

Read as the company's marketing manager gives the managing director a progress report about the development of the new model. Who is in charge of marketing: Keith or Alan?

Alan Right, now, Keith. Let's turn to the new sports line that we're planning for the European market.

Keith Let's do that. I must say, I think this project is fascinating. We could never have guessed five years ago that the old-fashioned type of sports bikes we've been making for years would help us get into the European market.

Alan No, but the fashion for city sports bikes is continuing to grow. A few years ago it was just a kind of cult in big cities like Berlin and Stockholm. But what made us decide to get into this market is the fact that now almost every major manufacturer on the Continent is selling bikes like these. And at enormous prices.

Keith OK, then. So where are we up to?

Alan Well, I would say that the marketing mix for the new bike line is coming together well. In terms of deciding upon the four Ps, we've made …

Keith Eh, product, price, place, promotion, right?

Alan Right. We've made good progress there. Let's look at the product first. If you just look at these design drafts here … OK, here you see that we've changed the look of our traditional sports design a bit. In effect, we're creating a new model using brighter, more modern colours and logos. Our market research shows that these are the important features of the single speeds which are selling well.

Keith Right. All looks very nice. Though I must say, I am old-fashioned. I prefer the traditional and very British look of the bikes we normally make.

Alan I know. But don't forget that the image of traditional, British quality is at the centre of our marketing strategy for the product.

Keith And quality at a fair price, right?

Alan Exactly. That brings us to the next P: price. Research among the young people who make up the market segment for the new product has convinced us that we have to go into the market at a lower price than the competition. Most of our competitors are selling their bikes at a price point somewhere between 700 and 900 euros. We want to price our single speeds at between 500 and 600 euros. That should almost guarantee us good sales.

Keith I'm very pleased to hear that. And what about place and promotion? What have you decided there?

Alan The report from our marketing consultants about which distribution channels we should be using – place – will be on my desk tomorrow. And I'm meeting with our advertising agency sometime this week to hear their recommendations regarding promotion. I should be able to give you more information on Monday.

Keith Very good, Alan. Thank you.

3 Understanding the dialogue

A Read the dialogue again and do the following tasks.

1 Say why Kendal Cycles has decided to market its single speed bikes in Europe.
2 Explain what the four Ps are.
3 Say in which ways the company is changing the look of its bikes for the European market.
4 Describe what role 'quality' will play in marketing the bikes.
5 Describe how the company wants to price its bikes in comparison with its competitors.
6 Explain what information the marketing consultants' report will contain.

B Match five of the definitions (1–7) to the appropriate terms highlighted in the dialogue. Two definitions are not needed. Discuss your results with your partner.

1 the level at which the price for a product is set
2 activities aimed at uncovering data from the market
3 a company hired by other companies to develop advertising for a product

4 independent advisors hired by companies to provide advice about specific marketing issues
5 a specific portion of the market at which a product will be aimed
6 the combination of activities and factors which are put together to sell a product
7 a clearly laid out plan for how to market a product

C Find two other two-word expressions in the dialogue which can be matched to the remaining definitions.

4 Which P?

WEBCODE **TRMU0601**

A Copy the table and decide which of the eight extracts below (from a text explaining the four Ps) belongs to which P.

The four Ps			
Product	Price	Place	Promotion

1 This is also known as a distribution channel.
2 There would be little point in carefully thinking through the design of a product, how to pitch it to potential customers, and where to make it available to them if you get this P wrong and ask the market to pay too much for it.
3 This has to be designed in the light of market research, which establishes what customers are likely to buy.
4 People in a position to buy exclusive, high-quality goods, for instance, may not respond well to being asked to pay what they consider too little.
5 This P also includes the public relations efforts that you engage in as well as the personal approaches of the sales people whose job it is to sell the product.
6 The question here is, are you going to sell your product through retail shops, direct to customers, by means of mail order catalogues, or on the internet?
7 This P includes, of course, advertising in all its forms.
8 Ideally, it has to feature a characteristic which could be seen as a unique selling point which distinguishes it from similar products sold by competitors.

B Look at the photos (a–d) and decide which of the four Ps they each represent.

c

5 The marketing consultants' report

A Complete the report sent to Alan by the marketing consultants (1–12) with the words or expressions from the box.

advertising • catalogues • consumer • data • flyers • inexpensive • in total • online • purchases • reported • responded • trend

B Now decide which heading belongs to each part of the report (a–e).

1 Consumer perceptions
2 Channels to market
3 Summary report
4 Types of promotion
5 Overview of findings

(a)

(b)

As agreed at the outset of the project, the market …[1] for the type of sports bikes in question is too new to allow research on the subject to rely on established sources of market data concerning consumer buying patterns. Due to this, …[2] for this survey was collected via a series of interviews with cyclists observed to be riding bikes of the type we are interested in. These …[3] interviews of 280 cyclists were held in six European cities in the course of June 20..: Paris, Berlin, Prague, Stockholm, The Hague and Copenhagen.

(c)

Unsurprisingly, 74% of interviewees …[4] having bought their bikes in bike shops. Interestingly though, 89% of those said that the bike shops where they made their …[5] were 'small and exclusive' as opposed to 'large and …[6]'. 19% of interviewees stated that they had bought their bikes …[7]. 7% of interviewees reported buying their bicycles from …[8].

(d)

…[9], some 63% of interviewees admitted buying their bikes directly in response to …[10]. Of these, 59% responded to advertisements in cycling magazines, 31% responded to outdoor advertising, such as …[11] and stickers, and 10% responded to internet advertising.

(e)

When asked to choose one of four expressions to describe themselves as cyclists, the interviewees …[12] in the following way:

Green and environmentally conscious biker: 21%
Sporty and fit: 17%
'Street' fashionable and cool: 36%
Road traffic militant: 26%

Recommendations

On the basis of these findings, which are covered in more detail in the course of this survey, we would like to make the following recommendations.

C **Work with a partner and read the list of recommendations below. Discuss which of them could be logically made on the basis of the survey's findings. Write down your results.**

1. The bulk of the advertising budget should be aimed at magazines for cyclists.
2. Every effort should be made to identify small bicycle 'boutiques' which sell exclusive bicycles.
3. Catalogues should be seen as the primary channel for marketing the new bikes.
4. Cyclists who regard themselves as green should be a key focus of any advertising.
5. By far the largest part of the advertising budget should be targeted at the internet.
6. Stickers which associate the bikes with street 'coolness' should be widely used.

D **Work with your partner to develop some further recommendations that could be made on the basis of the report. Discuss your results with the class.**

6 Designing a logo for the new bikes

Aspire Design, the company given the job of designing a logo for the sports bikes, send their suggestions to Kendal Cycles.

Read the excerpt from the brief given to Aspire Design and decide which logo best fits the brief and why.

> Our aim is to create a brand for our 'One more bike' sports bike range, which combines two basic elements:
> 1. the idea of traditional, British quality
> 2. street-level, alternative coolness
> There must be a balance between these factors in the brand image.

7 Arranging an appointment with the advertising agency KMK

Sie sind Fiona/Philip Watson und arbeiten bei Aspire Design. (Das ist die Firma, die für das Design des Logos und die Promotion der neuen Kendal-Fahrräder zuständig ist.) Verfassen Sie eine E-Mail an Alan Johnson (alan.johnson@kendal.cycles.co.uk), um einen Termin für die Präsentation Ihrer Ideen zu vereinbaren. Berücksichtigen Sie folgende Punkte:

- Anrede
- Tag: Mittwoch ist für Sie am Besten (am Liebsten Vormittags)
- Datum: Sie hätten am 4., 11. und am 24. des Monats Zeit
- Am 18. haben Sie leider einen anderen ganztägigen Termin
- Dauer der Präsentation: nicht länger als eine Stunde
- Ort: Gerne bei Ihnen in der Firma (29 Crawford Street, M3 2RT, Manchester) oder bei Kendal Cycles. Was immer für den Empfanger am Einfachsten ist
- höfliche Schlussformel

8 Aspire Design present their ideas to Kendal Cycles

Fiona from Aspire Design comes to Kendal Cycles to present their ideas.

16

A Listen to the first part of the dialogue and say which of the following audio-visual tools Fiona needs for her presentation.

a

b

c

d

e

f

17
KMK

B Hören Sie sich Fionas Präsentation an und beantworten Sie anschließend die folgenden Fragen auf Deutsch. Sie hören den Dialog zwei Mal.

1 Für welchen Bereich sollte man den größten Teil des Advertising-Budgets ausgeben?
2 Wo sollte man die Werbesticker platzieren?
3 Beschreiben Sie, wie die Cartoonfigur gemalt sein sollte.
4 Was für andere Beispiele dieser Art der Werbung kennt Alan?
5 Was schlägt Fiona vor, wie man die Sticker verwenden könnte?
6 Welche Rolle spielt das Internet bei dieser Kampagne?
7 Auf welche Art wird die englische Sprache auf den Werbestickern verwendet?

C Listen again and complete the recommendations from the dialogue with the words from the box.

advise • feel • recommend • recommendation • suggest • urge

1 We … that most of the advertising budget should be aimed at outdoor advertising.
2 The first … I want to make is that the sticker ads should feature a cartoon character who can be easily recognized.
3 We'd … you to do this as it will create an element of excitement.
4 There's another element to this idea which we would … you to use.
5 We … that you give them a reason to be interested.
6 We … you should use English on the stickers.

9 Language of presentations

PAGE 141

A The following list contains useful phrases for giving a presentation. Copy and complete the table below with appropriate phrases from the list.

Welcoming the audience	Introducing your topic	Structuring your presentation	Moving on to the next point	Describing visuals	Dealing with questions	Conclusion
…	…	…	…	…	…	…

1 I'd like to finish my presentation with … / That leads me on to my last point …
2 If you have any questions, please feel free to interrupt.
3 As you can see from the graph/chart/diagram/table, …
4 Thank you very much for listening.
5 The purpose/aim/objective of my presentation is to …
6 If you look at this slide, …
7 Hello everyone. It's good to see you all here.
8 I have divided my talk into three main parts. Part one deals with …
9 And now, let's move on to the next step/stage/point.
10 Ladies and gentlemen, I would like to welcome you to this presentation.
11 I'd prefer to answer any questions after finishing my presentation. / If you have any questions, I'd prefer to take them at the end.
12 Now let's take a look at … / Now let's turn to … / Now, moving on to our next point …
13 The first thing I want to talk about is … / Firstly …
14 Today I'm going to talk about …
15 My presentation consists of three parts. I'll begin with …, then move on to … and after that I'll tell you …
16 And finally, … / In conclusion … / To sum up … / That was a brief overview of …
17 I'd like to draw your attention to this chart.

17

B Which of the phrases does Fiona use in her presentation?

10 A quick feedback round

The day after the presentation, Alan sends Fiona some short feedback on her presentation.

Read his email and use some of the words in it to complete the handout on page 68.

As requested, here's some quick feedback on your presentation. First of all, I really liked some of your ideas and think that, on the whole, you were very well prepared.

A small point would be that I feel it would have been helpful to have been given a handout at the end. After all, 75% of what an audience hears will be forgotten within 24 hours – although I'm sure that won't apply in this case! Your slides were great as visual aids – very effective in keeping the audience's attention. You're going to email those to us, right?

My only real criticism is your intonation. I mean, you spoke loudly and slowly enough, but you could vary your speech more, and use stress and intonation effectively. But that's just a minor point.

Otherwise I was very impressed with how structured and direct your presentation was. You gave a good overview of what you wanted to talk about, and then got straight to the point. It was the perfect example of KISS!

10 TIPS FOR PREPARING AND GIVING A SUCCESSFUL PRESENTATION

1 …[1] thoroughly. Some experts say that one hour of preparation is needed for every minute of …[2].

2 Prepare …[3] for people to read after the presentation. Seventy-five per cent of what an …[4] hears will be forgotten within 24 hours.

3 Structure your presentation well. Try to give it a clear, three-part structure: introduction, main section and conclusion. The introduction should provide an …[5] of what you are going to say, the main section should lay this out in detail, and the conclusion should sum up what you said.

4 Use visual aids like graphs, flow charts and pictures to make your presentation more interesting. Visual aids have been found to be very …[6] in keeping your audience's …[7] and helping them to remember what you have said. An audience is 43% more likely to be persuaded by your arguments if you use good visual aids. Make sure that your slides are not overloaded with text, that everyone in the room can see them and that they can read the font on your slides.

5 Speak loudly and …[8] enough for everyone to hear.

6 Use your voice effectively. Vary the volume, pitch and pace of your voice, put stress on important words, and use …[9] to make your presentation sound lively and interesting enough to make sure your audience stays awake!

7 Keep it short and simple. The most effective presentations are as short as possible. In fact, one of the worst mistakes of a poor speaker is 'stealing' the listeners' time. You can best reach your objective by the principle of …[10]: 'Keep It Short and Simple'.

8 Take account of cultural differences. Many presentations to people from other countries or cultures fail because the presenter does not take such differences into account.

9 Make eye contact with your audience and only read from prompt cards.

10 Finally, practise your presentation. This builds your confidence and helps you to check your timing so that you don't 'steal' any of the listeners' time.

11 Designing and presenting the sticker ad campaign

Work in a small group and complete the following tasks.

1 Design an eight-part story about Bob and his bike on eight 'stickers'. You can use the stickers here to help you; these can appear at any point in your story. Keep the text on the stickers to a minimum.

2 Present your story to the class. Make recommendations as to why this will be the best way to market the bikes. The language for presentations (exercise 9) and the tips above will help you.

GRAMMAR

Modal verbs

1 We **can** spend more on internet advertising next year when the budget's bigger.
2 **Could** we think about doing some more market research?
3 We **will be able to** monitor how effective the online ads are by measuring clicks.
4 The ad is great. You **must** buy the product once you've seen it.
5 We **won't be allowed to** put up stickers in all areas.
6 We **should** talk about the results of the final market research.
7 The ads were so popular that we **had to** increase production to meet demand.
8 There was a spelling mistake on our advert. This **mustn't** happen again.

Modale Hilfsverben haben folgende Eigenschaften:

- Sie haben in allen Personen dieselbe Form.
- Bei der Verneinung gibt es zusammengezogene Kurzformen (5, 8).
- Alle außer *be able to* und *have to* werden mit dem Infinitiv ohne *to* verwendet.
- Wenn andere Zeitformen nötig sind, benutzt man die Ersatzverben *be able to* (für *can*), *be allowed to* (für *may*) und *have to* (für *must*) (3, 5, 7).
- Achtung: *must not* = nicht dürfen; *doesn't/don't have to* = nicht müssen.

Hilfsverb	Ersatzverb	Entsprechung
can	*be able to*	können
could		könnten/konnten
may		könnten
may	*be allowed to*	dürfen
might		dürfen
must	*have to*	müssen
shall		sollen
should		sollten
must not	*not be allowed to*	nicht dürfen
need		brauchen
needn't		nicht brauchen

12 Practice

Replace the German modal verbs in brackets with the most suitable modal verbs from the box above.

1 We … be sure that we have got the right price point before we launch the product. *(müssen)*
2 You … assume that you know what the market wants until you've carried out proper research. *(nicht dürfen)*
3 We … start market research as soon as we've decided which questions we need to ask. *(können)*
4 Management will … increase our advertising budget if we want to keep up with the competition. *(müssen)*
5 Tell Garry he … call me back until tomorrow morning. *(nicht brauchen)*
6 … I ask you to explain why you think we should change our brand image after so many years of success with it? *(könnten)*

13 Mediation

Zeigen Sie die Unterschiede von viralem Marketing und Guerilla-Marketing im Vergleich zu konventionellen Marketing-Strategien (Poster, Werbespots usw.).

MARKETING: THE FUTURE

Where it's all heading

Marketing is a straightforward business, right? You have a product, and know which markets to aim it at. Your advertising agency develops an ad campaign. And then you sit back and wait for customers to buy your product.

But if this summarizes how you understand the marketing process, you may need to think again. That's because there are several new approaches to marketing which are becoming increasingly important. Get up to speed with two of these by reading on.

Viral marketing

Marketeers have discovered people's willingness to pass on marketing messages to friends online, providing the message is packaged in an interesting way. The cost savings of this are clear. Viral marketing messages can take the form of videos, photos or soundclips which people send on to contacts for their entertainment value. It's often not made clear that these contain advertising and many people who post a viral marketing videos on their social networking site would be surprised that they have passed on an advertisement.

Nevertheless, this technique has been proved to work, and a company which successfully markets in this way will guarantee getting a "buzz" for its product.

Guerilla marketing

The idea here is to change the form in which marketing messages are presented and to get them out of the conventional advertising media. The technique aims at presenting marketing messages in a form that people do not expect to see them.

Guerilla marketing campaigns can take many forms and include, for example, putting your message on crudely produced (but cool) stickers or hiring groups of actors to play out a scene in public spaces which conveys your marketing message.

Even if these approaches to marketing are too unconventional for many companies, they offer significant cost savings over more conventional approaches. For this reason alone they are certain to be used by increasing numbers of companies.

►►►The changing face of marketing

1960s marketing executives were a glamorous lot who seemed to do most of their business over lunch, toasting their deals with Martini on ice. Marketeers in the 60s undoubtedly regarded themselves as the creators of powerful messages. At the same time, they saw consumers as being more than a little stupid and obedient.

But if the same approaches to marketing were used today, they would be ignored instantly by consumers. The latter are, of course, a good deal savvier than they were given credit for in the 1960s. As a result of realizing this, marketeers have changed their approaches, and marketing is carried out differently these days.

A quick glance at an ad from the 1960s and you can instantly see the literalness of its message. Back then, ads normally just spelled out what a product was and what it would do. Such was the marketeer's confidence in the power of their message to sway the consumer that this was thought to be enough. No attempt was made to engage with the consumer on an emotional level. At no point was it made clear that the consumer was an intelligent being who could make their own decision on the basis of their needs.

These days, of course, successful marketing campaigns put the consumer – and not the product – at the centre of their thinking. They do this not only at the level of designing products with specific categories of consumer in mind, but also at the level of getting consumers actively involved in creating the marketing buzz. If you need proof of this, just look at the use of social networking media on the internet which allows customers to display their affinity with products of their choosing.

In fact, some companies have taken consumer input a large step further. In recent years for instance, Ford has promoted its Fiesta brand by asking customers to contribute feedback about their cars in the form of photos, videos and blog posts on social networking sites.

Marketing and advertising certainly have changed a lot since the 1960s. Perhaps the key reason for this is the realization that consumers are in charge of the 'off' switch; they can change TV channels, turn the page, or close down that pop-up window faster than a 60s ad man could order another Martini. Marketeers have realized that, if they have this power, then consumers also need to be given a greater role in the marketing process.

14 Understanding the text

Answer the questions about the text in your own words.

1. How did marketeers in the 1960s view (a) themselves and (b) consumers?
2. Why is marketing carried out differently nowadays?
3. What were advertisements like in the 1960s and why?
4. Who or what do marketeers think about first nowadays when developing an advertising campaign? How do we know this?
5. What role can social networking sites play for companies in terms of advertising?
6. Why has the role of the consumer changed so much since the 1960s?

UNIT 7

Negotiating a deal

- Beginning negotiations
- Setting out terms
- Agreeing and disagreeing

1 Warm-up

A **Look at the cartoon. Then, in pairs, discuss other situations in which you have had to 'negotiate' (e.g. with your parents, with your friends, in your working life).**

B **Work with a partner and put this list of things you should do to prepare for a negotiation in order of importance. Say why you put them in this order.**

a Assess what your negotiating partner's aim in the negotiation might be – what does your negotiating partner want you to do?
b Assess whether your negotiating partner has the authority to make the final decision about the deal – can they sign the deal off?
c Think about where the possible areas of conflict might be – what are you and your negotiating partner potentially going to disagree about?
d Decide what your aim is in the negotiation – what do you want your negotiating partner to do for you?
e Make sure you have a 'fall-back position' – in which areas are you prepared to be flexible?
f Assess your negotiating partner's possible 'fall-back position' – in which areas will they potentially be prepared to be flexible?

C **What other things might you have to think about to prepare yourself for a negotiation?**

2 Making first contact

Sebastian Schaar is Sales Manager of Straßentaschen (Manufaktur) GmbH, a manufacturer of trendy shoulder bags and rucksacks based in Leipzig. He receives an email from an Australian wholesaler of sports fashion enquiring about his company's products.

A Read the email. Then explain in your own words ...

1 ... what Scott is enquiring about.
2 ... where a possible problem might lie and why.
3 ... what Scott wants Sebastian to do.

B Find words and expressions in the email which have the same meaning as these German words and expressions.

1 im Auftrag von
2 vorläufige Anfrage
3 Bedingungen
4 Absatzpotenzial
5 Rabatt
6 Versand
7 Zahlungsbedingungen

To: Sebastian Schaar
Copy:
Subject: **Enquiry about terms of a potential order**
From: Scott McGregor **Signature:**

Dear Sebastian Schaar

I am writing to you on behalf of my company, Inbound Sports Fashion Pty Ltd, to make initial enquiries about the terms of a potential order of your products.

I noticed on your website that the bags you produce are rather different from anything that can currently be found in the Australian market. That applies to the materials, colours and designs that you use. Due to this, I certainly feel that your products have sales potential here in Australia, which is why I'm enquiring about them.

One potential problem is that your list prices are rather high. The Australian market does not tend to tolerate high prices. The combination of your products being unknown and rather expensive could put us at an immediate disadvantage. They would also have to compete with all the usual well-known, high-quality sports brands. I would, therefore, like to enquire about the possibility of us receiving a discount on your list prices in order for us to try out your products in our marketplace.

Details of your shipment, credit and payment terms would also be appreciated.

I would be grateful if you could provide this information I am requesting as soon as possible, and look forward to hearing from you.

Yours sincerely

Scott McGregor

Purchasing Manager
Inbound Sports Fashion Pty Ltd

KMK **C** **Lesen Sie die Email erneut und entscheiden Sie ob die Aussagen (1–4) richtig oder falsch sind. Geben Sie jeweils eine kurze Begründung auf Deutsch. Beantworten Sie anschließend die Verständnisfragen (5–6) in kurzen Stichworten auf Deutsch.**

1. Scott hat bereits Anfragen an Sebastians Firma gestellt.
2. Scott ist sich sicher, dass man derzeit ähnliche Artikel in Australien kaufen kann.
3. Scott fürchtet, dass der hohe Preis zum Problem werden kann, weil man in Australien nicht viel Geld verdient.
4. Scott möchte wissen, ob Sebastian bereit wäre, ihm einen Sonderpreis für die Taschen zu machen.
5. Welche weitere Informationen benötigt Scott?
6. Wann benötigt er die Informationen?

D **In your own words, write down the positive and negative aspects of Straßentaschen's products for the Australian market.**

3 Beginning negotiations

A **A week later, Sebastian calls Scott. Read their conversation and say why it took Sebastian so long to contact Scott.**

Scott Scott McGregor here. What can I do for you?

Sebastian Hello, Scott. This is Sebastian Schaar from Straßentaschen in Germany.

Scott Ah, Sebastian. Good evening. Thank you for calling me.

Sebastian Well, it's my pleasure to call you. I found your enquiry really interesting but, unfortunately, I couldn't get back to you immediately since I was on holiday.

Scott No worries. We've caught up with each other now. I'm really keen to explore the points I raised in my email with you.

Sebastian Well, let's start with the price of our products. If you think about it, they are actually quite reasonably priced considering the quality of the material used in them and how detailed the design is. We could even come up with some exclusive designs for Australia.

Scott That would be great and, to be honest, I find your bags extremely interesting. They're really different to what's generally available here – great colours, great designs. And the materials you use certainly are unusual. But you have to admit that the prices are just too high for a market that has never even heard of the brand.

Sebastian Yes, but you could market them as being "exclusive" products, which they would be in this case.

Scott That's true, Sebastian, but you're missing the point – your products are more expensive than most of the high-end sports brands that sell well here.

Sebastian Hmm. I see what you mean. Listen, perhaps I can make this easy. We have a discount package which we offer importers who want to try out our bags in their domestic markets. Basically, if you order 4,000 bags – and it doesn't matter which models you choose – I can give you a discount on our list prices of 4%. We could wrap up a deal now and I could have your bags with you by next …

Scott Sebastian. Come on now, don't try to hard sell me. It just won't work. You won't be able to stampede me into saying yes right now, you know.

Sebastian All right. How would you like to play this, Scott?

Scott Basically, if you want to get into the Australian market, I'd say you do not only have to think about offering us discount, but you have to rethink your pricing strategy and bring down your prices.

Sebastian Hmm. Under normal circumstances I wouldn't really consider it, but in this case, we are obviously very interested in entering the Australian market, so as an exception, I'm willing to consider bringing down our prices more than usual for you to make this possible. But before I can do that, I'll need an idea of the size of order you'd be placing so that I can work out how much discount I'm able to offer.

Scott I'm afraid that won't be possible right away. Our Marketing Director is still looking at the issue. I'll have to wait for her decision before I can be specific about order size.

Sebastian Would it be possible to give me even just a ballpark figure?

Scott I'm afraid not. I really have to wait for that decision. I should be in a position to let you know by the end of next week.

Sebastian If you get back to me by the end of this week, while it's fresh in my mind and I'm still feeling generous, the discount might just be bigger!

Scott I hear what you're saying. Well, the ball certainly seems to be in my court, doesn't it?

Sebastian I'm afraid so.

Scott OK. Well, why don't we do it this way? I'll do my best to get back to you by the end of the week with a firmer idea of how many bags we'd order. Then we could speak again on the phone next week.

Sebastian That sounds good to me. I look forward to hearing from you again, Scott.

Scott And I look forward to speaking to you again, Sebastian.

B Match the words and expressions to the highlighted words in the dialogue.

1 to panic sb into doing sth
2 a rough idea/estimate
3 top-of-the-range
4 to investigate
5 mentioned
6 to force sb into buying sth

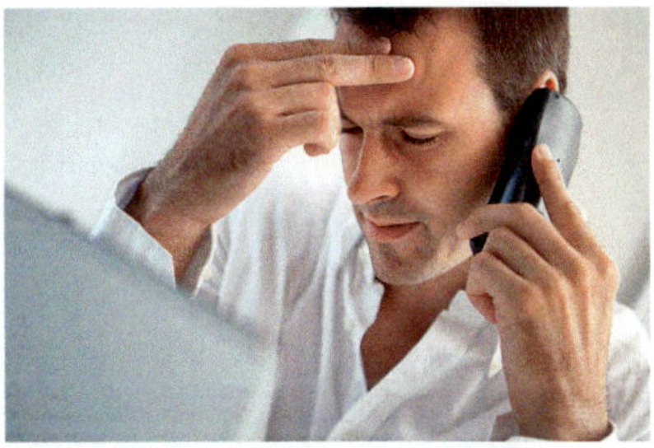

C Read again and finish these sentences in your own words. Try to use several facts for each one.

1 Sebastian thinks the price of the Staßentaschen products is reasonable because …
2 The two reasons that Scott gives for the price of the products being too high are that …
3 Sebastian tries to offer Scott …
4 Scott suggests that Sebastian …
5 Sebastian can't offer Scott a firm discount until …
6 It's up to Scott to …

4 Expressions for negotiating: key phrases

A Rearrange the words to make key phrases used in the dialogue.

1. this / can / easy / make / perhaps / I
2. possible / won't / that / afraid / be / away / right / I'm
3. me / it / possible / would / just / figure / to / give / even / a / ballpark / be / ?
4. next / should / be / in / a / I / to / position / end / week / you / know / the / of / let / by
5. hear / I / saying / you're / what
6. the / my / certainly / court / ball / to / back / be / in / seems
7. this / don't / why / we / way / it / do / ?

B Read the dialogue again and make a list of all of the expressions for negotiating that are useful to you in your exercise book. Include the phrases in exercise A.

Expressions for negotiating

Yes, but ...
That's true, but ...

TIP

Finding the right tone

Business people often negotiate in a robust fashion. This can be reflected in the language they use:
Come on now, ***don't try to hard sell me.***
You won't be able to ***stampede me into saying yes*** *right now, you know.*

It is possible to use sentences like these during negotiations; the key to doing so is *not* to sound hostile or unfriendly. Provided you keep your tone of voice friendly, you will not upset your negotiating partner.

On the other hand, if you are going to reject an offer, do not simply say "No". This can come across as being rude. Instead, add other words to soften the tone:
No, I'm afraid that won't be possible.
No, unfortunately I can't really agree to that.

5 Role-play: negotiating

Work with a partner and act out the role-play. Aim to use at least four of the phrases from exercise 4 and remember to keep your tone friendly but firm.

Student A: read the partner file on this page.
Student B: turn to partner file 6 on page 118.

Student A

You are a buyer for a German chain of sports shops and are interested in buying some sports shoes from Urban Terrain based in the UK. Call the sales manager of Urban Terrain and make an enquiry.

- Ask how much discount you could expect
- Enquire about credit and payment terms
- Let your negotiating partner know that you cannot be pressured into making a quick decision
- You are not in a position to say how many pairs of shoes you want to order at the moment

6 Setting out the terms

KMK

Sebastian beschließt Scott eine Email zu senden, in der er seine Bedingungen nennt, bevor sie wieder telefonieren.

Verwenden Sie die Notizen, die Sebastian sich gemacht hat, um die Email zu schreiben.

Email an Scott McGregor
Folgendes kann angeboten werden:

- *14 % Rabatt, wenn er 2000 Taschen bestellt*
- *Zahlungsbedingungen: 50 % Vorauszahlung (cash in advance) und 50% der Zahlung innerhalb von 30 Tagen – abgesichert durch Dokumentenakkreditiv (documentary credit)*
- *Spezielles Verkaufs-Set für Geschäfte erhältlich*
- *Clubmitgliedschaft im TaschenClub für Kunden möglich*
- *Rabatte für Limited Editions höher*

7 Let's get down to business ...

WEBCODE **TRMU0701**

18

Scott organizes a video conference with Sebastian to negotiate the terms of his order.

Listen to their negotiation, take notes and use them to answer these multiple choice questions.

1 Scott can't accept Sebastian's offer because he disagrees with …
a … one point included in it.
b … several points included in it.
c … all the points in it.

2 Initially, Scott does not want to order more than …
a … 1,500 bags.
b … 1,400 bags.
c … 1,900 bags.

3 He also wants an initial …
a … 80% discount and payment terms of 16 days.
b … 18% discount and payment terms of 60 days.
c … 8% discount and payment terms of 16 days.

4 To get a 15% discount, Scott would have to increase the order size to …
a … 1,150 bags.
b … 1,850 bags.
c … 1,085 bags.

5 Scott points out that the purpose of the first order is to …
a … try out the new bags in Australia.
b … promote the new bags in Australia.
c … fill up their stocks.

> **TIP**
> ### Figures
> When dealing with figures in English, remember that commas and dots are used differently:
>
> BE: 8,270 (comma after thousands)
> DE: 8.270 (point after thousands)
>
> BE: 7.85 (point in decimals)
> DE: 7,85 (comma in decimals)

8 Expressions for negotiating 2: agreeing and disagreeing

18

A Complete the expressions for agreeing and disagreeing from the dialogue with the words from the box. Then listen to the CD again to check your answers.

afraid • afraid not • agree to • agree with • go along with • management • no way • option • position • understand

1 I'm afraid I don't … some of the conditions you set out.
2 I can't … the volume of the order you're suggesting.
3 There are also a number of points I'm not in a … to agree to.
4 I'm afraid there's … I could offer you 18% discount on only 1,500 bags.
5 I'm … I couldn't say yes to 1,800 units.
6 I'm sorry, but I don't feel I can … that.
7 OK. I ... your position.
8 My … won't agree to that.
9 I'm …, no.
10 That means that 60 days is not really an … .

B Now copy the language box below into your exercise books and complete it using the expressions in exercise A. Add your own ideas.

LANGUAGE

Expressions for negotiating: agreeing and disagreeing

Agreeing	Disagreeing
That's absolutely correct.	I'm afraid I don't agree with you.
You're right.	I can't agree to the …
I couldn't agree more.	

C In pairs, take turns formulating and turning down offers using the information below. Use as many phrases from exercise A as possible.

Example: give 10% discount – order 1,500 units.

1 pay 70% cash up front – give 60-day payment terms on the remainder
2 pay cash up front – give 12% discount
3 increase discount by 5% – increase order size to 4,000 units
4 17% discount – agree to 60-day payment terms
5 pay cash on delivery – give 3% discount
6 order 2,400 units – give 14% discount

9 Contracts and warranties

When Sebastian and Scott finally settle their negotiations, Sebastian sends Scott through the warranty for the products and the contract between the two companies.

Read the definition of a contract and a warranty and then do the tasks below.

contract a legally binding agreement between two or more persons or parties. One party makes an offer (with specific terms and agreements) that the other party accepts.

warranty a written agreement in which a company selling something promises to repair or replace the product free of charge if there is a problem with it. This, however, must take place under certain conditions and within a given period of time.

A **How would you translate *contract* and *warranty* into German?**

B **Read the sentences below and decide whether they are from the contract or the warranty that Sebastian sends to Scott.**

1 The buyer agrees to the purchase of said goods for the sum of 75,652 euros (in words – seventy five thousand, six hundred and fifty-two).

2 Locks and fasteners are intended only to prevent accidental opening, and cannot necessarily prevent theft of product or its contents.

3 This does not cover damage that results from accident, misuse, abuse (including damage caused by airlines or other carriers), normal wear and tear, or theft.

4 Straßentaschen (Manufaktur) GmbH (hereafter the seller) and Inbound Sports Fashion Pty Ltd (hereafter the buyer) agree to the following terms and conditions regarding the purchase of 1,800 (in words – one thousand eight hundred) bags from the City and Trend range (hereafter the goods) as binding.

5 This covers any defects in materials or workmanship for two years from date of purchase.

6 The goods shall be delivered CFR in two separate shipments.

7 The first shipment shall consist of 1,000 (in words – one thousand) bags from the City and Trend range (full details below).

GRAMMAR

If-sentences

if-clause	main clause
1 simple present	**will-future**
If you **order** 200 units more,	I **will be able to** increase your discount by 3%.
2 simple past	**conditional (would + infinitive)**
If you **increased** the order size to 1,850 bags,	I **would be able to** offer you a discount of 15%.
If you **said** yes to a smaller discount,	I **might be able to** offer you better payment terms.
3 past perfect	**past conditional (would + present perfect)**
If you **hadn't raised** your prices,	we **wouldn't have asked for** a discount.

- *If*-Sätze vom Typ 1 drücken eine erfüllbare Bedingung aus. Beachten Sie die Zeitenfolge: Der *if*-Nebensatz steht im **simple present**, im Hauptsatz steht das **will-future** (1).
- *If*-Sätze vom Typ 2 drücken eine möglicherweise erfüllbare Bedingung aus. Beachten Sie die Zeitenfolge: Der *if*-Nebensatz steht im **simple past**, im Hauptsatz wird das **conditional (would + infinitive)** verwendet (2), wobei *would* durch *could*, *might*, oder *should* ersetzt werden kann.
- *If*-Sätze vom Typ 3 drücken eine Bedingung aus, die nicht erfüllt wurde. Beachten Sie die Zeitenfolge: Der if-Nebensatz steht im **past perfect**, im Hauptsatz wird das **past conditional (would + present perfect)** verwendet (3).
- Steht der *if*-Nebensatz an erster Stelle, wird er vom Hauptsatz durch ein Komma getrennt.

10 Practice

A Put the verbs in brackets into the correct form to complete the sentences.

1 I would have to rethink my offer if you … delivering Ex Works. (insist on)
2 If you agreed to longer payment terms, we … finalize the deal more quickly. (might be able to)
3 The 5% discount will not be a problem if you … pay cash in advance. (decide to)
4 If you send me the details by email this afternoon, I … show them to my boss tomorrow morning. (be able to)
5 If you had agreed to a meeting with me, we … the size of our order. (increase)
6 There … a delay in payment if you had sent me the contract by Wednesday. (not be)

B Translate the following into English using if-sentences. Remember to use commas where necessary.

1 Ich würde öfter bestellen, wenn Sie den Preis um 12 % senken würden.
2 Wenn wir uns heute Nachmittag in diesen Punkten nicht einig werden *(agree on)*, kommen wir nicht zu einem Vertragsabschluss.
3 Wir könnten besser verhandeln, wenn wir wüssten, welchen Preis unsere Konkurrenten anbieten.
4 Wenn Sie den Preis nicht senken, werde ich nicht bei Ihnen bestellen können.
5 Wenn Sie die Informationen früher geschickt hätten, hätte ich die Bestellung schon abschicken können.
6 Wenn die Bestellung größer gewesen wäre, hätte Ihnen meine Kollegin 15 % Rabatt angeboten.

11 Interaktion

Work with a partner and act out the role-play.

Situation

Karl/a Edmonsson, a buyer for a chain of sports shops in Denmark comes to Germany for a meeting with Steffen/Stefanie Görtz, who works in the sales department of Get Inline GmbH, which manufactures inline skates. They discuss an order that the Danish sports chain wishes to place with the company. Each of them has an aim for the discussion and they negotiate hard to try to get what they want.

Karl/Karla Edmonson

Your aim in the negotiation as well as your fall-back positions are detailed below.

- Wholesale price of skates: €42.00
- Aim:
  - order of initial 200 pairs of skates at 20% discount on wholesale price
- Fall-back positions (areas of flexiblity):
  - 200 pairs of skates at only 15% discount and secure payment terms for the entire bill of 30 days
  - or: 60% cash on delivery, with the remaining 40% payable within 30 days
- Negotiate hard and try to get the best deal for your company.

Steffen/Stefanie Görtz

Your aim in the negotiation as well as your fall-back positions are detailed below.

- Wholesale price of skates: €42.00
- Aim:
  - to sell a minimum of 200 pairs of skates at a maximum of 15% discount
  - entire bill should be settled upon delivery of the skates
- Fall-back positions (areas of flexiblity):
  - no flexibility on order size and discount, but some flexibility regarding payment terms
  - ideally: 80% cash on delivery with the remainder payable within 30 days, but you could accept 60% cash on delivery, with the remaining 40% payable within 30 days
- Negotiate hard and try to get the best deal for your company.

12 Produktion

Sie arbeiten bei der BikeAway GmbH in Oldenburg. Die Interessiertin Frau Bridges möchte von Ihrer Firma Kinder-Fahrräder bestellen. Sie haben die Zahlungs- und Lieferbedingungen sowie eventuelle Rabatte mit ihr am Telefon bereits besprochen. Jetzt schreiben Sie ihr eine E-Mail.

Ihre Aufgabe besteht darin, die Anrede sowie die E-Mail einschließlich Betreff zu formulieren. Berücksichtigen Sie in Ihrer E-Mail folgende Punkte:

- Datum, Anrede, Betreff
- Bedanken Sie sich für das Telefonat und bestätigen Sie die Bestellung und Zahlungsbedingungen:
  - Bestellung: 100 Fahrräder à 55,00€
  - Zahlungsbedingungen: 12% Rabatt, wenn die Kundin 80% des Gesamtbetrags gegen Nachnahme und den Rest innerhalb von 30 Tage bezahlt
- Informieren Sie die Kundin, dass Sie den Rabatt auf 15% erhöhen können, wenn sie ihre Bestellung auf 150 Fahrräder erhöht und die Bestellung innerhalb 48 Stunden bestätigt wird
- Informieren Sie die Kundin über einen weiteren Vorteil einer Kundschaft bei Ihrer Firma:
  - Kein Mindestbestellwert nötig. Es kann bestellt werden, was und wann man will
- Formulieren Sie einen geeigneten Schlusssatz und verdeutlichen Sie, dass das Rabatt-Angebot nur 48 Stunden gültig ist

Negotiating in the global business environment

A story of what can go wrong when negotiators forget about cultural differences

Our story begins when Seonel, a South Korean electronics company, was looking for a logistics company to handle the European end of its operations. It turned first to LogEx, a large logistics provider based in Rotterdam.

Kim Khan, Seonel's distribution manager, takes up the story: "We wanted to do business with a logistics company which was experienced enough in the European context to handle all our distribution there. We were looking for a partner who could do this effectively and minimize the chance of service disruptions."

Things seemed to get off to a good start. The Seonel team travelled to Rotterdam to meet LogEx managers at their headquarters. "We were impressed by the extent of their operations and their obvious expertise," reports Mr Khan.

However, when the two negotiating teams sat down at the conference table, things started to go wrong. "The LogEx team seemed to have decided that we needed them more than they needed us. They moved straight into a hard-nosed negotiating mode which really took our breath away. They got down to business immediately and offered terms which left no room for discussion. We found them more than a little rude."

Yes, but business is business. Isn't this the way it's done the world over? Mr Khan disagrees. "In the end, business partnerships are always based on hard bargaining. The problem was, we were just at the very beginning of our relationship, and expected something else."

Business people from South Korea and its neighbouring countries are used to a relatively long getting-to-know-you phase before hard negotiating starts, explains Mr Khan. "Personal relationships are important to us. We need to be able to answer the question: 'Is this a person I would like to do business with?' before negotiations can progress. LogEx's aggressive attitude almost put us off the whole deal."

So how does the story end? "Well, we told the LogEx negotiators that we wanted to break for something to eat. It was almost time for dinner anyway, so we suggested going to a Korean restaurant we had seen on the way from the airport. After a good dinner – and a few rounds of rice wine – we were able to say: 'Yes, these are guys we would like to work with.' LogEx now run our European logistics to our enormous satisfaction. And they did, in the end, concede a number of points at the negotiating table, by the way."

13 Thinking about cultural differences in negotiations

A **Make a list of the mistakes made by the LogEx negotiators in their dealings with Seonel and explain to your partner why these mistakes happened.**

B **Work in a group and think about what problems people from other cultures might have when operating in the German market. Then brainstorm a list of tips you could give to business people who want to do business in Germany.**

Examples: *calling people by their last name, shaking hands on arrival, etc.*

Exports and insurance

- Transporting goods and services
- Understanding shipping documents
- Insurance

1 Warm-up

A Describe the pictures (a–f) with the help of the words from the box.

costs • documentation • export regulations • packing • risks • transport

a

b

c

d

e

f

B With a partner, write down what experience you have had with each of the six categories above.

2 Transporting goods and services

A With a partner, make a list of as many means and modes of transport as you can think of and what they are used for. Compare your results with others.

B Copy the table below into your exercise book and complete it with the advantages and disadvantages of the modes of transport that you listed in exercise A.

Mode of transport	*Advantages*	*Disadvantages*
air	*fast* *safe* *…*	*airports expensive to build* *pollution (carbon footprint)* *…*

C **Choose two of the modes of transport and make word spiders to show what sort of things they are used to transport. Use the words in the box and your own ideas.**

a barge • bulky objects • cable cars • chemicals • data • food • gas • heavy objects • livestock • oil • people • raw materials • sand • vehicles

3 Packing the goods

A **Use a dictionary to match the words with the photos (a–h).**

1 bale
2 barrel/cask
3 chest
4 drum
5 pallet
6 sack/bag
7 plastic wrap
8 canister

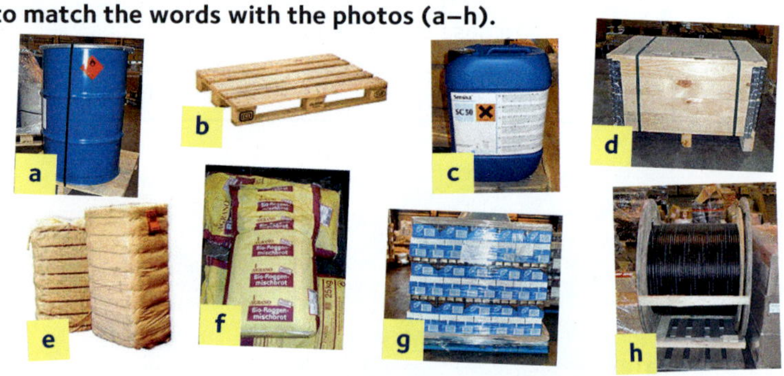

B **In groups, discuss what the various containers and materials can be used for.**

4 Dealing with a purchase order

TURCK
Industrielle Automation

Joanna Masters is studying business at York College in the UK. This week she has come to Hans Turck GmbH & Co. KG in Mülheim to shadow Cornelia Schweiger in the export department.

A **Read the conversation between Joanna and Cornelia about an order that Hans Turck has just received. Then say which three companies are involved.**

Cornelia … and now we're going to look at a purchase order we've received from India for goods to be supplied to Saudi Arabia.

Joanna How complicated! Is it always like this?

Cornelia It's nothing special these days. We have production facilities in 27 countries and representatives in another 60, so we're pretty international. In this case we've got a purchase order from ABB Limited in India. They want us to supply sensors to be used in a steel mill in Saudi Arabia.

Joanna But why is the order from India if the mill is in Saudi Arabia?

Cornelia ABB India is supplying some of the technology for the steel mill in Saudi Arabia. It's going to be built by a big Indian steel company called Arcelor Mittal in Saudi Arabia.

Joanna So is Arcelor Mittal the buyer?

Cornelia No, the buyer is ABB in India.

Joanna Ah yes, of course!

Cornelia As you said, it's complicated. But don't worry, you'll see what I mean when you've studied the purchase order. Here's a copy of the most important part with all the details. As you can see, it's a third party order, which means we don't supply to the company which places the order, but to another one.

Joanna I see.
Cornelia Now let's take a closer look at the details on the purchase order. We got it yesterday on 10 May, so we have to confirm it by 13 May. Now, can you find the terms of delivery?
Joanna Yes, here they are. They're Free Carrier.
Cornelia Yes, very good. The exact Incoterm is FCA – Free Carrier Mülheim an der Ruhr. This means the carrier comes to us and collects the goods at our works.
Joanna But isn't that Ex Works?
Cornelia No, there's a big difference. I'll explain it to you later.

B **Take notes on the following points and then use the information to write a summary of the purchase order. Begin like this:** ***ABB Limited in India has ordered ...***

1. *the goods ordered*
2. *the company supplying the goods*
3. *the company ordering and paying for the goods*
4. *the company which will use the goods*
5. *the terms of delivery*

5 Understanding a purchase order

KMK **A** **Lesen Sie das Versanddokument auf S. 86 und entscheiden Sie, ob die folgenden Aussagen (1–4) richtig oder falsch sind. Begründen Sie Ihre Antwort. Beantworten Sie anschließend die Verständnisfragen (5–8) in kurzen Stichworten auf Deutsch.**

1. Die Bestellung wird in Rupien bezahlt.
2. Der Käufer hat mehr als 30 Tage, die Rechnung zu bezahlen.
3. Die Versicherungskosten sind in der Incoterm®-Regel FCA inbegriffen.
4. Die Speditionsfirma ist schon bekannt.
5. Wie viele Sensoren wurden bestellt?
6. In welchem Land werden die Sensoren hergestellt?
7. Wer bezahlt die Zollgebühren?
8. Wie hoch wird die Strafe sein, wenn die Ware 16 Wochen zu spät geliefert wird?

B **Find words or phrases in the purchase order to match the following.**

1. the money used in a country
2. the person or company that sells the goods to the customer
3. the tax paid on goods brought into a country
4. a document showing how much the customer must pay for goods or services
5. a transport company
6. guarantee
7. punishment
8. a document showing where the goods are from
9. putting goods from different purchase orders in the same container
10. a transport document for goods sent by air

ABB						
Purchase Order – Direct Material – Third Party						
PO Number: 3195589			PO Date: 05 May 20..			Currency: EUR
Supplier: Hans Turck GmbH & Co. KG Postfach 45466 Mülheim Germany						
Item	**Quantity**	**Description**	**Item No.**	**Unit Price EUR**	**Discount**	**Value EUR**
1	132	BI15-CP40-VPX2/S100 Inductive sensor Country of origin: DE	15045	107.74		14,221.68
Total value						

Customer:	Arcelor Mittal Jubail, PO Box 100000, SA-31952 Jubail 2 Industrial City, Saudi Arabia
1 Price basis:	INCOTERM - FCA Mülheim a.d. Ruhr ABB LIMITED dispatch instructions
2 Customs duties:	By end customer
3 Terms of payment:	100% payment within 30 days from date of invoice
4 Contractual delivery date:	As per order confirmation date
5 Packing, forwarding, freight, insurance:	Included in FCA price. Details of freight forwarder will be communicated with dispatch instructions
6 Warranty:	24 months from date of dispatch OR 18 months from date of commissioning, whichever is earlier
7 Inspection at supplier's works:	Not applicable. Routine test certificates to be sent to ABB and approval from ABB required prior to dispatch
8 Shipping marks:	INABB/PAMC-SCM/PO#3191369468
9 Penalty for late delivery:	0.5% per week; Maximum 7.5% of total order value
10 Documents required for payment:	a. FCR (forwarder's certificate of receipt) b. invoice copy c. packing list d. certificate of origin e. test certificates
11 Order acknowledgement:	Please send your order acknowledgement within 3 days of receipt of purchase order
12 Contact person:	Mr Nirogi Chowdhury, Project and Engineering Management, Peenya, India
13 Bundling:	Not permitted
14 Dispatch documents:	Three sets of invoices, packing instructions, air waybills and test reports shall be sent to us directly
15 Address for communication:	ABB Limited, Peenya Industrial Estate, Peenya, Bangalore 560058, India

6 Organizing a freight forwarder

The consignment of sensors is now ready to be shipped, but Hans Turck have still not received details of the freight forwarder, so Cornelia Schweiger phones ABB in India.

A Complete the dialogue with the words from the box.

airworthy • consignee • dimensions • freight • gross • Incoterm • LCL • net • packages • tare • volume • width

Yamini Good morning, ABB Limited. How can I help you?
Cornelia Good morning, it's Cornelia Schweiger from Hans Turck in Germany. Could I speak to Mr Chowdhury, please?
Yamini I'm sorry, he's off sick this week. I'm standing in for him. My name is Yamini Rawat.
Cornelia Oh, I see. Well, I'm calling to ask for the name of the freight forwarder who will be picking up the consignment of sensors for Archelor Mittal in Saudi Arabia.
Yamini Could I have the order number, please?
Cornelia Yes, it's 3195589 dated 5 May.
Yamini Oh yes, Mr Chowdhury left me a note to contact a forwarder, so I'll do that today. We normally use Kühne and Nagel for Germany. Let me just make a note of the details. So we're the consignor and Arcelor Mittal is the …[1]. OK, so is it a full container load or less than a container load?
Cornelia …[2] – less than a container load.
Yamini And how many …[3] are there?
Cornelia Just the one.
Yamini OK, can you give me the …[4] weight and the …[5] weight, please?
Cornelia Yes, 100 kilos and 72 kilos.
Yamini So that gives us a …[6] weight of 28 kilos. Right. Now what about the …[7]? Length by …[8] by height?
Cornelia It's 80 by 80 by 80 centimetres.
Yamini OK, and the …[9]?
Cornelia Nought point three eight four cubic metres.
Yamini Fine, I've got that. What's the …[10], please?
Cornelia FCA Mülheim an der Ruhr.
Yamini Oh yes, I can see that in the system. And will the goods be in …[11] packing?
Cornelia Oh yes, because you'll probably fly them to Saudi Arabia, won't you?
Yamini Yes, we'll send them to Dammam Airport in Saudi Arabia as air …[12].
Cornelia Good. Could you let me have the final details in writing as soon as possible?
Yamini Yes, I'll do that. I'll email you the details …

B Write Yamini's email to Cornelia listing all the important details and explaining that Hans Turck will be contacted by Kühne + Nagel in the near future.

TIP

British and American measures

In the UK and the USA measures differ from the German metric system:

1 inch = 25.4 mm	1 sq foot = 929.03 cm^2	1 cubic inch = 16.4 cm^3
1 foot = 30.48 cm	1 sq yard = 0.836 m^2	1 cubic foot = 0.028 m^3
1 yard = 0.914 m		1 cubic yard = 0.765 m^3
1 mile = 1.609 km		

7 Measures, weights and dimensions

Look at the container and the figures and do the tasks below.

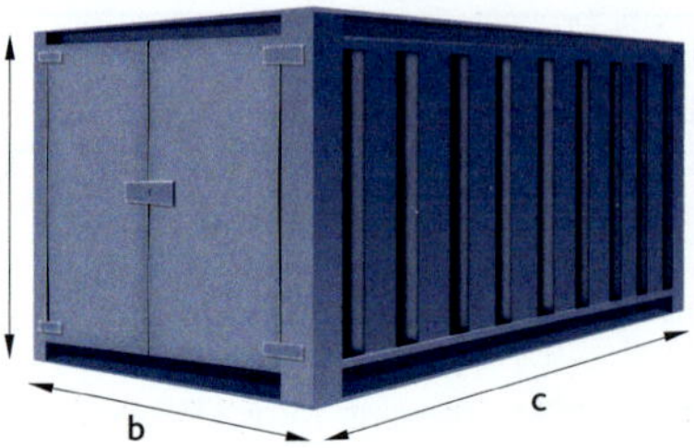

Internal measurements		
Length 5890 mm	Width 2340 mm	Height 2370 mm
External measurements		
Length 6050 mm	Width 2430 mm	Height 2590 mm
Weight		
1,980 kg		
20' Container		
max gross weight	20,320 kg	44,800 lbs
tare	1,980 kg	4,365 lbs
max net weight	18,340 kg	40,435 lbs max payload
FCL	Full container load	
LCL	Less than a container load	

1 Label the dimensions (a–c) of the container shown.
2 Give the volume of the container in cubic metres (m^3).
3 Explain how to work out (a) the tare and (b) the maximum payload.

8 Shipping documents

PAGE 121–126

A **Read the table opposite showing information about the most used documents in international trade. Then explain which ones Hans Turck GmbH & Co. KG will need for this consignment and why.**

B **Use the information from the table and the words from the box to complete this description of a bill of lading (B/L).**

apparent • carriage • clean • condition • foul • negotiable • receipt • title

The bill of lading is a document of … 1, which means the holder can sell the goods to someone else. Documents which can be traded are described as … 2. A B/L is also a contract of … 3 and a … 4 for the goods. Before shipping the goods, it is important to make sure that they are in … 5 good order and … 6. If nothing is missing and there is no sign of damage, the B/L is … 7. If the goods are not in order, the B/L is … 8.

C **Use the information in the table opposite to decide if the following statements are true or false. Explain each of your answers.**

1 A bill of lading can be sold.
2 Goods sent by road are accompanied by a B/L.
3 A B/L, an air waybill and a consignment note have three features in common.
4 A multimodal B/L isn't always a document of title.
5 The certificate of origin is issued by the buyer's chamber of commerce.
6 The buyer pays the commercial invoice.
7 The packing list shows where the goods were manufactured.

Document	German	Features
Bill of lading (B/L) – sea transport	*Konnossement*	▪ document of title (negotiable – ownership is transferable) ▪ receipt for the goods ▪ contract of carriage ▪ The B/L is "clean" if the goods are in apparent good order and condition. It is "foul" if they are not.
Air waybill (AWB) – air transport	*Luftfrachtbrief*	▪ not a document of title (non-negotiable – ownership is not transferable) ▪ receipt for the goods ▪ contract of carriage
Consignment note – rail or road transport	*Frachtbrief*	▪ not a document of title (non-negotiable – ownership is not transferable) ▪ receipt for the goods ▪ contract of carriage
Multimodal B/L – sea, air, rail or road transport	*Multimodaler Ladeschein*	▪ can be document of title (negotiable or non-negotiable) ▪ receipt for the goods ▪ contract of carriage
Insurance certificate	*Versicherungs-schein*	▪ proves that goods are insured ▪ used in documentary credit transaction (see terms of payment on page 130)
Certificate of origin	*Ursprungszeugnis*	▪ shows where goods are from ▪ issued by Chamber of Commerce in exporter's country
Commercial invoice	*Handelsrechnung*	▪ request for payment ▪ shows the price the buyer has to pay for the goods
Pro-forma invoice	*Proforma-Rechnung*	▪ not a request for payment ▪ shows how much the buyer will have to pay for the goods
Packing list	*Packliste*	▪ contains details of goods (number of packages, weights, dimensions)

9 Shipping labels

Match the labels in the box to the shipping symbols (a–h).

Do not use forklift • Do not stack • Flammable • Fragile • Keep dry •
This way up • Toxic • Use no hooks

10 Who pays for …?

PAGE 128 WEBCODE TRMU0801

A Study the three Incoterms® 2010 Rules on this page. Then copy the table below into your exercise book and complete it with the words *buyer* or *seller*.

EXW – EX WORKS (… named place of delivery)
The seller makes the goods available at his premises in the customary packing.
The seller assists the buyer in obtaining any documentation needed at the buyer's expense.
The buyer is responsible for loading the goods, transporting them to their destination, customs clearance and insurance.

FCA – FREE CARRIER (… named place of delivery): Multimodal transport
The seller is not responsible for the main carriage of the goods. The seller delivers the goods at his own expense and risk, in the customary packing, cleared for export to the carrier nominated by the buyer. The seller provides the commercial invoice and, if requested, a certificate of origin at the buyer's expense. If the goods are collected at the seller's premises, the seller loads the goods. The seller bears the risks until the goods are in the custody of the first carrier. Thereafter, the buyer bears all the costs and risks of transporting the goods to their destination.

CIP – COST AND INSURANCE PAID TO (… named place of destination): Multimodal transport
The seller pays for the main carriage of the goods. The seller delivers the goods in the customary packing, cleared for export to the carrier which he nominates. The seller bears the risk until the goods have been delivered into the custody of the first carrier. The seller pays the transport costs (including transport insurance) for the goods up to the named destination. The buyer pays all import duties and taxes.

	Who pays for …						
	packing?	loading?	insurance?	export documents?	import documents?	main carriage?	customs duties?
EXW	…	…	…	…	…	…	…
FCA	…	…	…	…	…	…	…
CIP	…	…	…	…	…	…	…

B What costs will Hans Turck GmbH & Co. KG have to cover when sending the consignment of sensors to Saudi Arabia?

11 Insurance terminology

The words in the box can be used after 'insurance' to form important two-word phrases. Write the phrases and match them with the German definitions below.

broker • claim • company • cover • policy • premium

1 Versicherungsgesellschaft
2 Prämie
3 Deckungssumme
4 Police/Versicherungsschein
5 Versicherungsmakler
6 Schadensmeldung

TIP

Documentary credit

The safest method of payment in international trade is by 'irrevocable' and 'confirmed' documentary credit.
'Irrevocable' means that no details of the sales contract can be changed without the agreement of all parties.
'Confirmed' means that the seller's bank will pay the seller if it receives the shipping documents stipulated in the sales agreement.

12 Terms of payment and insurance

PAGE **126 & 130** KMK

19

Cornelia beantwortet Joannas Fragen zu Lieferung und Zahlung.

Hören Sie sich den Dialog an und beantworten Sie die Fragen auf Joannas Liste in vollen Sätzen. Beziehen Sie sich auch auf das *Certificate of air cargo insurance* auf Seite 126.

Joanna Masters

Ein Tag bei der Hans Turck GmbH & Co. KG, Mülheim-Ruhr, Germany – Fragen

1 *Warum bevorzugen Käufer FCA statt EXW?*
2 *Welchen Incoterm verwendet die Hans Turck GmbH beim Versand von Waren an ihren neuen chinesischen Kunden?*
3 *Für welchen Teil der Reise nach China muss die Hans Turck GmbH die Waren versichern?*
4 *Welche Unterlagen benötigt man für die Bezahlung per Dokumentenakkreditiv?*
5 *Was muss der Verkäufer seiner Bank aushändigen, um Bezahlung für die Ware zu erhalten?*
6 *Wer bezahlt die Bankgebühren?*

GRAMMAR

The passive

Passive	Active
1 The risk **is borne** by us.	We **bear** the risk.
2 The goods **have been packed** by us.	We **have packed** the goods.
3 The goods **will be collected** by Lufthansa.	Lufthansa **will collect** the goods.
4 The documents **could be used** by the buyer's bank.	The buyer's bank **could use** the documents.
5 The goods **are handed over**.	The seller/Somebody **hands over** the goods.
6 A draft **is used**.	The buyer/importer/customer **uses** a draft.
7 The goods **were insured**.	An insurance company **insured** the goods.

- Das **passive** wird verwendet, wenn die Handlung im Mittelpunkt steht (1–7 links).
- Möchte man den Verursacher der Handlung angeben, benutzt man *by* (1–4).
- Ist der Verursacher der Handlung unbekannt, zweitrangig oder selbstverständlich, wird er weggelassen (5–7).
- Das *passive* wird mit einer Zeitform von *be* (1–7) oder einem Modalverb + *be* (4) + Partizip Perfekt (3. Form) des Vollverbs gebildet.

13 Practice

A Read the following instructions from the insurance policy about what must be done if a consignment is damaged during shipment. Then complete the sentences in the passive using the verbs in brackets.

1 If damage ..., write what the damage is on the shipping documents. (find)
2 When delivery ... by container, ensure that the container ... immediately. (make, check)
3 If the container ... damaged, note the damage on the shipping documents. (deliver)
4 If damage can be seen, shipping companies must ... to come to an inspection. (ask)
5 Care ... to minimize damage. (must take)
6 The Survey Report ... immediately. (should check)
7 A full set of shipping documents ... to the insurance company. (need to present)
8 No claims ... if they ... by the insurance company within 15 months after the end of the insurance policy. (accept, not receive)

B Make the following sentences passive. Leave out the agent *(Verursacher)* if necessary.

1 Freight forwarders transport large quantities of goods.
2 In the future, they will transport even more goods.
3 Thieves have stolen too many goods this year.
4 Thieves stole a lot of designer handbags.
5 They sold the bags on the black market.
6 They should employ more security guards.
7 Exporters will spend more money on security next year.
8 The police have caught a few of the thieves.
9 They will send some to prison.
10 Newspapers publish their pictures every day.

14 Produktion

Sie sind Sachbearbeiter/-in in der Verkaufsabteilung der Firma Riedel Medizintechnik-Handels GmbH Hamburg. Ihr Unternehmen exportiert medizinische Geräte in die ganze Welt. Heute erhalten Sie eine E-Mail von Ms Fiona Johnson, der Einkaufsleiterin der australischen Firma *Medical Supplies Pty Ltd.* Sie bittet um ausführliche Informationen über das neue Röntgengerät XJ-400 *(X-ray machine)*, welches sie im vergangenen Monat am Stand Ihrer Firma auf der Internationalen Fachmesse für Medizintechnik in Stuttgart gesehen hat.

Verfassen Sie ein Angebot (E-Mail) für Ms Fiona Johnson (f.johnson@mspl.au). Berücksichtigen Sie folgende Punkte:

- Anrede und Dank für Anfrage
- Kurze Beschreibung Ihres Unternehmens
- Verweis auf Katalog zum Downloaden unter www.riedel-mth.de
- Listenpreis des Röntgengerät XJ-400 beträgt 12.000,– €
- Ihre Preise verstehen sich FCA Hamburg
- Großhändlern wird ein Handelsrabatt von 10% eingeräumt
- Zahlungsbedingungen: bei Erstaufträgen Kasse bei Auftragserteilung oder per Dokumentenakkreditiv
- Lieferung erfolgt ca. 30 Tage nach Auftragseingang
- Sie würden sich freuen, mit der australischen Firma in Geschäftsbeziehungen zu treten
- höflicher Schluss

15 Interaktion

Work with a partner and act out the following role-play.

Situation
Lars/Lara Wiese from Schenker AG calls Morrison Frieght plc to organize the transport of a consignment from England to Germany. Adam/Alice Lamont takes the call.

Lars/Lara Wiese

Introduce yourself and make small talk.
Say why you're calling.
Give the following details when asked:
- Container of fruit: 20' container
- Consignor: Ambridge Market, Colchester, UK
- Consignee: E Reichelt, Grünerstr. 20, 10179 Berlin
- Pick-up date: Urgent – 14 May
- Delivery date: 16 May – must be delivered
- Volume: 25 m^3
- Weight: 15 tonnes
- Incoterm: FCA Colchester

Ask for the freight price.
Thank the person for their help.

Adam/Alice Lamont

Introduce yourself and make small talk.
Ask how you can help.
You require the following information:
- Type of consignment + no. of packages
- Consignor
- Consignee/destination (ask to spell)
- Pick-up date
- Delivery date – any room for change?
- Volume
- Weight
- Incoterm

You have to calculate the freight price and will call back.
Thank the caller.

The specialty insurance market

Bruce Springsteen's voice ($6 million), Heidi Klum's legs ($2.2 million), Mariah Carey's legs (*$1 billion), a food critic's taste buds (Egon Ronay: $400,000), the Titanic, the San Francisco earthquake, the Space Shuttle, Concorde … Who insures such risks?

The answer is always the same – Lloyd's of London. Lloyd's started in the 1680s as a humble coffee house owned by Edward Lloyd in Tower Street near the docks. Rich merchants met there to share the risk of insuring their vessels for long sea voyages. Each merchant accepted part of the risk by writing his name on a piece of paper called a slip. As they wrote their names under each other, they were called 'underwriters', and the term is still used today to mean 'an insurer'.

Lloyd's of London is a uniquely organized insurance market. It is a society of individuals – and, since 1994, corporations – able to insure almost any type of risk. Clients first contact a Lloyd's broker, who represents one of the 164 underwriting syndicates specializing in different types of risk. The broker then negotiates the insurance premium with members of the syndicate, whereby each member accepts a fraction of the risk. When all the risk has been accepted, the premium is paid by the client to the underwriters. If the insured event happens – e.g. shipwreck, plane crash or offshore oil rig explosion – the underwriters must pay compensation, often immediately. The main categories of risk are marine, aviation, motor, non-motor and credit.

Until 1994, the members of Lloyd's were individuals. Lloyd's members were always rich and sometimes also famous, and it is for this reason that they were called 'Names'. 'Names' had unlimited personal liability for the risks they underwrote, and received high premiums for making their capital available. However, as their liability was unlimited, they risked having to sell everything they possessed to pay insurance claims. Until the late 1980s Lloyd's 'Names' made good profits, and in 1988 there were 32,433 of them. Then, between 1988 and 1992, a string of large claims came and brought massive losses to Lloyd's, which amounted to £7.9 billion (US$12.4 billion). Many 'Names' went bankrupt and were unable to pay. Since then, however, Lloyd's has been reformed and has now returned to profit. 'Names' with unlimited personal liability are no longer admitted to Lloyd's. Limited liability was formally introduced in 1993, and most risks are now insured by corporations.

*This is not a misprint!

16 Comprehension and discussion

Answer the following questions in your own words.

1. What sort of risks were first insured at Lloyd's?
2. When was Lloyd's founded and how did it start out?
3. What proportion of a risk does a member of a syndicate accept?
4. Who were the 'Names' and why do they no longer exist?
5. How much of their personal wealth could 'Names' at Lloyd's lose in the event of an insurance claim?
6. Against what sort of risks must most businesses insure themselves?
7. What are the consequences for a business if insurance companies refuse to insure it?
8. What sort of insurance do you have for yourself and when did you last make a claim?

A problem at Best Buy Großhandel GmbH

- Dealing with complaints
- Apologizing
- Communication problems

1 Warm-up

A **Make a list of things that can go wrong when goods are delivered to a customer.**

B **Imagine that a consignment has been broken on the way to a customer. In groups of three or four, make a mind map to show what action should be taken and what the consequences of the action will be. Each group should represent either the seller or the customer.**

C **Compare your mind map with those of other groups. Note the points on which you agree and disagree.**

2 A consignment is delayed

Jana Lorenz works in the purchasing department of Best Buy Großhandel GmbH in Dortmund, which supplies wholesalers all over the EU. Five weeks ago, her company ordered a consignment of ladies' T-shirts from a Chinese supplier in Shanghai, and was promised delivery within 30 days after receipt of order. The goods are now four days late, so she contacts the supplier.

Read Jana's complaint on page 96 and find phrases for the following headings.

1. reference to delay
2. request for explanation
3. request for delivery by a given deadline
4. consequences of further delay

An: chen-yu-lan@632tradingchina.cn
Kopie:
Betreff: **Delay in delivery of order no. LTS36B dated 13 February 20..**
Von: jana.lorenz@bbgh.de
Signatur: Ohne

Dear Ms Chen Yu Lan

On 13 February 20.. we placed the above-mentioned order for ladies' T-shirts for delivery by 16 March.

The consignment is now 4 days overdue.

We would welcome your explanation of the delay, but must be sure that the consignment will reach our premises by 30 March at the latest, as several customers are now threatening to cancel their orders and look elsewhere.

We trust that we will hear from you in the very near future. Prompt delivery is all that is needed to settle this matter.

Yours sincerely

Jana Lorenz
Purchasing Department
Best Buy Großhandel GmbH

3 Reassuring the customer

Ms Chen Yu Lan replies to Jana's email immediately.

To: jana.lorenz@bbgh.de
Copy:
Subject: **Re: Delay in delivery of order no. LTS36B dated 13 February 20..**
From: chen-yu-lan@632tradingchina.cn
Signature:

Dear Ms Lorenz

Thank you for your email, which we received this morning, regarding your order for ladies' T-shirts.

We are sorry to note that the goods have not arrived yet, but must point out that the delay has been caused by a rush of incoming orders for our goods.

Since receiving your email, we have spoken to our freight forwarder and have been assured that you may count on delivery within 7 days.

Please accept our apologies for the inconvenience, and do not hesitate to contact us if there are any further delays.

Yours sincerely

Chen Yu Lan
Export Sales Department
632 Trading Company China

A **Explain how soon Chen Yu Lan replied to Jana Lorenz's email and what impression this would make with Best Buy Großhandel GmbH.**

B **Write down the polite expressions Chen Yu Lan uses to apologize for the delay.**

4 Working with words

Find synonyms in the two emails to match the words or expressions in the box.

delivery • late • arrive at • clients • somewhere else • quick • concerning • sudden large number • transport company • rely on

5 Complaining about a delay

PAGE 143 KMK

Sevda Yildiz ist Einkaufsleiterin bei der Best Buy Großhandel GmbH in Dortmund. Heute möchte sie eine überfällige Lieferung Haushaltsporzellan beim chinesischen Lieferanten, Man Sang Trading Limited in Hongkong, anmahnen und hat sich Notizen aufgeschrieben.

Schreiben Sie Sevdas E-Mail an Mr John Zheng (j.zheng@mansang.org) in der Exportabteilung. Berücksichtigen Sie folgende Punkte:

- *Ware vor 3 Wochen am ... mit Auftrags-Nr. HHC/46 bestellt*
- *Lieferung inzwischen 7 Tage überfällig*
- *Grund für Verspätung?*
- *Kunden drohen inzwischen, ihre Aufträge zu stornieren und sich anderswo einzudecken*
- *letzte Frist für Lieferung: heute in 5 Tagen (genauen Termin angeben)*
- *passender Schluss*

6 A phone call from a dissatisfied customer

20

As soon as the T-shirts from China arrive at Best Buy Großhandel in Dortmund, the company sells them on to TopStyle Bazaar in Copenhagen, Denmark. Unfortunately, there is a problem with the consignment.

A Listen to the phone call between Gunner Kristoffersen in Denmark and Jacqueline Romberg in Best Buy's export sales department and explain what the problem is.

Jacqueline Best Buy Großhandel GmbH. Sie sprechen mit Jacqueline Romberg. Was kann ich für Sie tun?

Gunner Good morning. It's Gunner Kristoffersen from TopStyle Bazaar in Copenhagen. I hope you speak English.

Jacqueline Yes, I do, Mr Kristoffersen. How can I help you?

Gunner Well, we ...[1] ladies' T-shirts supplied by your company yesterday, and when we checked them, we ...[2].

Jacqueline Oh dear, I'm sorry to hear that! Can I have the order number, please?

Gunner Yes, it's CS3824T and we ...[3] on the fifteenth of last month.

Jacqueline Let me just check. OK, I've got it here. A trial order for 50 ladies' T-shirts. Could you tell me why they're unsatisfactory?

Gunner Basically, they're …[4]. We visited your stand at the Copenhagen International Fashion Fair in February, and the sample you showed us was good, but the ones you've sent …[5] and the colours are too dark. We wanted bright colours. Goods …[6] the Danish market. Is this a new supplier?

Jacqueline No, it's a good company we know very well. They normally manufacture the T-shirts very efficiently, so I'm not sure what's happened in this case.

Gunner Well, our customers here in Denmark are very careful buyers. They …[7]. Basically, we …[8] as soon as possible.

Jacqueline Yes, I understand. Can I get back to you on this, Mr Kristoffersen? We take all customers' complaints very seriously here, and I'm sure we can find a solution.

Gunner I hope so. We need …[9] for the summer season.

Jacqueline I'll talk to my boss, Herr Schäfer, today. You'll be hearing from us very soon and sorry again about the inconvenience.

Gunner Fine. I …[10].

Jacqueline Thanks for calling, Mr Kristoffersen. Bye.

Gunner Goodbye.

B **Now read the dialogue and complete it with the expressions (a–j). Then listen to the CD to check your answers.**

- **a** are poorly finished
- **b** of inferior quality are unsuitable for
- **c** look forward to hearing from you
- **d** look at the products very carefully before they buy them
- **e** not up to sample
- **f** took delivery of a consignment of
- **g** the T-shirts urgently
- **h** found they were sub-standard
- **i** placed the order
- **j** need better quality replacements

C **Listen to or read the dialogue again and do the following tasks.**

1. Explain when and where the customer first became interested in the goods.
2. Say what is wrong with the goods he has received.
3. Find words or expressions in the dialogue to describe what is wrong with the goods.
4. Say why TopStyle Bazaar needs the T-shirts so quickly.
5. Explain what Gunner Kristoffersen now expects Best Buy Großhandel to do.

D **Find five words and expressions in the dialogue to mean *bad* or *not good enough*.**

*Expressions for saying **bad** or **not good enough***
…
…

GRAMMAR

Adjectives and adverbs

1 I'd be grateful for a **quick** reply.
2 The sample you showed us seemed **good**.
3 Our customers here in Denmark are **careful** buyers.
4 They ***normally*** manufacture the T-shirts ***efficiently***.
5 We ***really*** need the T-shirts.
6 She works very ***hard***.
7 We know the company ***well***.

- **Adjektive** werden verwendet, um Personen oder Sachen näher zu beschreiben (1–3).
- Sie haben keine besondere Endung.
- Adjektive stehen unmittelbar vor Substantiven (1, 3) oder unmittelbar nach einer Form von *be* (oder Verben wie *become, feel, seem, smell, sound, taste* usw., die *be* ersetzen können) (2).

- **Adverbien** werden verwendet, um ein Verb näher zu beschreiben (4–7).
- Regelmäßige **Adverbien** haben die Endung *-ly*. (4, 5). Wenn das Adjektiv auf -Mitlaut *+y* endet, endet das Adverb auf *-ily* (z. B. *happy – happ**ily** / noisy – nois**ily***).
- Eine kleine Anzahl von Adverbien hat dieselbe Form wie Adjektive: *early, fast, hard, high, late, low, straight* (6).
- Das Adverb von **good** lautet ***well*** (7).
- Adverbien stehen entweder vor dem Verb (4, 5) oder danach (4, 6, 7).

! In English "hardly" means *kaum*!

7 Practice

A Complete the sentences with the adjective in brackets or its form as an adverb.

1 Jack Longfellow is a … businessman and always chooses his markets … . (clever)
2 He's old now and walks …, but he certainly isn't a … thinker! (slow)
3 He also … needs a holiday because of his … back, but he still goes to work. (bad)
4 Last week he was at his … warehouse watching lorries … come and go when he got a shock. (noisy)
5 There was a … explosion and a lorry just outside … caught fire. (sudden)
6 Jack realized that everyone was in … danger and … evacuated the warehouse. (immediate)
7 They were lucky because it was raining …, so the … lorry only burned for a few minutes. (heavy)
8 A … mechanic had caused a fire by … throwing away a lit cigarette. (careless)

B Use the words in brackets to complete the text. Make any necessary changes.

John was … (angry)**1** because he couldn't find his keys. He didn't want to arrive at work … (late)**2** again. He …(quick)**3** looked at his watch. It was dark so it was … (hard)**4** to see what time it was. He was … (tired)**5** when he arrived at the office. He had just sat down when he heard a … (loud)**6** noise. It was his telephone. It was ringing … (loud)**7**. He picked it up … (angry)**8**. "Don't work too … (hard)**9**, darling," said his wife. "I hope your interview goes … (good)**10** today, darling," said John.

8 Complaining about unsatisfactory goods

PAGE 143 KMK

Die Firma Just Jeans KG in Stuttgart (Kronprinzstraße 40, 70173 Stuttgart) hat heute von der chinesischen Firma Guangzhou Garment Factory (2 Sixth Street, Guangzhou, China 510000), eine Sendung Jeansjacken erhalten, die Anlass zu Beanstandungen gibt.

Verfassen Sie für Ihre Einkaufsleiterin, Frau Christina Toledano, die den Brief selbst unterschreiben wird, eine Mängelrüge an die Exportleiterin der chinesischen Firma, Ms Juanjuan Wan. Berücksichtigen Sie folgende Punkte, die Frau Toledano für Sie aufgeschrieben hat:

- *heutiges Datum und Anrede*
- *Bezug auf Lieferung (Auftrag Nr. JJ106/CH von vor 14 Tagen)*
- *Inhalt bei Ankunft nass wegen mangelhafter Verpackung*
- *Farbe und Qualität weichen erheblich von dem Muster ab (Fotos beigefügt)*
- *Bitte um umgehenden Ersatz, da Jeansjacken dringend benötigt werden*
- *ohne beträchtliche Ermäßigung nicht bereit, die minderwertige Ware zu behalten*
- *Bitte um Stellungnahme*
- *Fortsetzung der Geschäftsbeziehung von der Regelung der Beschwerde abhängig*
- *passender Schluss*

9 Responding to Gunner's complaint

Jacqueline Romberg's boss, Harald Schäfer, responds to Gunner Kristoffersen's complaint by email.

A **Arrange the parts of his email (1–9) in the correct order.**

B **Find two ways of saying "I'm sorry" in the email.**

An: g.kristoffersen@ts_bazaar.com

Betreff: ...

Von: harald.schäfer@bbgh.de   Signatur: Ohne

1 I have just been informed of your phone call regarding the above-mentioned consignment of T-shirts, and am dismayed to hear that the goods are sub-standard.

2 I hope this solution will meet with your approval and would ask you to accept our apologies for the inconvenience caused.

3 Dear Mr Kristoffersen

4 In the meantime we are sending you replacements at no extra charge by return.

5 Since hearing from you, we have contacted the manufacturer and are waiting for their explanation.

6 Harald Schäfer
Export Sales Manager
Best Buy Großhandel

7 **Unsatisfactory consignment / Order no. CS3824T dated 15 March 20..**

8 We look forward to doing further business with you in the future.

9 Yours sincerely

TIP

Making apologies

In English, it is quite usual to apologize more than once for a mistake or an unfortunate event of some sort, e. g. arriving late for a meeting:
Sorry. I do apologize. You must have been waiting for ages. Sorry about that.

At the end of the meeting the apology is repeated: *Sorry again for keeping you waiting.*

Apologies are made even if the speaker is not responsible for the event or guilty in any way, e. g. picking up a visitor at the airport: *Sorry about the awful weather!*

An apology is not necessarily an admission of guilt or responsibility. It often simply means that the speaker regrets that something unfortunate has happened. For this reason, make sure you apologize more than once when responding to a customer's complaint, even if your company is not at fault.

10 Apologizing for a faulty consignment

PAGE **143**

Several days ago the Me2 Mode GmbH fashion company in Hamburg (Haldesdorfer Straße 98, 22179 Hamburg) supplied a consignment of polo shirts (order no. BT106/D dated one month ago) to the Tiptop Trading Company in Birmingham (77 Commercial Road, Birmingham BM7 8FD, UK). Today, however, the German company receives a complaint because 250 polo shirts too many have been delivered in XL and 250 in L are missing.

As the Export Sales Manager at Me2 Mode GmbH, write a response to the customer's complaint. Include the following points:

- Contact person: Ms Gemma Murry, Purchasing Director
- Confirm receipt of letter/email
- Express regret about unsatisfactory goods
- Give explanation: error in dispatch department
- Apologize
- Promise delivery of missing goods carriage paid within 48 hours
- Offer 50% discount on extra T-shirts
- Hope that customer agrees with suggestions
- Polite ending

LANGUAGE

Apologizing

Spoken
Sorry.
Sorry I'm late.
Sorry about/for …
We're really sorry about …
I'd like to apologize for …

Written
I am / We are sorry (to hear) that …
I/We very much regret that …
I/We note to my/our regret that …
I am / We are dismayed to hear that …
I/We (sincerely) apologize for …
Please accept my/our (sincerest) apologies for any inconvenience caused.

11 Role-play: trouble-shooting

KMK

Situation: Ein/e Vertreter/in der Firma Best Buy Großhandel GmbH besucht zur Zeit Kunden in Irland. Heute hat er/sie einen Termin bei Ronan/Rosie O'Connell, dem/der Geschäftsführer/in der irischen Fitnessstudiokette O'Connell's Gyms Ltd in Dublin.

Benutzen Sie den folgenden Ablauf, um ein Gespräch zu führen.

Ronan/Rosie O'Connell

Sie begrüßen Ihren Besuch freundlich und machen Small Talk.

Vertreter/in – Eigener Name

Sie antworten freundlich, machen Small Talk und fragen, ob der Kunde / die Kundin zufrieden ist.

Sie erklären, dass Sie immer noch auf eine Sendung Fitnessuhren und Pulsmesser warten.

Sie sind überrascht, entschuldigen sich für den Lieferverzug und fragen nach der Auftrags-Nr.

Die Auftrags-Nr. lautet FWHRM/68 (vor 14 Tagen bestellt). Sie erklären, dass die Nachfrage nach den Geräten groß ist und fragen, wann mit der Lieferung gerechnet werden kann.

Sie bitten um Entschuldigung und sehen im System auf Ihrem iPhone, dass die Sendung vor genau einer Woche verschickt wurde.

Sie danken dem/der Vertreter/in, dass er/sie sich sofort nach der Sendung erkundigt.

Inzwischen haben Sie herausgefunden, dass der Hafen in Rotterdam bestreikt wird.

Sie fragen, wie lange der Streik noch andauern wird.

Man weiß es nicht. Sie fragen, ob Mr/Ms O'Connell mit einer Teilsendung (*part-delivery*) von 50 % der Ware per Luftfracht einverstanden wäre.

Sie fragen, wer dafür die Mehrkosten übernimmt.

Ihre Firma würde hierfür aufkommen. Die Ware würde in 48 Stunden ankommen.

Sie sind mit diesem Vorschlag einverstanden und bedanken sich.

Sie entschuldigen sich nochmals, geben Mr/Ms O'Connell Ihre Visitenkarte und sagen, er/sie möge Sie anrufen, falls es noch Probleme gibt.

Sie bedanken sich und verabschieden sich.

Sie verabschieden sich.

12 Dealing with communication problems

WEBCODE **TRMU0901**

A Study the survey below and complete the following sentences.

1 When speaking to non-native speakers of English, the biggest problem is that …
2 The biggest problem when speaking to native speakers is that …
3 The mistakes made by non-native speakers are mainly …
4 People who have learned English as a foreign language often speak with …
5 The same percentage of people found that native speakers … and …

Factors which can cause communication problems for you in English at work	with native speakers	with non-native speakers
They speak too fast	86%	10%
They use unknown expressions	60%	10%
They use too much idiomatic language	57%	3%
They use difficult words	56%	11%
They don't speak clearly enough	56%	61%
They have a heavy accent	45%	58%
I can't make myself understood	16%	24%
They make grammar mistakes	2%	53%

Source: Business Spotlight Survey

B Read the tip box below and then say which of the expressions you would use in the following situations.

1 A native speaker says: "Expediency should definitely not be the only criterion for decision-making."
2 You feel that some people haven't understood everything in a meeting.
3 Someone at a meeting says: "I think we should leave that to the powers that be."

TIP

Making sure you've understood

German business people routinely do business in English with non-native and native speakers, but surveys have shown that there are still communication problems (*see table*). To maximize understanding, e.g. in telephone conversations or at telephone conferences and meetings, it is important to do the following:

- Ask the speaker to repeat something if necessary: *Could you just repeat that, please?*
- Ask for clarification if something is unclear: *I'm not quite sure what you mean. Could you explain that, please?*
- Don't be afraid to ask someone to speak more slowly: *Please could you slow down?*
- Don't be afraid to ask speakers to use less difficult language: *I didn't quite understand that. Could you say that again more simply, please?*
- Include a chance to give feedback at the end of a meeting: *Is there anything that needs more discussion?*

C Describe any difficulties you have experienced when speaking English with native and non-native speakers.

13 Rezeption: Hörverstehen

21

Sie arbeiten in der Exportabteilung der Firma Best Buy Großhandel GmbH in Dortmund. Während Ihrer Abwesenheit ruft ein englischer Kunde an und hinterlässt eine Nachricht.

Hören Sie sich die Nachricht an und notieren Sie die erforderlichen Angaben für Ihren Abteilungsleiter.

Anruf für:	...
Anrufer (Name, Firma, Stadt, Land):	...
Kontaktdaten:	...
Grund und Ergebnis des Anrufes:	...

14 Rezeption: Hörverstehen

22

Ihr Unternehmen, die Herzog & Rau AG in Wuppertal, stellt Aufzüge und Rolltreppen *(lifts and escalators)* her und hat vor ca. 12 Monaten einen Teil der Produktion nach China ausgelagert. Während einer Geschäftsreise zu Ihrem chinesischen Partner in Shenzhen findet eine Besprechung mit der Geschäftsleitung statt. Ihr Vorgesetzter, Herr Dr. Lindemann, bittet Sie das Protokoll zu führen.

Hören Sie sich die Besprechung an und schreiben Sie die fehlenden Informationen zu jedem TOP auf.

PROTOKOLL

Besuch in Shenzhen, China
Besprechung am 15. Mai 20..

Anwesende:
Mr Li Wei Long, Managing Director,
Shenzhen Manufacturing Company Limited
Dr Lindemann, Produktionsleiter

TOP 1
Aussichten für das kommende Jahr: ...

TOP 2
Grund für Verzögerung bei der Auslieferung von 10 Rolltreppen für das neue Einkaufszentrum in Duisburg: ...

TOP 3
Verbesserungsvorschläge: ...

TOP 4
Nächster Besuch: ...

15 Understanding your business partner

A very large proportion of the West's trade is with China, so it is vital for business people to understand the basic values of Chinese society.
Yang Liu, a young artist, who was born in Beijing and has a company in Berlin, has published a number of designs contrasting the cultural differences between Germany and China. The Germans are blue, the Chinese red.

Look at the illustrations and do the following tasks.

1. Write one or two sentences to describe each contrast. Compare your results with those of other members of your class.
2. Find examples of behaviour you have observed for two or three of the contrasts.
3. Make a list of any other cultural differences you have noticed.

1 Punctuality

2 Attitudes toward anger

3 Problem-solving

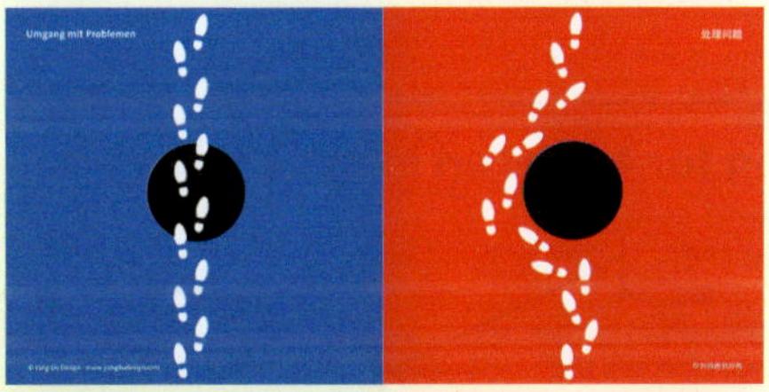

4 Approaching new things

5 How they imagine the other culture

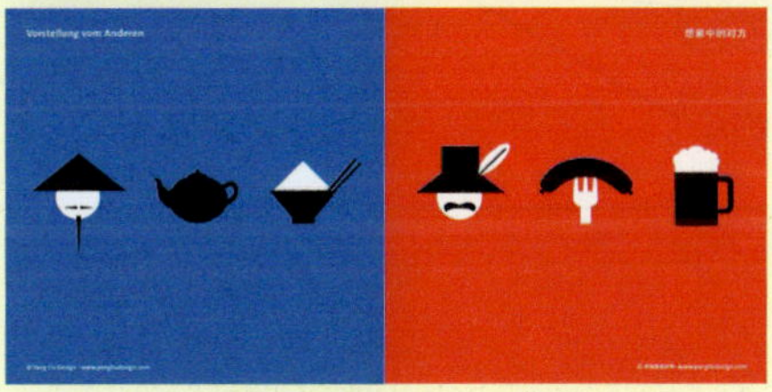

Source: Yang Liu Design, Berlin

UNIT 10

Applying for a job abroad

- Understanding job advertisements
- Writing CVs and cover letters
- Preparing for a telephone interview

1 Warm-up

a

b

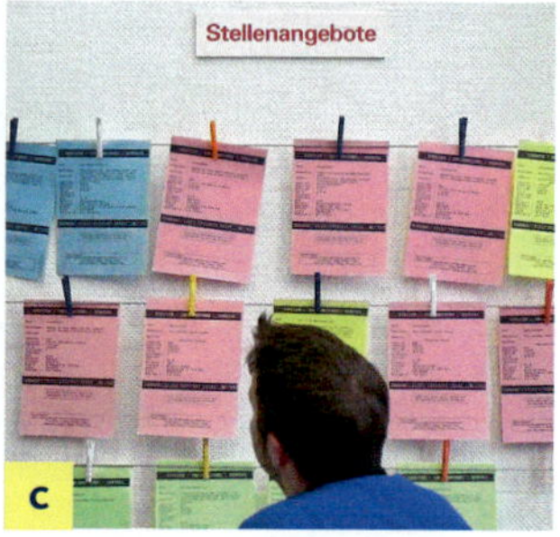

c

A **What do you need to think about before looking for a job? Look at the photos and the language box for help.**

B **How do you look for a job in …**

1 Germany? **2** abroad?

C **How did you find your job?**

LANGUAGE

Applying for a job/an internship/a work placement

source of job
- job centre (BE)
- employment centre (AE)
- recruitment agency
- advertisement
- on the internet
- in a publication (newspaper/magazine)

job application
- CV/curriculum vitae (BE)
- résumé (AE)
- certificate(s)
- reference(s)
- an applicant
- to apply for …
- a post/position/job as
- a work placement/an internship

2 Advice about job hunting

Sebastian Hartmann is a trainee at Metro AG in Mülheim an der Ruhr. He plans to work abroad after finishing his traineeship and today he is talking to his friend Jessica Bell on Skype about job applications.

A Read their conversation. Then say why Jessica is so stressed.

Jessica Hi, Sebastian.

Sebastian Hi, Jess. How are things?

Jessica Let's just say I'll be feeling a lot better this time tomorrow!

Sebastian Oh?! Why's that?

Jessica I'm stressed out at the moment. I've got my interview tomorrow and I'm afraid they'll ask me horrible questions I can't answer!

Sebastian They will, but I'm sure you're well prepared, Jess. What sort of job is it?

Jessica It's a job in sales at Morrison Supermarkets plc. I was very surprised I was short-listed for the job.

Sebastian They must have liked your application. Can you give me any tips? I want to apply for some jobs abroad soon myself, and I'd like to make my application more attractive.

Jessica Well, over here most employers use a recruitment agency. The agency publishes advertisements on its website, selects the best applications, and sends them to the employer.

Sebastian Oh really! Can't you just write to the employer directly?

Jessica You can, but companies get so many applications for a job these days that they prefer to get a recruitment agency to make a short-list for them.

Sebastian Is that how you got your interview tomorrow?

Jessica Yes, that's right, but first I got expert advice from the college careers advisor, and she told me I had to tailor my CV to each job I applied for. I then registered with some recruitment agencies, looked at the advertisements, and researched the companies thoroughly before I started writing my CV. Each time I found an interesting job, I looked at every word of the description and made sure my profile fitted exactly what they wanted.

Sebastian I'm sorry but I'm not quite sure what you mean by 'profile'.

Jessica A British CV has a section called "Profile" at the beginning. It's the part of the CV you see first, and in it you show that you are the perfect person for the job. If your profile's good, the recruitment agency reads the rest of the CV. If it isn't, they bin it. In Britain they look at your CV for about 20 seconds. That's how much time you've got to make a good impression.

Sebastian So you need a really good photo and good paper too, I suppose.

Jessica There's no photo on a CV here because that could prejudice the employer and most communication is by email, so the paper is less important than the layout – just keep it simple.

Sebastian Well that's very different from Germany.

Jessica Oh really? The hardest thing about my CV was getting all the important facts onto two pages. I had to choose the right headings and sell myself. Anyway, I've got three interviews now.

Sebastian Wow, that's great! Listen, I don't want to keep you, so good luck tomorrow!

Jessica Thanks. Bye.

Sebastian Bye.

B **Complete the following sentences about the dialogue in your own words.**

1 Sebastian tries to reassure Jessica that …
2 We know that there are still other applicants for the job Jessica wants because …
3 Sebastian would like Jessica to …
4 Sebastian was surprised to hear that …
5 Jessica was advised to …
6 The "profile" section of a British CV is …

3 Understanding job advertisements

A **Read the job advertisement for Trade International plc and then complete the statements with a, b or c.**

1 The job is in …
a Germany.
b England.
c North America.

2 The pay is about £ 25,000 …
a per month.
b per project.
c per year.

3 The person employed will …
a help the team leader.
b be the team leader.
c work in Germany.

4 The person employed will …
a translate complaints.
b deal with complaints.
c make complaints.

5 The person employed …
a must have experience of customer services.
b needn't have experience of customer services.
c will receive training in customer services.

6 The job advertised is …
a never stressful.
b always stressful.
c sometimes stressful.

Trade International plc –
safe solutions in a fast-moving world

German-speaking Customer Services Specialist

Location	London, UK
Salary	£23,000–£27,000 per annum
Sector	Customer services
Job type	Permanent

Job description: duties include
– Supporting sales team and team leader for German market on a day-to-day basis
– Dealing with customer enquiries
– Ensuring accurate order processing from order to invoice
– Resolving complaints quickly and efficiently

Person specification
– Customer services experience essential
– Good MS Office knowledge essential
– Excellent spoken and written English
– Fluent German speaker
– Excellent soft and teamwork skills
– Confident and calm under pressure
– Learns and adapts quickly
– Builds rapport with customers and staff

Submit your application to
Ms J Winters, Recruitment Manager,
Trade International plc, Century House,
99 Prince William Street

B **Match the highlighted words in the job ad to their German equivalents.**

1 erforderlich
2 selbstbewusst
3 gute Beziehungen
4 Reklamationen
5 Aufgaben
6 fließend
7 Rechnung
8 Bewerbung

GRAMMAR

Comparatives and superlatives

1 My working hours are **shorter** than yours, but Paul's are the **shortest**.
2 Jane's boss is **happier** than mine, but Zara's is the **happiest**.
3 I hope I feel a lot **better** after my job interview tomorrow.
4 He wore his **best** clothes to the interview.
5 I always feel **worst** the night before an interview.
6 The layout of your application is just **as important as** the content.
7 For me, a job in sales is **more attractive than** a job in financial controlling.

- Einsilbige Adjektive werden mit *-er* und *-est* gesteigert (1).
- Zweisilbige Adjektive, die auf *-y* enden, werden auf ähnliche Weise gesteigert, wobei auf die Schreibweise zu achten ist (2).
- Zweisilbige Adjektive, die nicht auf *-y* enden, und längere Adjektive werden mit *more/less* und *most/least* gesteigert (7).
- Einige Adjektive haben unregelmäßige Steigerungsformen (3–5).
- Vergleiche bildet man mit *as … as* (so … wie) (6), und *than* (als) (7).

4 Practice

Employer	Europartners Ltd	Trade International plc	Leeds Cash & Carry Ltd
Working hours per week	40 (45-minute paid break)	38 (30-minute unpaid break)	42 (45-minute paid break)
Hourly rate	£18	£20	£25
Overtime pay	Time off (or) 25% for first five hours 50% for any longer	Time off (or) 25% for first two hours 50% for any longer	Time off (or) 50% more per extra hour
Holiday days p.a.	20	25	30

Read the table and then complete the sentences with the comparative or superlative of the adjectives from the box.

attractive • bad • few • generous • good • healthy • high • long • low • short

1 Working hours at Leeds Cash & Carry Ltd are … at Trade International.
2 Working hours at Europartners Ltd aren't … at Trade International.
3 A paid lunch break is … an unpaid one.
4 Lunch-break arrangements are … at Trade International.
5 The hourly pay rates at Europartners Ltd are the … .
6 Overtime pay at Europartners Ltd is … at Trade International. Leeds Cash & Carry Ltd have the … overtime pay.
7 Doctors say that taking time off work is … getting payment for overtime.
8 Leeds Cash & Carry Ltd have the … holiday arrangements, whereas employees at Europartners Ltd are given the … holiday days per year.

5 Writing a CV

WEBCODE **TRMU1001**

Sebastian applies for the job at Trade International plc and models his CV on Jessica's.

A **Use Sebastian's CV and the Skype dialogue in exercise 2 to list the differences between a British and a German CV.**

B **Which differences surprise you? Explain why to your partner.**

Sebastian Hartmann
Lichtstraße 44, 40235 Düsseldorf, Germany
Landline: 0049 209 36549931 Mobile: 0049 176 3960024
Email: sebastian.hartmann@linkall.de

PROFILE

Final year commercial trainee about to obtain a professional qualification from the Düsseldorf Chamber of Commerce as a Management Assistant in Wholesale and Foreign Trade. Offering problem-solving skills, able to work both independently and in a team, and deliver results under pressure. Seeking to use existing skills and education in sales and customer services with opportunities for development.

KEY ACCOMPLISHMENTS

- Member of winning team in trainees' Team Project Management Competition at Metro AG, a major German wholesaling and retailing company with sales divisions all over the world.
- Optimized intranet webpages for Metro trainees
- Played a key role in organizing a programme for Norwegian trainees visiting Metro AG

KEY SKILLS

Professional
- Accountancy, Business Studies, Human Resources, Economics
- Excel, Microsoft Word, PowerPoint

General
- Experienced in planning and coordinating projects during traineeship and at school
- Native speaker of German
- Fluent written and spoken English
- Excellent command of written and spoken French

PROFESSIONAL TRAINING

Aug 2009 – present **Trainee Management Assistant in Wholesale and Foreign Trade**
Metro AG, Düsseldorf, Germany

- 2 ½-year dual system traineeship programme
- Block release attendance of Düsseldorf Vocational Training College
- Subjects taken: Business Studies, Accountancy, IT, Commercial English, Business Processes

EDUCATION

June 2009 **German Higher Education Entrance Qualifications *(Abitur)***
Max-Planck Gymnasium (grammar school), Düsseldorf,
Germany (2000–2009)

- Final grade: 2.0 (merit)
- Major subjects: English, Physics
- Minor subjects: German, French, Mathematics, Social Studies, History, Biology, Sport, Literature
- Awarded Appolinaire Prize in French

WORK EXPERIENCE

June 2010	**Commercial Services, University of York, UK** Gained valuable professional and personal insights into English working life and culture
July 2008	**Peek & Cloppenburg, Düsseldorf (major German retail chain)** Became skilled in negotiating with a range of domestic and international suppliers

HOBBIES & INTERESTS

Climbing, skiing, reading, music, travel

PERSONAL DETAILS

Date of birth:	26 January 19..
Nationality:	German
Marital status:	Single
Driving licence:	Full driving licence

REFERENCES

Available on request

TIP

Sell yourself

You should use as many positive statements in your CV as possible; each one should boost your application.

To boost his image, Sebastian uses two positive headings in his CV (*key accomplishments* and *key skills*) and a number of positive words and expressions such as *able to, boosted, experienced in, offering, optimized, troubleshooter,* etc. Remember: *"Your application is a product with a price tag. Make sure it sells."*

6 Language for CVs

A Use the words from the box to complete the following profile.

awarded • boosted • challenging • experienced in • key • optimized • powerful • wide

Profile

Team player ...[1] working in many different fields. Able to find solutions in ...[2] situations. Offering a ...[3] range of skills and abilities. ...[4] sales by 50% last year. Played a ...[5] role in setting up the company's intranet. Developed a ...[6] online tool to deal with FAQs. ...[7] order procedures resulting in greater efficiency. ...[8] a Grade A for a Fair Trade project in final year of traineeship.

B Match the CV headings (1–9) with the meanings (a– i).

1	profile	**a**	what you do in your free time
2	key accomplishments	**b**	your qualifications from school, further and higher education
3	key skills	**c**	the temporary jobs you have had
4	professional training	**d**	age, nationality, etc.
5	education	**e**	the section of the CV in which you say who you are, what you can do and what you want to do
6	work experience	**f**	the most important things you have done so far
7	hobbies & interests	**g**	people who think you will do the job well
8	personal details	**h**	the job you have learned to do
9	references	**i**	your most important abilities

7 Sebastian's cover letter

Use the expressions (a–j) to complete Sebastian's cover letter.

- **a** Although I have been offered
- **b** I look forward to
- **c** became proficient in
- **d** has confirmed my interest in
- **e** I am a native speaker of
- **f** I am available for interview
- **g** I was extremely interested
- **h** it has taught me to
- **i** I quickly adapted to
- **j** Vacancy for

Sebastian Hartmann
Lichtstraße 44
40235 Düsseldorf
Germany

16 April 20..

Ms J Winters
Recruitment Manager
Trade International plc
Century House
99 Prince William Street
EC4V 4DD
LONDON
ENGLAND

Dear Ms Winters

…[1] **customer services specialist with fluent German**

…[2] to read your advertisement for a fluent German speaker in customer services, since this precisely fits my career plans.

…[3] German and first became interested in the wholesale trade when I did a four-week work placement in the purchasing section of Peek & Cloppenburg in Düsseldorf, Germany during the summer vacation in 2008. Before my traineeship at Metro AG, I completed a further work placement in the Commercial Services department of the University of York, where I enjoyed the hands-on approach to delivering services and …[4] spoken English. …[5] the new English-speaking working environment and enjoyed it immensely.

My traineeship at Metro AG …[6] the fields of wholesaling and exports, and enabled me to use my skills in working with people, both as a team player and service provider. In particular, …[7] be customer-focused and get the best out of a team within a tight time frame, which helped my team to win the Team Project Management Competition for Trainees.

…[8] a permanent contract at Metro AG, I wish to make use of both my professional and linguistic skills and feel sure that the vacancy at your company would be ideal for me.

…[9] at any time except for the first two weeks of June when my final examinations take place. My CV is enclosed for your consideration, and …[10] hearing from you at your earliest convenience.

Yours sincerely

Sebastian Hartmann

Sebastian Hartmann

Enc

LANGUAGE

Writing a cover letter

Showing interest and suitability

I was extremely interested to see/read your advertisement for the post of …
I wish to gain experience in … / make use of my foreign language skills.
I feel sure that your company/organization has the post I am looking for.
I believe I am particularly suited for the post advertised because …

Describing your skills

As a native speaker of French/German/Spanish/English, …
I am fluent in (spoken and written) …
I have a good knowledge of …

Talking about previous experience

Before/After my traineeship, I completed a work placement at … in the … department.
My experience/traineeship at … has confirmed my interest in …
My traineeship has enabled me to use/develop my skills in …

Expressing availability for an interview / the job

I am available for an interview immediately / at short notice / at a week's notice / as from …
I would be able to start work any time after …
I very much look forward to hearing from you at your earliest convenience.

8 Tailoring your application

A **Tailor your own CV to fit the vacancy advertised by Recruitnet. It is at Europartners Ltd. Make sure you use positive language to boost your image and most of the headings in Sebastian's CV.**

B **Use the contact details and the expressions in the language box above to write a cover letter to Europartners Ltd in the form of a letter or an email to accompany your CV.**

Our client has an excellent opportunity for a German-speaking credit controller to join their team reporting to the office manager. Your duties for this role will include general administration, resolving account queries, making credit decisions regarding the dispatch of goods and chasing customers for overdue monies whilst building rapport with both customers and internal branch staff. The job would ideally suit a good team player able to work well under pressure. The successful candidate must be fluent in both written and spoken German. If you are a fluent German speaker send us your CV. We promise to respond within 48 hours.

Contact details: Mrs Deborah Sharples, Human Resources Director, Europartners Ltd, 40 Tanners Drive, MILTON KEYNES, MK14 5BW, ENGLAND
email: deborah.sharples@europartners.co.uk.

9 Choosing the right candidate

23

Jennifer Winters, Head of Human Resources at the British company Trade International plc, carries out telephone interviews with candidates applying for the job of German-speaking Customer Sales Representative.

A Listen to the interviews and complete the table below.

	Interview 1	Interview 2	Interview 3
Name	*Tobias Klein*	*Bianca Tiemeyer*	*Sebasatian Hartmann*
Present employer?	*Atlas Trading in Frankfurt*	*Tiemeyer Import/ Export in Dortmund*	*Metro AG in Mülheim/Ruhr*
Strengths?	*- good at work and school* *- team …*[1]	*- good at English* *- …*[2] *- honest* *- hard-working*	*- teamwork* *- taking the …*[3] *- working indepen-dently* *- …*[4]
Weaknesses?	*- forgets important things*	*- …*[5] *- own standards too high*	*- lack of …*[6]
Why this job?	*- wants to work in Manchester*	*- thinks she is best …*[7] *- would like to work …*[8]	*- has the necessary skills* *- link with Germany* *- likes working in UK*
Future plans?	*- wants a …*[9] *- wants to be independent and free*	…[10]	*- wants to develop in job, gain experience and study in evenings*
Own questions?	-	*- would like some help with …*[11]	*- …*[12]

B In your exercise books, add another column to the table with the heading 'Interview 4 – Me'. Then fill in your own answers to the interviewer's questions.

Interview 1	Interview 2	Interview 3	Interview 4 – Me

C Explain why you think each applicant is suitable/unsuitable for the job.

10 Interaktion

Work with a partner and act out the role-play.

Situation
There is a job vacancy at Trade International plc. Jennifer/John Winters, Head of Human Resources, calls an applicant for a telephone interview. Take turns to act out each role with the help of the points below.

Jennifer/John Winters

- Introduce yourself.
- Suitable time for phone call?
- Ask the candidate to talk about their CV.
- How would the candidate describe themselves?
- How would the candidate's colleagues describe him/her?
- Is the candidate a team player? Examples?
- Hobbies?
- Strengths and weaknesses?
- Reason for deciding to train as …
- Expectations of the job?
- Why should this particular candidate be chosen?
- Questions?

Applicant

- Introduce yourself.
- Say that this is a suitable time for phone call.
- Talk about your CV.
- Describe yourself from your own point of view and from that of your colleagues.
- Give examples of how you are a team player.
- Describe your hobbies.
- Describe your strengths and weaknesses.
- Give reasons for choosing this career.
- Describe what you expect from the job.
- Justify why you should be chosen for the job.
- Ask any questions you may have.

Virtual job-hunting: Technology fills situations vacant

By Rory Cellan-Jones, Technology correspondent, BBC News

Ready for your close-up? Graeme Anthony's video CV got him the job he was looking for.

Looking for a job – or trying to find a new employee? Then prepare for a technological revolution. New tools, many of them related to the explosion in the use of social media, are transforming the recruitment world.

Until recently, the process of seeking a job followed a familiar routine – scan the newspaper recruitment pages, or visit an agency, then despatch your carefully prepared CV (or résumé if you're American) in all directions. Now though, those who want to stand out in a crowded job market are resorting to more sophisticated approaches. A search on YouTube throws up plenty of examples of the new breed of job-seeker, promoting themselves with video offerings. Among them is Graeme Anthony, who needed to get a new job in PR in a hurry when he moved from Manchester to London. His YouTube C.V.I.V. – curriculum vitae interactive video – is simple but effective. He sits behind a table pitching his skills, and then links appear to more videos giving greater detail. "It brings me to life in a completely new way," he explains, "It shows off my personality in a way a paper CV can't. It's got the wow factor."

It worked. When London's Frank PR agency saw the video, Graeme was quickly invited for an interview, and got the job. Graham Goodkind, chairman and founder of Frank PR, says he's surprised that so few candidates resort to hi-tech tricks. "It's always amazed me in this day and age, that when things are moving so quickly from a technological point of view, CVs and résumés are really the same as they were 10, 15 or even 20 years ago. So this really opened up our eyes to how it really could be done, and we wanted to meet the guy straight away."

Source: adapted from: www.bbc.co.uk/news/business-12194581

11 Understanding the text

Do the following tasks based on the text.

1. Outline the traditional method of looking for a job.
2. Describe how Graeme Anthony looked for a job.
3. Explain what he means by the "wow factor".
4. Describe Graham Goodkind's reaction when he saw Graeme Anthony's video CV.

12 Videos about yourself

Graeme Anthony made six videos of himself, each 1–3 minutes long. He also used background music. In groups of three to four, make a series of videos of each group member. Use Graeme Anthony's ideas or your own ideas to structure your videos.

Video 1 – About me / **Video 2** – Contact / **Video 3** – Introduction / **Video 4** – Portfolio / **Video 5** – Timeline / **Video 6** – Skills

File 1: Unit 2, Exercise 11, page 25

Student B:

You work for in the sales department of Skater Styles GmbH. You receive a phone call from a customer in the UK who would like to order some baseball caps from you.

- Details of the order?
- Reference to website on page 25 to see availability of items
- Suggest alternatives if items not currently not available
- Take order (will be sent out tomorrow)
- Thank the customer for his/her business

File 2: Unit 3, Exercise 5, page 31

Student A:

You are Nina Wittstock. Use your diary below to help you arrange a day and a time for the meeting with Marlon Gibson.

Terminkalender: Nina Wittstock

Donnerstag
07.00: Abflug 07.20 Uhr Dortmund, Ankunft 07.20 London-Luton, easyJet U2 2172
10.00 – 13.00: Meeting mit Marketing-Team
13.00 – 15.00: Mittagessen mit Marketing Direktor
16.00 – 18.00: Shopping? (Oxford Street)
20.00 – 23.00: Abendessen mit Jessica Sutherland (Marketing Consultant) im Savoy Grill
Freitag
10.00 – 12.00: Kundenbesuch im Londoner Studio (Pierre Jardin Fashion Designer)
12.00 – 14.00: Mittagessen mit Pierre Jardin
18.00: Checkin London-Luton
19.00: Abflug 19.20 Uhr London-Luton, easyJet U2 2177

File 3: Unit 4, Exercise 4, page 41

Student A:

You are responsible for making travel reservations for your colleagues.
A colleague calls you. Answer the phone using your own name and offer your help.
You require the following information:

- Destination
- Departure date
- Return date

You will take care of the reservations and pass on the details.

File 4: Unit 5, Exercise 9, page 57

Student C:

You are a trainee at your company (own name).

- Introductions and small talk
- Exams in Germany in June
- September best for English trainees' visit
- Room in your house (sister – own flat)
- Can take boy or girl trainee
- Promise to ask friends, family, workmates to find three more families
- German class tests and exams in summer
- Soon after Easter best for visit to UK
- Own ideas

File 5: Unit 4, Exercise 9, page 45

Student B:

You are a receptionist at the Avon View Hotel in Bristol in the UK. Take a phone call and make a reservation using the information below.

- Rooms available: single room: 22, 23, 24 September; double room only available: 22, 23 September; twin room: 23, 24 September
- Prices: single room: £100 per night; double room: £170 per night; twin room: £90 per person, per night
- Payment methods available: Visa / MasterCard
- Hotel facilities: squash court (closed for repairs), small gym, swimming pool and sauna

File 6: Unit 7, Exercise 5, page 76

Student B:

You are the Sales Manager of Urban Terrain, a sports shoe manufacturer in the UK. You receive a call from a buyer working for a German sports chain.

- Listen to their enquiry
- Offer a 2.5% discount for an initial order of 200 pairs of shoes (if placed quickly)
- Try to convince the caller to place the order straight away
- You are not in a position to offer a further discount until you know what size of order they are likely to place
- Try to get your partner to find out about the order size as quickly as possible

File 7: Unit 5, Exercise 9, page 57

Student A:

You are the training officer at your company (own name). You lead the meeting.

- Introductions and small talk
- Welcome the visitor (Ms Jane / Mr Jack Seymour from the Watermill Brewery in Cumbria, UK) Number of English students coming?
  - Age?
  - Knowledge of German?
- Arrival date?
- Preferred accommodation (host family / guest house / hotel)?
- German side will find accommodation
- Date of return visit to UK?
- Will send minutes to all participants
- AOB?
- Finish/Close the meeting

File 8: Unit 2, Exercise 11, page 25

Student A:

You work for a clothing chain in the UK. Call up Skater Styles to order some baseball caps. Ask to be put through to the right person.

The baseball caps you are interested in ordering are:

- 30 KoolKult Caps – 10 in blue (No. 493828), 10 in black (No. 673982) and 10 in yellow (No. 983726).
- 60 Street Style Caps – 25 in blue (No. 387197), 15 in red (No. 329876), 20 in orange (No. 887282).

You would like to have the colours in the quantities specified above. If this is not possible, you are prepared to compromise as you would like the order to be delivered as soon as possible.

File 9: Unit 5, Exercise 9, page 57

Student B:

You are Jane / Jack Seymour, Training Officer at the Watermill Brewery in Cumbria, UK.

- Introductions and small talk
- Thanks for allowing students to shadow
- 4 trainees to come to Germany
  - 2 boys, 2 two girls, 18+
  - No knowledge of German
- Good dates: June or September next year
- Homestay accommodation preferred – chance to experience family life in Germany
- German visit to UK: just before or just after Easter the following year
- Own ideas

File 10: Unit 3, Exercise 5, page 31

Student B:

You are Marlon Gibson. Use your diary below to help you arrange a day and a time for the meeting with Nina Wittstock.

Appointments diary: Marlon Gibson

Thursday
8 a.m. – 9 a.m.: Working breakfast
11.00 a.m. – 12.00 p.m.: Meeting with Managing Director
4.00 p.m. – 7.00 p.m.: Factory visit
Friday
8.00 a.m.: Take children to school
4.00 p.m.: Buy birthday present (30 mins)
7.00 p.m. - ?: Wife's birthday dinner at The Gun Restaurant, London Docklands

1 Certificate of origin

1 Consignor
The Black Horse Co Ltd
Ache Road
Moorgate, LONDON

No. PQ 74459 | ORIGINAL

2 Consignee
The Importing Co Ltd
Queensway
New York, United States of America

3 Country of Origin
European Union - United Kingdom

EUROPEAN UNION

4 Transport details (Optional)
Ship - Filly Noir

5 Remarks

CERTIFICATE OF ORIGIN

6 Item number, marks, numbers, number and kind of packages; description of goods			7 Quantity
10 Cases	Horse New York 1 - 10	Power Units	310 kilos

Specimen

8 THE UNDERSIGNED AUTHORITY CERTIFIES THAT THE GOODS DESCRIBED ABOVE ORIGINATE IN THE COUNTRY SHOWN IN BOX 3

THE HERTFORDSHIRE CHAMBER OF COMMERCE AND INDUSTRY

Place and date of issue; name, signature and stamp of competent authority

Hatfield

....

....
The Hertfordshire Chamber of Commerce and Industry

2 Irrevocable letter of credit

Advice for the beneficiary

NAME OF ISSUING BANK
ABC Bank Plc, International Division,
1, Broadway, London EC27

Place and date of issue
London 15th April 1998

Irrevocable documentary credit

Number 62340

Place and date of expiry
at counters of advising bank 31st August 2011

Applicant –
Playtime Toys Limited
Blisset Street
London W36

Beneficiary –
The Orient Toy Company
Cornwall Road North
Hong Kong

Advising Bank –
Bank XYZ
Duke Road
Hong Kong

Ref. No. –

Amount –
HK$ 9,000 (Hong Kong Dollars nine thousand)

Availability

☐ by sight payment ☒ by acceptance ☐ by negotiation

☐ by deferred payment at

against the documents detailed herein

☒ and beneficiary's draft at 90 days sight
on Bank XYZ, Duke Road, Hong Kong

Partial Shipments
☐ allowed ☒ not allowed

Transhipment
☐ allowed ☒ not allowed

Shipping/despatch/taking in charge from/at Hong Kong

for transportation to: Heathrow Airport, London

INVOICE IN THREE COPIES ALL ORIGINALLY SIGNED certifying that the goods are in accordance with Playtime Toys Limited Order Number 51 dated 4.2.1998.

AIR WAYBILL evidencing goods dispatched to Playtime Toys Limited London W36 marked "Freight Paid".

PACKING LIST IN TRIPLICATE

We are informed that insurance is being arranged by our principals.

DESCRIPTION OF GOODS

Plastic toy cars

CFR Heathrow Airport, London.

Specimen

Documents to be presented within 21 days after the date of issuance of the transport document(s) but within the validity of credit.

We hereby issue the Documentary Credit in your favour. It is subject to the Uniform Customs and Practice for Documentary Credits (2007 Revision International Chamber of Commerce, Paris, France, Publication No. 500) and engages us in accordance with the terms thereof. The number and the date of the credit and the name of our bank must be quoted on all drafts required. If the credit is available by negotiation, each presentation must be noted on the reverse of this advice by the bank where the credit is available.

ABC Bank Plc, International Division
1, Broadway, London EC27

This document consists of signed page(s)

3 Commercial invoice

The Black Horse Co Ltd
Ache Road
Moorgate, London

The Importing Co Ltd
Queensway
New York
United States of America

Invoice No: 6789

2	15 HP "Power Units" @ £345.00 each		
	Total value ex works	£690.00	
	FOB Charges plus Insurance Premium	£127.00	
	Sea Freight Charges	£ 90.00	
Marks & Nos.	Total CIF NEW YORK	STG£907.00	
Horse New York 1 - 10	Goods manufactured in UK by A. Power Co. Ltd. Power Road, Peterborough UK Total No. of pieces: 10 cases Net Weight: 292 kilos Gross Weight: 310 kilos Cube: 1.35 cubic metres Despatched per vessel - Filly Noir Certified True & Correct for THE BLACK HORSE CO LTD		

4 Bill of lading

Bill of Lading for Combined Transport shipment or Port to Port shipment

Shipper
P&O NEDLLOYD LTD
BERTH 204/205/206
WESTERN DOCKS,
SOUTHAMPTON

B/L No.: PONLBHX23009678
Reference: LGM0099535

Consignee or Order (for U.S. Trade only: Not Negotiable unless consigned 'To Order')
YUSIF BIN YUSIF FAKHRO
P.O.BOX 214
MANAMA
BAHRAIN

Notify Party/Address (It is agreed that no responsibility shall attach to the carrier or his Agents for failure to notify (see clause 20 on reverse))
YUSIF BIN YUSIF FAKHRO
P.O.BOX 214
MANAMA
BAHRAIN

Place of Receipt (Applicable only when this document is used as a Combined Transport Bill of Lading)
SOUTHAMPTON

Vessel and Voy. No.
OOCL FREEDOM OFM0234

Place of Delivery (Applicable only when this document is used as a Combined Transport Bill of Lading)
PORT OF MINA SULMAN
STATE OF BAHRAIN

Port of Loading
SOUTHAMPTON

Port of Discharge
BAHRAIN

Undermentioned particulars as declared by Shipper, but not acknowledged by the Carrier (see clause 11)

Marks and Nos; Container Nos;	Number and kind of Packages; Description of Goods	Gross Weight (kg)	Measurement (cbm)
POCU0432963 SEAL: 000204	1x20'GP CONTAINER SAID TO CONTAIN		
	20 C/S FCL/FCL	6240.0000	
TEST DATA TEST DATA TEST DATA	TEST DATA FOR REMOTE BILL PRINTING FREIGHT COLLECT SHIPPERS LOAD, STOW & COUNT SHIPPED ON BOARD PER OCEAN VESSEL OOCL FREEDOM AT SOUTHAMPTON ON XXXXXXXXXXXXXXXX FOR P&O NEDLLOYD LIMITED		

TOTAL: PART OF 1x20' CONTAINER(S) ONLY

FREIGHT AND CHARGES:

ORIGIN INLAND HAULAGE CHARGE	P	HAI
ORIGIN TERMINAL HANDLING/LCL SERVICE CHARGE	P	HAI
OCEAN FREIGHT	C	BAH
DESTINATION TERMINAL HANDLING/LCL SERVICE CHARGE	C	BAH
DESTINATION INLAND HAULAGE CHARGE	C	BAH

* Total No. of Containers/Packages received by the carrier	Movement	Freight Payable at
1 PART	FCL/FCL	KANOO, BAHRAIN

Received by the Carrier from the Shipper in apparent good order and condition (unless otherwise noted herein) the total number or quantity of Containers or other packages or units indicated in the box above entitled "*Total No. of Containers/Packages received by the Carrier" for Carriage subject to all the terms and conditions hereof (INCLUDING THE TERMS AND CONDITIONS ON THE REVERSE HEREOF AND THE TERMS AND CONDITIONS OF THE CARRIER'S APPLICABLE TARIFF) from the Place of Receipt or the Port of Loading, whichever is applicable, to the Port of Discharge or the Place of Delivery, whichever is applicable. If the acknowledged tally is of Containers, this indicates that the Container has been packed and sealed by the Merchant at his premises without the Carrier being represented and able to check or verify either the tally of Goods or the stowage, which are consequently unknown to him (See Clause 8). The Merchant accepts that, except by special arrangement or pursuant to Clause 9 hereof, Containers are not weighed by the Carrier at any time. If the Carrier so requires, before he arranges delivery of the Goods one original Bill of Lading, duly endorsed, must be surrendered by the Merchant to the Carrier at the Port of Discharge or at some other location acceptable to the Carrier. In accepting this Bill of Lading the Merchant expressly accepts and agrees to all its terms and conditions whether printed, stamped or written, or otherwise incorporated, not withstanding the non-signing of this Bill of Lading by the Merchant. Without prejudice to the generality of this reference, attention is drawn, inter-alia, to Clause 12 (Shipper's/Merchant's Responsibility), 19 (Dangerous Goods) and 24 (Law & Jurisdiction).

Number of Original Bills of Lading	Place and Date of Issue	
2/TWO	PONL BIRMINGHAM	23/09/00

IN WITNESS of the contract herein contained the number of originals stated opposite has been issued, one of which being accomplished, the other(s) to be void.

EXCESS VALUATION: REFER TO CLAUSE 7(3) ON REVERSE SIDE (U.S. TRADE ONLY).....

*** ORIGINAL ***

This Bill of Lading has been printed remotely via the Internet, at the customer's premises.

5 Documentary credit

Deutsche Bank
Musterstadt Branch
P.O. BOX 222777
D-12345 Musterstadt

TELEX : 888833
SWIFT : DEUTDEDE987
PHONE : 0123/456-789 MEIER

PER SWIFT ERLEDIGT
14. FEB 2003

DOCUMENTARY-CREDIT ISSUANCE
PAGE 1 OF 2

Ihre Nr./Your No.		
Unsere Nr./Our No.	7770550128IA	
+05%/-05%	Währung/Currency EUR	Betrag/Amount 45.130,00

PUSAN BANK
P.O. BOX 5555

SEOUL
KOREA, SUED

BY ORDER OF

FREIZEIT & WELLNESS GMBH
STADTGARTEN 15
D-12345 MUSTERSTADT

WE ISSUE OUR IRREVOCABLE DOCUMENTARY CREDIT IN FAVOUR OF
SUN FUN & WIRELESS LTD.
7TH FLOOR, DONGWOO BLDG.
123 YEOKSAM-DONG, KANGNAM-KU
SEOUL, KOREA 987654
FOR AN AMOUNT OF EUR 45.130,00
AMOUNT IN WORDS
****** ****** ****** ****** ****** FOUR** FIVE** ONE*** THREE* ZERO**
DECIMAL PLACES, IF ANY, AS STATED ABOVE.
UP TO AN AMOUNT OF 05 PERCENT MORE OR 05 PERCENT LESS
AVAILABLE WITH US
BY DEFERRED PAYMENT AT 30 DAYS AFTER BL-DATE.
THE FOLLOWING DOCUMENTS ARE TO BE PRESENTED:

1) SIGNED COMMERCIAL INVOICE 1 ORIGINAL AND 3 COPIES
2) PACKING LIST IN 3-FOLD CONFIRMING THAT ALL PACKING INSTRUCTIONS AS PER APPLICANT'S LETTER DATED 11. FEB 2011 HAVE BEEN COMPLIED WITH
3) FULL SET (3-3) OF CLEAN ON BOARD SHIPPING COMPANY MARINE BILLS OF LADING ISSUED TO ORDER, BLANK ENDORSED, MARKED: FREIGHT PREPAID TO HAMBURG AND NOTIFY APPLICANT WITH FULL ADDRESS.
4) INSPECTION CERTIFICATES ACC. EN13456-4.2B FOR EACH ITEM SHOWING THE FIGURES OF THE ACTUAL ROPE-DIAM, THE ACTUAL BREAKING LOAD AND THE CHEMICAL ANALYSIS OF THE ROPING WIRES

CERTIFICATE OF ORIGIN
EVIDENCING SHIPMENT OF THE FOLLOWING GOODS:
XYZ AS PER ORDER SPECIFICATION NO. 24681359
QUALITY AISI 124 / ...... = 18.000 M +/- 5 PCT,
QUALITY AISI 236 / ...... = 114.000 M +/- 5 PCT.
DDP 20359 HAMBURG

Dokumenten-Akkreditive unterliegen den Einheitlichen Richtlinien und Gebräuchen für Dokumenten-Akkreditive, Revision 2007 , ICC
Documentary credits are subject to Uniform Customs and Practice for Documentary Credits, 2007 Revision, ICC Publicatio
Inkassi unterliegen den Einheitlichen Richtlinien für Inkassi, Revision 2007 ICC Publikation Nr. 522. /
Collections are subject to Uniform Rules for Collections, 2007 Revision, ICC Publication No. 522.

Deutsche Bank
Musterstadt Branch
P.O. BOX 222777
D-12345 Musterstadt

TELEX : 888833
SWIFT : DEUTDEDE987
PHONE : 0123/456-789 MEIER

PER SWIFT ERLEDIGT
14. FEB 2003

DOCUMENTARY-CREDIT ISSUANCE
PAGE 2 OF 2

Ihre Nr./Your No.		
Unsere Nr./Our No.	7770550128IA	
+05%/-05%	Währung/Currency EUR	Betrag/Amount 45.130,00

PUSAN BANK
P.O. BOX 5555

SEOUL
KOREA, SUED

FROM ANY SOUTH KOREAN PORT
TO ANY NORTH SEA PORT SHOWING PLACE OF DELIVERY DDP 20359 HAMBURG
ON 30. APR 2003 AT THE LATEST.
THE CREDIT IS VALID UNTIL 21. MAY 2003.
PRESENTATION OF DOCUMENTS WITHIN 21 DAYS AFTER THE DATE OF SHIPMENT, BUT WITHIN THE VALIDITY OF THE CREDIT.
PARTIAL SHIPMENTS ARE NOT ALLOWED.
TRANSHIPMENT IS ALLOWED.
ADDITIONAL CONDITIONS:
A FEE OF EUR 175,00 OR EQUIVALENT WILL BE DEDUCTED FOM THE PROCEEDS FOR EACH FULL SET OF DOCUMENTS EVEN IF PRESENTED UNDER ONE REMITTANCE LETTER WHEN IT IS NECESSARY TO CONTACT THE APPLICANT VOR APPROVAL OF DISCREPANT DOCUMENTS.
FURTHERMORE WE WILL DEDUCT OUR SWIFT/TELEX CHARGES FOR EACH ADVICE OF PAYMENT.
AN ADDITIONAL FEE OF EUR 50,00 OR EQUIVALENT PER MONTH WILL BE DEDACTED FOR UNPAID DOCUMENTS IN OUR CUSTODY.
PLEASE SEND DOCUMENTS TO THE FOLLOWING ADDRESS: DEUTSCHE BANK AG, MUSTERSTADT BRANCH, FINANZPLATZ 24, 12345 MUSTERSTADT, GERMANY.
PLEASE ADVISE THIS CREDIT TO THE BENEFICIARY WITHOUT ADDING YOUR CONFIRMATION.
PLEASE ADVISE THROUGH
PUSAN BRANCH, KANG NAM BRANCH
1923-33 SEOCHO-KU, SEOCHO-DONG
SEOUL, KOREA
ACC. 012-34-56789-9
ALL CHARGES OTHER THAN OURS ARE FOR ACCOUNT OF THE BENEFICIARY.

PLEASE FORWARD THE DOCUMENTS TO US BY REGISTERED AIRMAIL. PROVIDED THE TERMS AND CONDITONS OF THIS CREDIT HAVE BEEN FULLY COMPLIED WITH AND WE HAVE RECEIVED THE DOCUMENTS; WE SHALL EFFECT PAYMENT AT MATURITY IN ACCORDANCE WITH YOUR INSTRUCTIONS.

DEUTSCHE BANK AG
MUSTERSTADT BRANCH

Dokumenten-Akkreditive unterliegen den Einheitlichen Richtlinien und Gebräuchen für Dokumenten-Akkreditive, Revision 2007 , ICC Publikation Nr. 500. /
Documentary credits are subject to Uniform Customs and Practice for Documentary Credits, 2007 Revision, ICC Publication No. 500.
Inkassi unterliegen den Einheitlichen Richtlinien für Inkassi, Revision 2007 , ICC Publikation Nr. 522. /
Collections are subject to Uniform Rules for Collections, 2007 Revision, ICC Publication No. 522.

6 Certificate of air cargo insurance

Exporter
Hans Turck GmbH & Co. KG, Mülheim-Ruhr, Germany

CERTIFICATE NUMBER: TUR1448-4001-118064-1096

NBB Risk Services
(International) Ltd
Harzard House 80 Fenchurch
Street
London EC3 4JX
UK

Exporter's reference
SCAMONJ

Forwarder's reference

Consignee
NANNING Engineering, Liuzhou, China

Settling agent
Huatai Insurance Agency & Consultant Service Ltd
Room 725, Jan Yuan Mansion
155 Tian He East Road
510620 Guangzhou
China

CONDITIONS OF INSURANCE
☒ Institute Cargo Clauses (A)
☐ Institute Cargo Clauses (B)
☐ Institute Cargo Clauses (C)
☐ Institute Cargo Clauses (Air) (Excluding sendings by Post)
Further subject to Institute War Clauses and Institute Strikes Clauses (Cargo) (Air Cargo)
Insitute Classification Clause
Institute Radioactive Contamination Exclusion Clause
Other Special Conditions (see reverse)

Other transport details

Conveyance	**Place of shipment**
Air freight	Düsseldorf Airport

Port of discharge	**Final destination**	**Insured value**	**Premium**
Guangzhou Airport, China	Liuzhou, China	EUR 110,000.00 incl. 10%	Premium paid

Shipping marks; container numbers
Number and kind of packages; description of goods

COMMODITY: REMOTE I/O EQUIPMENT; DETAILS AS PER CONTRACT
QUANITITY: 1 SET
TERMS OF DELIVERY: CIP LIUZHOU, CHINA
PACKING: SUITABLE FOR LONG DISTANCE AIR TRANSPORTATION
7 PACKAGES
SHIPPING MARKS: SGTWWPS2 200008GDH-01
LIUZHOU, CHINA

DETAILS OF GOODS AND MARKS AS PER COMMERCIAL INVOICE NO. ARE/221288

ORDER NO: 220243376

DETAILS AS PER CONTRACT NO: SGTWWPS2 20008GDH-01

TOTAL AMOUNT: EUR 100,000.00

STIPULATIONS AS PER L/C:
CLAIMS PAYABLE IN CHINA IN CURRENCY OF THE DRAFT
COVERING AIR TRANSPORTATION ALL RISKS, WAR RISKS

Gross weight
1,835 kg

Net weight
1,610 kg

PROCEDURE IN EVENT OF CLAIM

1 It is the duty of the Assured and their agents to take such measures as may be reasonable for the purpose of averting or minimising a loss and to ensure that all rights against Carriers Bailees or other third parties are properly preserved and exercised.
2 Follow the procedures stated overleaf.
3 Apply immediately for survey of damaged goods to the Agent stated above or if none stated to the nearest Institute of London Underwriters or Lloyd's Agent or to NBB Risk Services (International) as shown above.

This is to certify that NBB Risk Services (International) has insured the above-mentioned goods for the voyage and value stated on behalf of:
Hans Turck GmbH, Mülheim-Ruhr, Germany
Under policy number
TUR1448-4001-118064-1096

This Certificate is not valid unless countersigned.
This Certificate requires endorsement by the Assured.

Signatory's company
Hans Turck GmbH; Mülheim-Ruhr, Germany

Name of signatory
Cornelia Schweiger

Dated
31 March 20..

For NBB Risk Services (International) Ltd
G. Wallis
Gerald Wallis, Managing Director

Signed
Schweiger

Business letters

Tel: +49 211 93288154
Fax: +49 211 93288150
www.top-act-event.de
nina.wittstock@top-act-event.de

TOP Act EVENT

Top Act Event Management GmbH[1]
Graf-Adolf-Str. 240
40210 Düsseldorf
Germany

NW/TT[2]
09 December 20..[3]

Modular Buildings Ltd[4]
99 Canterbury Road
FOLKESTONE
CT18 8HT
GREAT BRITAIN

Attn. Mr Donald Campbell, Export Sales Director[5]

Dear Mr Campbell[6]

Enquiry about modular buildings[7]

Your company has been recommended to us by Ms Sarah Parkinson of Catering Solutions in Newcastle, who tells us that you supply high-quality modular buildings at competitive prices.[8]

Please let us have details of your entire range of products and your current export price list, including all discounts. Details of your terms of delivery and payment would also be appreciated. Delivery would need to be made by 31 May 20.. at the latest.

For your information, a plan of the site with details of all the buildings needed is enclosed.

We look forward to hearing from you soon.

Yours sincerely
Top Act Event Management[9]

Nina Wittstock[10]

Nina Wittstock[11]
Purchasing Director

1 **Letterhead**

2 **Reference initials:** NW = signatory's initials TT = secretary's intials

3 **Date:** Always write the month as a word to avoid confusion. Write the year with four digits.

4 **Inside address:** Write the city in capital letters and the postcode on a separate line in a letter to the UK.

5 **Attention line**

6 **Salutation:** Linked with the complimentary close (no. 9).

7 **Subject line:** Underlined or bold

8 **Body of the letter:** Starts with a capital letter.

9 **Complimentary close:** Linked with the salutation (no. 6).

10 **Signature**

11 **Signatory's name** is written clearly under the signature. Signatory's initials are in no. 2.

12 **Enc** = Enclosure
Encs = Enclosures

Salutation line and complimentary close		
You open a letter with	**when you**	**and you close with**
Dear Sir or Madam	don't know the person's name	Yours faithfully
Dear Mr/Mrs/Miss …	know the person	Yours sincerely
Dear Ms …	know that the person is female but are not sure whether she is *Miss* or *Mrs*	Yours sincerely

In international trade the eleven Incoterms® 2010 Rules (international commercial terms) are used in contracts of sale to define the rights and obligations of the buyer and seller as regards risk, transport, insurance, packing, customs duty and documentation. They are terms of delivery.

INCOTERMS 2010

RULES FOR ANY MODE OR MODES OF TRANSPORT

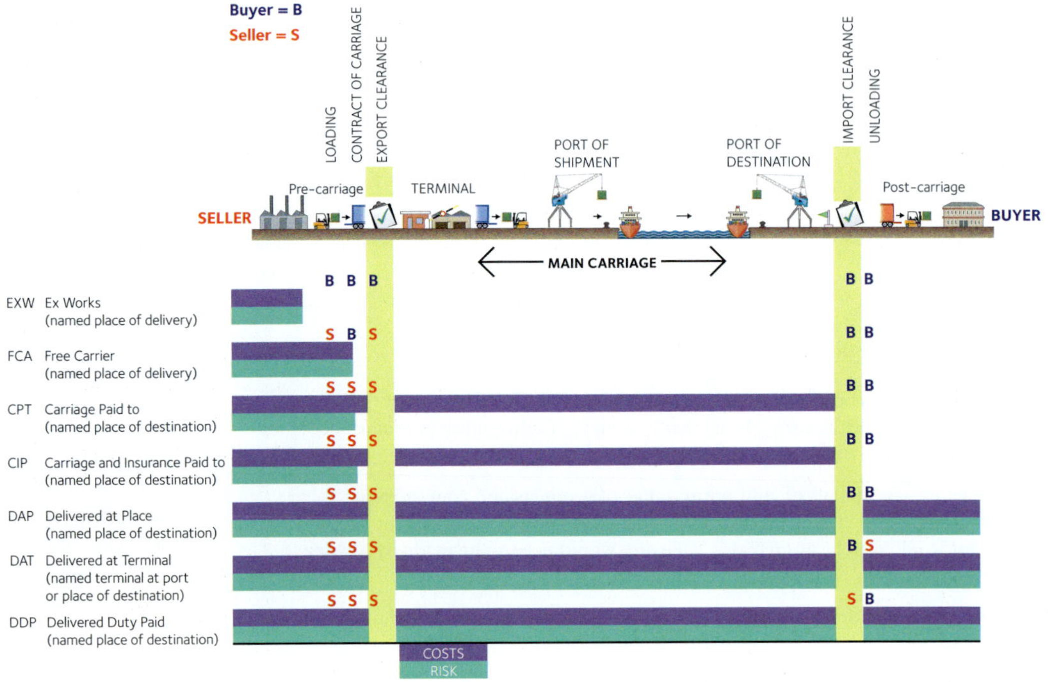

INCOTERMS 2010

RULES FOR SEA AND INLAND WATERWAY TRANSPORT

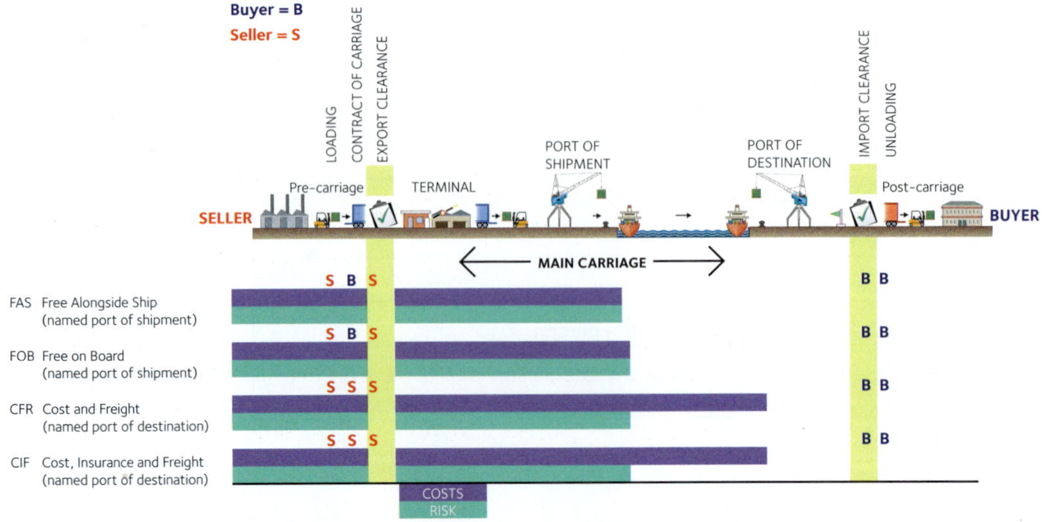

Rules for any mode or modes of transport

EXW – EX WORKS (... named place of delivery)
The seller makes the goods available at his premises in the customary packing. The seller assists the buyer in obtaining any documentation needed at the buyer's expense. The buyer is responsible for loading the goods, transporting them to their destination, customs clearance and insurance.

FCA – FREE CARRIER (... named place of delivery) Multimodal transport
The seller is not responsible for the main carriage of the goods. The seller delivers the goods at his own expense and risk, in the customary packing, cleared for export to the carrier nominated by the buyer. The seller provides the commercial invoice and, if requested, a certificate of origin at the buyer's expense. If the goods are collected at the seller's premises, the seller loads the goods. The seller bears the risks until the goods are in the custody of the first carrier. After that the buyer bears all the costs and risks of transporting the goods to their destination.

CPT – CARRIAGE PAID TO (... named place of destination) Multimodal transport
The seller pays for the main carriage of the goods. The seller delivers the goods, in the customary packing, cleared for export to the carrier which he nominates. The seller bears the risk until the goods have been delivered into the custody of the first carrier. The seller pays the transport costs for the goods, excluding transport insurance, up to the named destination. The buyer is responsible for insuring the goods for the main carriage and pays all import duties and taxes.

CIP – CARRIAGE AND INSURANCE PAID TO (... named place of destination) Multimodal transport
The seller pays for the main carriage of the goods. The seller delivers the goods in the customary packing, cleared for export to the carrier which he nominates. The seller bears the risk until the goods have been delivered into the custody of the first carrier. The seller pays the transport costs for the goods, including transport insurance, up to the named destination. The buyer pays all import duties and taxes.

DAP – DELIVERED AT PLACE (... named place of destination) Multimodal transport
The seller is responsible for the carriage of the goods in the customary packing, cleared for export to the named terminal at the destination by the carrier which he nominates. He bears the risk until the goods have been delivered to the named terminal. The buyer is responsible for unloading the goods at the place of destination and pays all import duties and taxes.

DAT – DELIVERED AT TERMINAL (... named terminal at port or place of destination) Multimodal transport
The seller is responsible for the carriage of the goods in the customary packing, cleared for export to the named terminal at the destination by the carrier which he nominates. He bears the risk until the goods have been delivered to the named terminal. The seller is responsible for unloading the goods at the place of destination. The buyer pays all import duties and taxes.

DDP – DELIVERED DUTY PAID (... named place of destination) Multimodal transport
The seller is responsible for the carriage of the goods in the customary packing, cleared for export to the named terminal at the destination by the carrier which he nominates. He bears the risk until the goods have been delivered to the named destination. The seller pays all import duties and taxes. The buyer is responsible for unloading the goods at the place of destination.

Rules for sea and inland waterway transport

FAS – FREE ALONGSIDE SHIP (... named port of shipment)
The seller is not responsible for the main carriage of the goods. The seller delivers the goods at his own expense and risk, in the customary packing, cleared for export, alongside the vessel selected by the buyer at the named port of shipment. Thereafter, the buyer bears all the costs and risks of transporting the goods to their destination.

FOB – FREE ON BOARD (... named port of shipment)
The seller is not responsible for the main carriage of the goods. The seller delivers the goods at his own expense and risk, in the customary packing, cleared for export, on board the vessel selected by the buyer unless otherwise agreed, at the named port of shipment. Thereafter, the buyer bears all the costs and risks of transporting the goods to their destination.

CFR – COST AND FREIGHT (... named port of destination)
The seller pays for the main carriage of the goods. The seller delivers the goods at his own expense and risk, in the customary packing, cleared for export, on board the vessel selected by the buyer, at the named port of shipment. The seller pays the transport costs for the goods, excluding transport insurance, up to the named port of destination. The buyer is responsible for insuring the goods for the main carriage and pays all import duties and taxes.

CIF – COST INSURANCE FREIGHT (... named port of destination)
The seller pays for the main carriage of the goods. The seller delivers the goods at his own expense and risk, in the customary packing, cleared for export, on board the vessel selected by the buyer, at the named port of shipment. The seller pays the transport costs for the goods, including transport insurance, up to the named port of destination. The buyer pays all import duties and taxes.

Terms of payment

payment in advance	Vorauszahlung/Vorkasse
cash with order (CWO)	Barzahlung bei Auftragserteilung
payment by irrevocable and confirmed documentary (letter of) credit	Zahlung durch unwiderrufliches und bestätigtes Dokumentenakkreditiv
documents against payment (D/P)/ cash against documents (CAD)	Kasse gegen Dokumente
cash on delivery (COD)	gegen Nachnahme
1/3 with order, 1/3 on delivery, 1/3 within 30 days after delivery	1/3 bei Auftragserteilung, 1/3 bei Lieferung, 1/3 innerhalb von 30 Tagen nach Lieferung
payment within 60 days from date of invoice	Zahlung innerhalb von 60 Tagen nach Rechnungsdatum
10 days 2%, 30 days net	Zahlung innerhalb 10 Tagen abzüglich 2 % Skonto oder innerhalb 30 Tagen netto
payment on receipt of goods	Zahlung bei Erhalt der Waren
payment on receipt of invoice	Zahlung bei Rechnungserhalt
documents against (three months') acceptance (D/A)	Dokumente gegen (Dreimonats)akzept
open account terms with monthly/quarterly settlement	offenes Zahlungsziel mit monatlicher/vierteljährlicher Abrechnung

Schriftliche Prüfung

Zeit:	**90 Minuten**
Hilfsmittel:	**allgemeines zweisprachiges Wörterbuch**
Maximale Punktzahl:	**100 Punkte**

Im Rahmen der schriftlichen Prüfung werden die Aufgabenanteile für die drei Kompetenzbereiche wie folgt gewichtet:

- **Rezeption 40 %**
- **Produktion 30 %**
- **Mediation 30 %.**

Im Folgenden werden vier Aufgaben vorgelegt, die Sie bearbeiten sollen. Die erste und die zweite Aufgabe beziehen sich auf Ihre Fähigkeit, englische Texte (gesprochene und geschriebene) zu verstehen = **Rezeption**. In der dritten Aufgabe sollen Sie ein Schriftstück erstellen = **Produktion** eines englischen Textes. Bei der vierten Aufgabe wird von Ihnen erwartet, dass Sie Texte von der deutschen oder englischen in die jeweils andere Sprache übertragen = **Mediation**.

Die Prüfung beginnt mit der Hörverständnisaufgabe. Alle weiteren Aufgaben können in beliebiger Reihenfolge bearbeitet werden.

Rezeption I: Hörverstehen

24

Teil I: Dialog — 10 Punkte

Situation: Brian Hopkins, 19, besucht die *European Vocational School for Office Professions (EVSOP)* in Bristol. Er hat im Rahmen eines Projekts der EU die Gelegenheit, deutsche Azubis nach ihren Erfahrungen im Arbeitsleben und speziell im Bereich des Groß- und Außenhandels zu befragen.

Aufgabe: Hören Sie aufmerksam zu und entscheiden dann, ob die nachstehenden Aussagen (1–8) richtig oder falsch sind und begründen Sie jeweils kurz Ihre Antwort. Beantworten Sie die Verständnisfragen (9–10) in kurzen Stichworten auf Deutsch.

1. Stefanie und Brian hatten bereits miteinander Kontakt.
2. Das Hotel, in dem die beiden deutschen Azubis übernachten, heißt „Severn Bridge".
3. Die deutsche Regierung hat Billionen von Euro für Arbeits-Qualifizierungsmaßnahmen ausgegeben.
4. Brian muss ein Busticket kaufen, um zur Arbeit zu kommen.
5. Brians Ausbildungsbetrieb wendet eine Probezeit für Azubis an.
6. Stefanie konnte vor dem Beginn ein Praktikum ableisten.
7. Stefanies Betrieb stellt Operationsgeräte her und vertreibt sie.
8. Die drei unterbrechen ihr Gespräch nach einer Weile.
9. Inwiefern hat sich Stefanies Arbeitsverhältnis seit Unterzeichnung des Vertrags verändert?
10. Wie beschreibt Stefanie das Preisniveau des ÖPNV in ihrer Region?

25

Teil II: Anrufbeantworter — 10 Punkte

Aufgabe: Sie hören Ihren Anrufbeantworter ab, auf dem eine Nachricht eines Geschäftspartners hinterlassen wurde.

- Schreiben Sie die persönlichen Daten des Geschäftspartners auf (siehe das unten stehende Notizblatt).
- Nutzen Sie dann den Notizzettel um den Inhalt des Gesprächs in Stichworten auf Deutsch aufzuschreiben.
- Sie hören die Nachricht zwei Mal.

Datum: ...
Anrufer: ...
Uhrzeit: ...
Kontakt: ...
Nachricht: ...

Rezeption II: Leseverstehen — 20 Punkte

Aufgabe: Lesen Sie den nachstehenden Text durch und bearbeiten dann die Verständnisfragen (1–5) in Stichworten auf Deutsch. Entscheiden Sie, ob die nachstehenden Aussagen (6–10) richtig oder falsch sind und begründen Sie jeweils kurz Ihre Antwort.

1 Für welche Gruppe von Verbrauchern ist der Aakash hauptsächlich gedacht? (2)
2 Nennen Sie 3 Eigenschaften des Aakash. (3)
3 Was erfährt der Leser über die zweite Version des Tablet Computers? (3)
4 Wo soll der Aakash eingesetzt werden? (2)
5 Was ist der Sakshat Computer? (2)
6 Der Computer wird im Moment im indischen Arbeitsministerium getestet.
7 Der Tablet Computer wurde vollständig in Indien entwickelt. (2)
8 Ziel der Firma DataWind war es auch einen Internetzugang anzubieten. (2)
9 In der Vergangenheit hatten billige Tablets häufig Probleme. (2)
10 Es gibt bereits einen günstigen Laptop von DataWind. (2)

India launches Aakash tablet computer priced at $35

Costing a fraction of Apple's iPad, the subsidized Aakash is aimed at students. It supports web browsing and video conferencing, has a three-hour battery life and two USB ports, but questions remain over how it will perform. Officials hope the computer will give digital access to students in small towns and villages across India, which lags behind its rivals in connectivity.

At the launch in the Indian capital, Delhi, Human Resource Development Minister Kapil Sibal handed out 500 Aakash (meaning *sky*) tablets to students who will test them. He said the government planned to buy 100,000 of the tablets. It hopes to distribute 10 million of the devices to students over the next few years. "The rich have access to the digital world, the poor and ordinary have been excluded. Aakash will end that digital divide," Mr Sibal said.

The Aakash has been developed by UK-based company DataWind and Indian Institute of Technology (Rajasthan). It is due to be assembled in India at DataWind's new production centre in the southern city of Hyderabad. "Our goal was to break the price barrier for computing and internet access," DataWind CEO Suneet Singh Tuli said. "We've created a product that will finally bring affordable computing and internet access to the masses." The company says it will also offer a commercial version of the tablet, called UbiSlate. It is expected to hit the shelves later this year, retailing for about $60.

Mr Sibal says the device will enhance learning in India. Experts say it does have the potential to make a huge difference to the country's education, particularly in rural areas where schools and students do not have access to libraries and up-to-date information.
But critics say it is too early to say how the Aakash will be received as most cheap tablets in the past have turned out to be painfully slow. "The thing with cheap tablets is most of them turn out to be unusable," Rajat Agrawal of technology reviewers BGR India told Reuters news agency. "They don't have a very good touch screen, and they are usually very slow." Critics also point out that an earlier cheap laptop plan by the same ministry came to nothing.

In 2009, it announced plans for a laptop priced as low as $10, raising eyebrows and triggering worldwide media interest. But there was disappointment after the "Sakshat" turned out to be a prototype of a hand-held device, with an unspecified price tag, that never materialized.

Source: adapted from: http://www.bbc.co.uk/news/world-south-asia-15180831

Produktion (Schriftstücke erstellen) 30 Punkte

Situation: Sie sind Auszubildende/r bei Computrade GmbH in Ludwigshafen. Diese Unternehmung vertreibt als Großhändler Computer, elektronische Bauteile sowie Mobiltelefone. Ihr Vorgesetzter (m.herrmann@computrade.de) plant einen Messestand auf der Messe AsiExpo in Indien. Sie sollen für diesen Stand die Eckdaten per E-Mail abklären.

Aufgabe: Ihre Aufgabe besteht darin, eine E-Mail zu erstellen. Formulieren Sie den Text einschließlich Anrede und Betreff. Formulieren Sie einen Schlusssatz, signieren Sie die Mail mit Ihrem Namen und schicken Sie Ihrem Chef eine offene Kopie der E-Mail. Schreiben Sie in vollständigen Sätzen und decken Sie folgende Punkte ab:

- E-Mail an info@delhiexpo.in
- Stellen Sie ganz kurz unsere Firma vor und hängen Sie die Dateien „engcomp.pdf" an
- Fordern Sie eine Preisliste der Messegesellschaft an
- Beziehen Sie sich auf einen 20 m² großen Stand
- Bitten Sie um Hilfe bei der Einrichtung (Regale, Teppiche, Sitzelemente)
- Fragen Sie nach der Internetversorgung (am besten wäre: WLAN und LAN-Verkabelung am Stand)
- Fragen Sie, ob Messestände in der Nähe eines Restaurants verfügbar sind und ob diese teurer sind
- Kann die Messegesellschaft bei der Zimmerbuchung behilflich sein?

To: info@delhiexpo.in
CC: ...
Subject: ...
Attachments: ...

Send Draft

Mediation (Übertragen eines Textes) 30 Punkte

Situation: Sie erhalten per Post die angeforderten Informationen über die Messe von Indien. Im Umschlag finden Sie unter anderem folgende Broschüre.

Aufgabe: Geben Sie Ihrem Vorgesetzten in Stichworten auf Deutsch nur die Informationen weiter, die für Ihre Firma von Bedeutung sind.

TCCI

The Trade Centre of Central India (TCCI) is located in the outskirts of the city of Bengaluru, Bangalore. It has a surface area of 50 acres, which is split up into six different exhibition areas, each of which extends to about 3,500 m^2 of exhibition halls and services.

Hall One is 4,890 m^2 and has ceiling heights which range from a minimum of 7 m to 10 m to allow free movement of all merchandise including heavy machinery. Just outside of Hall One is an extra 3,500 m^2 of conference rooms for 300 delegates and several restaurants.

The TCCI is the most modern exhibition complex in India, designed for all your needs. All halls are air-conditioned and can be used for exhibitions, conventions and conferences. We are open to all your wishes. The TCCI is located at a distance

of about 5 km from the airport and 15 km from the railway station in Bengaluru. We also have 20 five-star hotels, which are within walking distance or can be reached within 15 minutes by taxi.

To book exhibition space or to make general enquiries, please contact:

TCCI Trade Promotion Ltd
56/5, 3rd Floor, Maharja Building
Airport Road,
North Bangalore – 990 002

Tel.: 91-90-44211066
Fax: 91-90-4421107
Email:enquiries@tcci.bengaluru.in

Mündliche Prüfung

Die Prüfung ist eine Gruppenprüfung, bei der Sie Gespräche persönlichen und fachlichen Inhalts in der Fremdsprache führen sollen. Es wird von Ihnen erwartet, dass Sie der vorgegebenen Situation entsprechend sprachlich agieren und reagieren. Es kommt dabei vor allem darauf an, dass Sie sich spontan äußern, dass Sie versuchen, sich verständlich zu machen, und dass Sie gut zuhören.
Die Prüfung besteht aus zwei Teilen und dauert insgesamt ca. 20 Minuten. Zur Vorbereitung haben Sie 20 Minuten Zeit.
Im **ersten Teil** der mündlichen Prüfung werden Sie gebeten, sich zu persönlichen oder beruflichen Themen zu äußern.
Im **zweiten Teil** sollen Sie zusammen mit einem anderen Kandidaten ein Rollenspiel durchführen. Dazu erhalten Sie vom Prüfer Rollenkarten, auf denen eine Situation beschrieben ist, die Sie vorspielen sollen.

Hilfsmittel: allgemeines zweisprachiges Wörterbuch.

Mündliche Prüfung: Teil II — 15 Punkte

Kandidat/in A

Situation: Sie reisen gemeinsam mit Ihrem Ausbilder, Herrn Matthias Herrmann, zur AsiExpo, einer Messe in Indien. Dort treffen Sie auf einem Forum der indischen Handelskammer einen Auszubildenden aus Frankreich (Kandidat/in B: Martin/e).

Aufgabe: Unterhalten Sie sich mit Martin/e
- Stellen Sie sich vor und fragen Ihren Gesprächspartner nach seiner Person.
- Erkundigen Sie sich, woher in Frankreich Ihr Gesprächspartner stammt.
- Erzählen Sie von Ihrer Ausbildung in der Berufsschule und Ihrem Ausbildungsbetrieb.
- Erkundigen Sie sich nach der Produktpalette des französischen Betriebs.
- Führen Sie weiteren Small-Talk (Wetter in Indien, Essen, Flug, Hotel u. ä.).
- Fragen Sie, ob Martin/e Lust hat, nach der Messe in Europa weiter Kontakt zu halten.
- Wünschen Sie Martin/e einen schönen Aufenthalt und einen guten Rückflug.

Kandidat/in B

Situation: Sie sind Martin/e LeGrand und Azubi aus Frankreich. Sie reisen gemeinsam mit Ihrem Ausbilder zur AsiExpo, einer Messe in Indien. Dort treffen Sie auf einem Forum der indischen Handelskammer auf einen Auszubildenden aus Deutschland (Kandidat/in A).

Aufgabe: Unterhalten Sie sich mit Kandidat/in A
- Stellen Sie sich vor und fragen Ihren Gesprächspartner nach seiner Person.
- Erkundigen Sie sich, woher in Deutschland Ihr Gesprächspartner stammt und sagen Sie, dass Sie von der Côte d'Azur, aus Nizza (engl. *Nice*) stammen.
- Erzählen Sie von Ihrer Ausbildung in Ihrem Betrieb und in welcher Abteilung Sie arbeiten.
- Erzählen Sie von Ihrer Produktpalette (verwenden Sie dazu die Produktpalette Ihres eigenen Betriebs).
- Fragen Sie nach den Ausbildungsbedingungen in Deutschland.
- Erkundigen Sie sich nach der Produktpalette des französischen Betriebs.
- Führen Sie weiteren Small-Talk (Wetter in Indien, Essen, Flug, Hotel u. ä.).
- Wünschen Sie Kandidat/in A einen schönen Aufenthalt und einen guten Rückflug.

Useful phrases

Greeting people

Unit 1

Offering help	**Hilfe anbieten**
▪ How can I be of assistance to you?	▪ *Wie kann ich Ihnen behilflich sein?*
▪ What can I do for you?	▪ *Was kann ich für Sie tun?*
Introducing yourself	**Sich vorstellen**
▪ How do you do? My name is …	▪ *Wie geht es Ihnen? Mein Name ist …*
▪ Good morning/afternoon/evening. I'm …	▪ *Guten Morgen/Tag/Abend. Ich bin …*
▪ I work in the … department.	▪ *Ich arbeite in der …-abteilung.*
▪ Hi, I don't think we've met. I'm …	▪ *Hallo. Ich glaube nicht, dass wir uns kennengelernt haben. Ich bin …*
Greeting people you do not know	**Menschen, die man nicht kennt, begrüßen**
▪ I'm very pleased to meet you.	▪ *Es freut mich, Sie kennen zu lernen.*
▪ Nice to meet you too.	▪ *Ganz meinerseits.*
▪ Welcome to …	▪ *Herzlich willkommen bei …*
▪ Thank you. It's nice to be here.	▪ *Dankeschön. Es ist schön, hier zu sein.*
Introducing people who do not know each other	**Menschen, die sich nicht kennen, einander vorstellen**
▪ This is … / These are my colleagues, John and Mary.	▪ *Das ist …. Das sind meine Kollegen, John und Mary.*
▪ Let me introduce you to …, from the … department.	▪ *Darf ich Ihnen … aus der …-abteilung vorstellen?*
▪ I'd like you to meet …	▪ *Ich möchte Ihnen … vorstellen.*
▪ Have you met …?	▪ *Haben Sie … schon kennen gelernt?*
Offering your first name	**Das „Du" anbieten**
▪ Please, call me Brian.	▪ *Sie können mich ruhig Brian nennen.*
▪ It's Peter, by the way.	▪ *Ich bin übrigens Peter.*
Offering and accepting refreshments	**Getränke anbieten und annehmen**
▪ Can I offer you something to drink?	▪ *Kann ich Ihnen etwas zu trinken anbieten?*
▪ I'd love a glass of water, please.	▪ *Ich hätte gerne ein Glas Wasser, bitte.*
▪ What do you take in your tea/coffee?	▪ *Wie trinken Sie Ihren Tee/Kaffee?*
▪ Milk, please, but no sugar.	▪ *Bitte mit Milch, aber keinem Zucker.*

Showing a visitor around your company

Asking for directions	**Nach dem Weg fragen**
▪ Excuse me, I'm looking for …	▪ *Entschuldigung, ich suche …*
▪ Can you tell me where I can find …, please?	▪ *Können Sie mir sagen, wo ich … finde, bitte?*
▪ Could you tell me the way to …, please?	▪ *Können Sie mir den Weg nach … beschreiben?*
▪ Do you happen to know …?	▪ *Wissen Sie vielleicht …?*
Giving directions	**Den Weg beschreiben**
▪ Please take one of the lifts/elevators to the first floor.	▪ *Bitte nehmen Sie einen der Aufzüge in den ersten Stock.*
▪ When you come out of the lift, turn left/right.	▪ *Wenn Sie aus dem Aufzug kommen, gehen Sie nach links/rechts.*
▪ Continue to the end of the corridor.	▪ *Gehen Sie weiter bis zum Ende des Flurs.*
▪ Go straight ahead/on.	▪ *Gehen Sie geradeaus.*
▪ It's the first door on the right, just after …	▪ *Es ist die erste Tür auf der rechten Seite, gleich hinter …*
▪ to the right/left of …	▪ *nach rechts/links von …*
▪ You'll find it between the … and the …	▪ *Sie sehen es zwischen … und …*
▪ It's just next to …	▪ *Es ist genau neben …*
▪ Go upstairs/downstairs.	▪ *Gehen Sie die Treppe hoch/runter.*

Making a telephone call

Unit 2

Making a call	Telefonieren
▪ Good morning. My name is …	▪ *Guten Morgen. Ich heiße …*
▪ Good afternoon. This is … from …	▪ *Guten Tag. Hier spricht … von …*
▪ I'd like to speak to Mr/Mrs/Ms/Miss …	▪ *Ich hätte gern Herrn/Frau … gesprochen.*
▪ Could you put me through to the … department, please?	▪ *Könnten Sie mich zur …-abteilung durchstellen, bitte?*
▪ Is your Managing Director available at the moment?	▪ *Ist Ihr Geschäftsführer gerade zu sprechen?*
Making small talk	**Smalltalk halten**
▪ How are you?	▪ *Wie geht es Ihnen?*
▪ How's the weather today?	▪ *Wie ist das Wetter bei Ihnen heute?*
▪ Did you have a nice holiday?	▪ *Haben Sie einen schönen Urlaub gehabt?*
Saying what the call is about	**Sagen Sie, worum es bei dem Anruf geht**
▪ I'm interested in …	▪ *Ich interessiere mich für …*
▪ I was wondering if you could help me.	▪ *Ich wollte fragen, ob Sie mir weiterhelfen könnten.*
▪ I'm enquiring about …	▪ *Ich wollte mich nach … erkundigen.*
▪ I'd like some information on …	▪ *Ich möchte Informationen zu … erhalten.*
▪ The reason I'm calling is …	▪ *Der Grund, warum ich anrufe, ist …*
Answering the phone	**Ans Telefon gehen**
▪ Good morning, Fynton Industries Ltd. How can I help you?	▪ *Guten Morgen, Fynton Industries GmbH. Wie kann ich Ihnen weiterhelfen?*
▪ Hello, … speaking.	▪ *Hallo, hier ist … .*
Asking the caller for more information	**Den Anrufer nach mehr Informationen fragen**
▪ Could you tell me what it's about, please?	▪ *Könnten Sie mir bitte sagen, worum es geht?*
▪ May I ask why you're calling?	▪ *Darf ich fragen, warum Sie anrufen?*
Transferring the call	**Den Anruf weiterleiten**
▪ I'll put you through to …	▪ *Ich leite Sie an … weiter.*
▪ I'll connect you with …	▪ *Ich verbinde Sie mit …*
▪ Can you hold the line for a moment, please?	▪ *Könnten Sie bitte kurz in der Leitung bleiben?*
Explaining that someone is busy	**Erklären, dass jemand gerade keine Zeit hat**
▪ I'm afraid that … is in a meeting at the moment.	▪ *Es tut mir leid, … ist gerade in einer Besprechung.*
▪ I'm sorry, but … isn't available at the moment.	▪ *Es tut mir leid, aber … ist gerade nicht erreichbar.*
▪ I'm afraid his/her line is engaged.	▪ *Es tut mir leid, sein/ihr Anschluss ist besetzt.*
▪ Can I get him/her to call you back?	▪ *Kann ich ihm/ihr ausrichten, dass er/sie Sie zurückrufen soll?*
▪ Can I take a message?	▪ *Kann ich etwas ausrichten?*
▪ Would you like to leave a message?	▪ *Würden Sie gerne eine Nachricht hinterlassen?*
▪ What number can he/she reach you on?	▪ *Unter welcher Nummer kann er/sie Sie erreichen?*
Saying what you want to do	**Sagen, was Sie tun wollen**
▪ Can I leave a message?	▪ *Kann ich eine Nachricht hinterlassen?*
▪ I'll call again later.	▪ *Ich rufe später noch mal an.*
▪ There's a very urgent matter that I need to discuss with you.	▪ *Ich muss mit Ihnen über eine ganz dringende Angelegenheit sprechen.*
Asking the caller to repeat something	**Den Anrufer bitten, etwas zu wiederholen**
▪ Sorry, I didn't catch that.	▪ *Es tut mir leid, das habe ich nicht verstanden.*
▪ Could you say that again, please?	▪ *Könnten Sie das bitte noch einmal sagen?*
▪ Could you spell that for me, please?	▪ *Könnten Sie mir das bitte buchstabieren?*
Ending the call	**Das Telefongespräch beenden**
▪ Is there anything else I can do for you?	▪ *Kann ich noch etwas für Sie tun?*
▪ Thanks for your help/assistance.	▪ *Vielen Dank für Ihre Hilfe/Unterstützung.*
▪ You're welcome. Goodbye.	▪ *Kein Problem / Keine Ursache. Auf Wiederhören.*
▪ Have a nice day/evening.	▪ *Schönen Tag/Abend noch.*

Writing an enquiry

Unit 3

Source of address	Quelle der Anschrift
▪ I was most impressed by the products you showed me on your stand at the … trade fair.	▪ *Ich war von den Produkten, die Sie mir auf Ihrem Stand auf der … Messe gezeigt haben, sehr beeindruckt.*
▪ We note from your company's website that you sell a wide range of …	▪ *Wir entnehmen der Homepage Ihrer Gesellschaft, dass Sie eine breites Sortiment von … anbieten.*
Description of your company	**Beschreibung Ihrer Gesellschaft**
▪ We are a rapidly growing / leading importer and wholesaler of … with excellent business contacts all over … and beyond.	▪ *Wir sind ein schnell wachsender / führender Importeur und Großhändler für … mit hervorragenden Geschäftskontakten in ganz … und darüber hinaus.*
Reason for your enquiry	**Grund für Ihre Anfrage**
▪ At present we are particularly interested in … at reasonable prices.	▪ *Nun gilt unser besonderes Interesse … zu angemessenen Preisen.*
Your requirements	**Ihr Bedarf**
▪ Please send us a favourable quotation for these items / for …	▪ *Bitte schicken Sie uns ein günstiges (Preis)angebot für diese Artikel / für …*
▪ We would therefore/also be grateful if you would let us have a comprehensive catalogue on your entire range …	▪ *Wir wären Ihnen deshalb/auch dankbar, wenn Sie uns einen umfassenden Katalog über Ihre gesamte Produktpalette schicken würden …*
▪ … and your current export price list.	▪ *… zusammen mit Ihrer aktuellen Exportpreisliste.*
▪ … including all discounts granted.	▪ *… einschl. aller gewährten Rabatte.*
▪ … including details of your terms of delivery and payment.	▪ *… einschl. Einzelheiten über Ihre Liefer- und Zahlungsbedingungen.*
▪ Delivery would be required within 6 months.	▪ *Die Lieferung hätten wir gerne innerhalb 6 Monaten.*
References	**Referenzen**
▪ References are available on request.	▪ *Referenzen sind auf Wunsch erhältlich.*
Polite ending	**Höfliche Schlussformel**
▪ If your products meet our requirements, we will be in a position to place a substantial order.	▪ *Wenn Ihre Produkte unseren Anforderungen entsprechen, werden wir in der Lage sein, einen größeren Auftrag zu erteilen.*
▪ We look forward to your early reply with interest.	▪ *Über eine zeitnahe Antwort würden wir uns freuen.*

Writing an offer

Reference to enquiry	Bezug auf Anfrage
▪ We were delighted to receive your enquiry dated … about our …	▪ *Wir waren sehr erfreut, Ihre Anfrage vom … über unser(e) … zu erhalten.*
▪ I am pleased let you have details of our offer in writing.	▪ *Ich freue mich, Ihnen ein schriftliches Angebot zukommen zu lassen.*
▪ Many thanks for the above-mentioned enquiry / your enquiry dated …	▪ *Wir danken für die oben genannte Anfrage / Ihre Anfrage vom …*
Description of your company/goods/services	**Beschreibung Ihrer Gesellschaft/Waren/ Dienstleistungen**
▪ We are a major distributor of …	▪ *Wir sind ein bedeutender Großhändler für …*
▪ … with an excellent reputation throughout Europe.	▪ *… mit einem hervorragenden Ruf in ganz Europa.*
Sales material	**Verkaufsmaterial**
▪ We enclose our current catalogue and price list for your information.	▪ *Wir fügen unseren aktuellen Katalog und Preisliste zu Ihrer Information bei.*
▪ To download our latest comprehensive catalogue and export price list, please visit our website at …	▪ *Um unseren neuesten Gesamtkatalog und Exportpreisliste herunterzuladen, besuchen Sie bitte unsere Homepage unter …*
Price	**Preis**
▪ We will be pleased to supply you with … at €… each.	▪ *Wir liefern Ihnen gerne … zu je … €.*
▪ … at US$10 per unit.	▪ *… zu 10 US$ pro Stück.*

Terms and discounts	Geschäftsbedingungen und Nachlässe
▪ Our prices are quoted FOB Hamburg.	▪ *Unsere Preise verstehen sich FOB Hamburg.*
▪ … DDP your premises	▪ *… DDP Ihren Geschäftsräumen.*
▪ Wholesalers are granted a trade discount of …%.	▪ *Großhändlern wird ein Handelsrabatt von … % eingeräumt.*
▪ Our terms of payment for an initial order are CWO.	▪ *Unsere Zahlungsbedingung für einen Erstauftrag ist die Zahlung bei Auftragserteilung.*
▪ … or, with favourable references, 10 days 3%, 30 days net.	▪ *… oder bei günstigen Referenzen, 3 % Skonto bei Zahlung innerhalb von 10 Tagen, netto bei Zahlung innerhalb von 30 Tagen.*
▪ … payment on receipt of goods.	▪ *Zahlung bei Erhalt der Waren.*
Delivery	**Lieferung**
▪ … within … days after receipt of order	▪ *… innerhalb … Tagen nach Auftragseingang*
▪ while stocks last	▪ *solange der Vorrat reicht*
Polite ending	**höfliche Schlussformel**
▪ We feel sure that a trial order will convince you of the quality of our products and look forward to doing business with you.	▪ *Wir sind sicher, dass ein Probeauftrag Sie von der Qualität unserer Produkte überzeugen wird und freuen uns, mit Ihnen in Geschäftsbeziehung zu treten.*
Enclosure(s)	**Anlage(n)**
▪ Catalogue	▪ *Katalog*
▪ Price list	▪ *Preisliste*

Making an appointment

Suggesting a time	Eine Zeit vorschlagen
▪ When would suit you?	▪ *Wann würde es Ihnen passen?*
▪ Would … be convenient for you?	▪ *Wäre Ihnen um … recht?*
▪ How about … on …?	▪ *Wie wäre es am … um …?*
▪ Are you free on …?	▪ *Haben Sie am … Zeit?*
Responding	**Antworten**
▪ Let me just check my diary.	▪ *Lassen Sie mich kurz in meinen Kalender schauen.*
▪ Just let me see when I'm available.	▪ *Lassen Sie mich kurz nachsehen, wann ich Zeit habe.*
▪ Yes, that's fine with me.	▪ *Ja, das passt mir.*
▪ I'm sorry, but I've already got an appointment then.	▪ *Es tut mir leid, aber da habe ich schon einen Termin.*
▪ I'm busy all day until … .	▪ *Ich habe den ganzen Tag bis … keine Zeit.*
▪ I'm afraid not. I'm tied up all day.	▪ *Leider nein. Ich bin den ganzen Tag beschäftigt.*
Suggesting an alternative	**Eine Alternative vorschlagen**
▪ Could we arrange something else?	▪ *Könnten wir wann anderes vereinbaren?*

Making travel arrangements

Unit 4

Asking for help making travel reservations	Nach Hilfe zum Buchen einer Reise fragen
▪ Could you take care of our travel and hotel reservations?	▪ *Könnten Sie sich um unsere Reise- und Hotelbuchungen kümmern?*
▪ Can you look after the car rental for me, please?	▪ *Können Sie sich um den Mietwagen kümmern?*
▪ Could you book me a flight to …, please?	▪ *Könnten Sie mir einen Flug nach … buchen?*
▪ Could you possibly look after the arrangements of our trip?	▪ *Könnten Sie unsere Reise-Arrangements überprüfen?*
Asking for details about travel arrangements	**Nach Einzelheiten zu Reise-Arrangements fragen**
▪ What are the dates of your trip?	▪ *Was sind die Daten Ihrer Reise?*
▪ When are you planning to travel?	▪ *Wann wollen Sie verreisen?*
▪ When will you be returning?	▪ *Wann kommen Sie zurück?*
▪ What time would you like to depart?	▪ *Um wie viel Uhr möchten Sie gerne fliegen?*
▪ Is there anything special I need to know?	▪ *Gibt es irgendetwas Besonderes, das ich wissen sollte?*

Giving details about when you want to travel	Angaben darüber machen, wann man reisen möchte
We'd like to travel early on …	*Wir würden gerne früh am … abreisen.*
I'm going to stay until …	*Ich werde bis … bleiben.*
I'd like to catch a flight early/late in the evening.	*Ich würde gerne einen Flug früh/spät am Abend nehmen.*
Ideally, I'd like to fly out in the early afternoon.	*Im Idealfall würde ich am frühen Nachmittag fliegen.*

Writing an email — Unit 5

Salutation	Begrüßungsformel
Dear Mr/Mrs/Ms/Miss …	*Sehr geehrte(r) …*
Dear Sirs / Dear Sir or Madam	*Sehr geehrte Damen und Herren*
Dear Paul	*Lieber Paul*
Opening sentence	**Einleitungssatz**
How are things?	*Wie geht's dir/Ihnen?*
I hope you're well.	*Ich hoffe, es geht dir/Ihnen gut.*
I am writing to …	*Ich schreibe dir/Ihnen, um zu …*
Just a quick note/message to say …	*Nur eine ganz kurze Bemerkung/Nachricht, um zu sagen, dass …*
Answering or forwarding an email	**Eine E-Mail beantworten oder weiterleiten**
I was delighted to receive your email.	*Ich habe mich sehr über Ihre E-Mail gefreut.*
Thanks for your emails about …	*Vielen Dank für Ihre E-Mails zu …*
I've just received the email below from …	*Ich habe gerade untenstehende E-Mail von … bekommen.*
Giving information	**Auskunft geben**
Please refer to the attachment for …	*Bitte schauen Sie sich den Anhang an, um …*
Click on the link for more details.	*Klicken Sie auf den folgenden Link, um nähere Informationen zu erhalten.*
Closing sentence	**Schlusssatz**
Many thanks for your assistance/help.	*Vielen Dank für Ihre Hilfe.*
Looking forward to …	*Ich freue mich auf …*
I look forward to meeting you.	*Ich freue mich darauf, Sie bald zu treffen.*
Complimentary close	**Grußformel (am Briefende)**
Regards / Best wishes / *(fml)* Yours sincerely	*Mit freundlichen Grüßen*
(fml) Yours faithfully	*Hochachtungsvoll*
All the best / Best regards	*Liebe/Schöne Grüße*

Describing trends

to rise/grow negligibly from … to …	*geringfügig von … auf … ansteigen/wachsen*
to go up / increase slightly by … %	*leicht um … % (an)steigen*
to keep stable / remain constant at …	*gleich / konstant bei … bleiben*
to even out at …	*sich bei … ausgleichen*
to fall/drop significantly from … to …	*deutlich von … auf … fallen / zurückgehen*
to go down / decrease considerably by … %	*erheblich um … % sinken / abnehmen*

Giving a presentation — Unit 6

Welcoming the audience	Das Publikum begrüßen
▪ Good morning, ladies and gentlemen and welcome to …	▪ *Sehr geehrte Damen und Herren, ich begrüße Sie zu …*
▪ Hello, everyone. Thank you for coming today. It's good to see you all here.	▪ *Hallo zusammen. Vielen Dank für Ihr heutiges Erscheinen. Schön, dass Sie alle da sind.*
▪ Ladies and gentlemen, I would like to welcome you to this presentation.	▪ *Sehr geehrte Damen und Herren, ich möchte Sie zu diesem Vortrag willkommen heißen.*
Introducing your topic	**Ihr Thema vorstellen**
▪ The purpose of my presentation is to …	▪ *Das Ziel meiner Präsentation ist …*
▪ Today I'm going to talk about …	▪ *Heute werde ich über … sprechen.*
▪ I'd like to begin by giving you a presentation about …	▪ *Ich möchte mit einem Vortrag über … anfangen.*
Structuring the presentation	**Die Präsentation strukturieren**
▪ I have divided my talk into three main parts. Part one deals with …, part two …, part three …	▪ *Ich habe meinen Vortrag in drei Hauptteile unterteilt. Der erste Teil behandelt …, der zweite Teil …, der dritte Teil …*
▪ My presentation consists of three parts. I'll begin with …, then move on to … and after that I'll tell you …	▪ *Mein Vortrag setzt sich aus drei Teilen zusammen. Ich fange mit … an, gehe dann über zu … und danach erzähle ich …*
Moving on to the next point	**Zum nächsten Punkt überleiten**
▪ Now, let's move on to our next point …	▪ *Nun komme ich zum nächsten Punkt …*
▪ Let's now take a look at …	▪ *Schauen wir uns nun einmal … an.*
▪ Now let's turn to …	▪ *Wenden wir uns nun … zu.*
Describing visuals	**Illustrationen beschreiben**
▪ As you can see from this slide/chart/table/diagram …	▪ *Wie Sie an dieser Folie/Grafik/Tabelle / diesem Diagramm sehen können …*
▪ This pie chart shows … .You can see that the biggest segment indicates the …	▪ *Dieses Kuchendiagramm zeigt … . Sie können sehen, dass das größte Segment/Kuchenstück … angibt.*
▪ These illustrations show …	▪ *Diese Abbildungen zeigen …*
▪ I'd like to draw your attention to this organizational chart.	▪ *Ich möchte Ihre Aufmerksamkeit nun auf dieses Organigramm lenken.*
Dealing with questions	**Mit Fragen umgehen**
▪ If you have any questions, please feel free to interrupt.	▪ *Wenn Sie irgendwelche Fragen haben, unterbrechen Sie mich einfach.*
▪ I'd prefer to answer any questions after finishing my presentation.	▪ *Ich möchte Fragen lieber nach dem Vortrag beantworten.*
▪ Now if you'd like to ask any questions, I'd be delighted to answer them.	▪ *Wenn Sie noch Fragen haben, würde ich sie gerne jetzt beantworten.*
Conclusion	**Schluss**
▪ To sum up …	▪ *Zusammenfassend …*
▪ I'd like to finish my presentation with …	▪ *Ich würde meinen Vortrag gerne mit … schließen.*
▪ And finally, …	▪ *Und schließlich …*
▪ In conclusion …	▪ *Abschließend …*

Language of negotiations — Unit 7

▪ I'm afraid that won't be possible right away.	▪ *Es tut mir leid, das wird nicht sofort möglich sein.*
▪ Perhaps I can make this easy.	▪ *Vielleicht kann ich es Ihnen leicht machen.*
▪ Would it be possible to give me even just a ballpark figure?	▪ *Könnten Sie mir vielleicht eine grobe Schätzung anbieten?*
▪ I should be in a position to let you know by the end of next week.	▪ *Ich sollte in der Lage sein, Ihnen Ende nächster Woche Bescheid zu sagen.*
▪ I hear what you're saying.	▪ *Ich weiß schon, was Sie meinen.*
▪ The ball certainly seems to be back in my court.	▪ *Jetzt stehe ich unter ziemlichem Zugzwang.*
▪ Why don't we do it this way?	▪ *Warum machen wir es nicht so?*

Useful phrases

Agreeing and disagreeing

Agreeing	Sich einig sein
▪ That's absolutely correct.	▪ *Das ist absolut richtig.*
▪ You're right.	▪ *Sie haben Recht.*
▪ OK. I understand your position.	▪ *In Ordnung. Ich verstehe Ihre Position.*
▪ I think I can agree to that.	▪ *Ich denke, dem kann ich zustimmen.*
▪ That sounds fine.	▪ *Das klingt in Ordnung.*
▪ No problem. I see what you mean.	▪ *Kein Problem. Ich verstehe, was Sie meinen.*
▪ I couldn't agree more.	▪ *Ich bin ganz Ihrer Meinung.*
Disagreeing	**Sich uneinig sein**
▪ I'm afraid I can't agree to …	▪ *Es tut mir leid, ich kann … nicht zustimmen.*
▪ I'm sorry, but I don't agree with you there.	▪ *Es tut mir leid, aber dem kann ich nicht zustimmen.*
▪ I'm not in a position to agree to that.	▪ *Ich bin nicht in der Lage, dem zuzustimmen.*
▪ I don't think I can go along with that.	▪ *Dem kann ich mich leider nicht anschließen.*
▪ I'm afraid there's no way I can agree with you there.	▪ *Es tut mir leid, ich kann Ihnen da auf keinen Fall zustimmen.*
▪ I'm afraid not, no.	▪ *Leider nicht, nein.*
▪ Sorry, but that's not really an option.	▪ *Es tut mir leid, aber das kommt nicht wirklich in Betracht.*

Saying and writing numbers and figures

▪ 763 – seven hundred and sixty-three	▪ *763 – siebenhundertdreiundsechzig*
▪ 1,600 – one thousand six hundred	▪ *1.600 – eintausendsechshundert*
▪ 145,000 – one hundred and forty-five thousand	▪ *145.000 – einhundertfünfundvierzigtausend*
▪ 1,000,000 – one million	▪ *1.000.000 – eine Million*
▪ 1,000,000,000 – one billion	▪ *1.000.000.000 – eine Milliarde*
▪ 44.8 – forty-four point eight	▪ *44,8 – vierundvierzig Komma acht*

Taking down details of a consignment

Unit 8

▪ Let me just take a note of the details.	▪ *Lassen Sie mich kurz die Einzelheiten notieren.*
▪ Could I have the order number, please?	▪ *Könnte ich die Bestellnummer haben, bitte?*
▪ Can you give me the details of the consignor and the consignee – name and address?	▪ *Können Sie mir die Angaben von Absender und Empfänger geben – Namen und Adressen?*
▪ Is it a full container load or less than a container load?	▪ *Handelt es sich um eine ganze Containerladung oder weniger als eine Containerladung?*
▪ How many packages are there?	▪ *Wie viele Pakete sind da?*
▪ Can you give me the gross weight and the net weight, please?	▪ *Können Sie mir das Bruttogewicht und das Nettogewicht geben?*
▪ So that gives us a tare weight of … kilos.	▪ *Das macht also ein Verpackungsgewicht von … Kilo.*
▪ What about the dimensions – length by width by height?	▪ *Wie sind die Maße – Länge mal Breite mal Höhe?*
▪ What's the volume of the consignment?	▪ *Was ist das Volumen der Warensendung?*
▪ Can you tell me the Incoterm, please?	▪ *Können Sie mir bitte den Incoterm nennen?*
▪ Will the goods be in airworthy packing?	▪ *Werden die Produkte flugtauglich verpackt?*
▪ I'll email you the details as soon as I have them.	▪ *Ich e-maile Ihnen die Einzelheiten sobald ich sie habe.*

Making a complaint: Buyer

Unit 9

Refererence to goods	Bezug auf die Waren
▪ We have just taken delivery of the above-mentioned consignment and regret to inform you that we are dissatisfied with it.	▪ *Wir haben soeben die oben erwähnte Sendung erhalten und bedauern Ihnen mitteilen zu müssen, dass wir damit nicht zufrieden sind.*
Description of problem	**Beschreibung des Problems**
▪ Upon examining the goods we discovered that the contents were wet due to poor packing.	▪ *Bei Prüfung der Ware stellten wir fest, dass der Inhalt wegen mangelhafter Verpackung nass war.*
▪ We believe this is the result of rough handling in transit.	▪ *Wir glauben, dass dies das Ergebnis unsachgemäßer Behandlung im Transit ist.*
▪ We enclose photographs for your information.	▪ *Wir fügen Fotos zu Ihrer Information bei.*
Request for explanation	**Bitte um Erklärung**
▪ We would welcome your explanation of the damage.	▪ *Wir würden eine Erklärung Ihrerseits bezüglich des Schadens begrüßen.*
▪ Please explain how such a thing could happen.	▪ *Bitte erklären Sie, wie so etwas passieren konnte.*
Consequences for buyer and/or seller	**Folgen für den Käufer und/oder den Verkäufer**
▪ You will understand that we cannot sell these items at the normal price.	▪ *Sie werden verstehen, dass wir diese Positionen nicht zum normalen Preis verkaufen können.*
▪ If they do not arrive here by … we will have to obtain them elsewhere.	▪ *Wenn sie bis zum … nicht hier ankommen, werden wir sie woanders beziehen müssen.*
Request for suitable action	**Bitte um geeignete Schritte**
▪ We must therefore ask you to send replacements by return, as these goods are needed urgently.	▪ *Wir müssen Sie deshalb bitten, umgehend Ersatz zu schicken, da die Waren dringend benötigt werden.*
▪ We would (also) point out that …	▪ *Wir möchten Sie (auch) darauf hinweisen, dass …*
▪ We feel sure you will appreciate that we are only prepared to keep the sub-standard items if a considerable reduction in price is granted.	▪ *Sie werden sicherlich dafür Verständnis haben, dass wir nur bereit sind, die minderwertige Ware zu behalten, wenn ein erheblicher Preisnachlass gewährt wird.*
▪ … if the price is reduced by …%.	▪ *… wenn der Preis um … % reduziert wird.*
▪ Our future business relationship will depend on how this matter is dealt with.	▪ *Die Fortsetzung unserer Geschäftsbeziehung ist von der Regelung dieser Angelegenheit abhängig.*
Suitable ending	**Passender Schluss**
▪ We expect to hear from you in the very near future.	▪ *Wir erwarten, von Ihnen recht bald zu hören.*

Responding to a complaint / Apologizing: Seller

Acknowledgement of complaint	Empfangsbestätigung der Beschwerde
▪ We have received your email/letter regarding the above-mentioned consignment of …	▪ *Wir haben Ihre E-Mail / Ihren Brief bezüglich der oben erwähnten …-Sendung erhalten.*
▪ Your complaint is now being investigated.	▪ *Ihre Beschwerde wird jetzt untersucht.*
First expression of regret	**Erster Ausdruck des Bedauerns**
▪ We are sorry to hear the consignment was delayed and that the consignment is unsatisfactory.	▪ *Es tut uns leid zu hören, dass die Sendung verzögert eintraf und dass einige der Waren nicht der Qualität entsprachen.*
▪ We are dismayed to hear that the consignment is unsatisfactory.	▪ *Wir sind entsetzt zu hören, dass die Lieferung unzufriedenstellend ist.*
Action taken	**Unternommene Schritte**
▪ Since hearing from you we have contacted our freight forwarders and are waiting for their report.	▪ *Nach Erhalt Ihrer Nachricht haben wir uns mit unserem Spediteur in Verbindung gesetzt und erwarten seinen Bericht.*
▪ Having investigated the matter, we have now discovered that the wrong goods were delivered due to an error in our dispatch section.	▪ *Nach Untersuchung der Angelegenheit haben wir nun herausgefunden, dass auf Grund eines Fehlers in unserer Versandabteilung die falsche Ware geliefert wurde.*

Solution	Lösung
In the meantime, we are sending you replacements at no extra charge by return.	*Zwischenzeitlich schicken wir Ihnen umgehenden Ersatz ohne zusätzliche Kosten für Sie.*
The missing … will be delivered to you carriage paid within 48 hours.	*Die fehlenden … werden Ihnen innerhalb 48 Stunden frachtfrei geliefert.*
If you are prepared to keep …, we will grant you a reduction in price of …%.	*Wenn Sie bereit sind, die … zu behalten, gewähren wir Ihnen einen …%igen Rabatt.*
Under the circumstances, we are willing to offer you a replacement consignment or a reduction in price of …% on the unsatisfactory items.	*Unter diesen Umständen sind wir bereit, Ihnen eine Ersatzsendung oder eine Preisreduzierung von … % für die nicht zufriedenstellende Ware anzubieten.*
Second apology	**Zweite Entschuldigung**
Please accept our apologies for this.	*Bitte nehmen Sie hierfür unsere Entschuldigung an.*
In the meantime, please accept our apologies for the inconvenience caused, which was due to circumstances beyond our control.	*In der Zwischenzeit nehmen Sie bitte unsere Entschuldigung für die verursachten Unannehmlichkeiten an, die auf Umstände außerhalb unserer Kontrolle zurückzuführen sind.*
We assure you it will not happen again.	*Wir versichern Ihnen, dass es nicht wieder vorkommen wird.*
Polite ending	**höflicher Schluss**
We look forward to hearing from you soon.	*Wir freuen uns, bald von Ihnen zu hören.*
We hope this suggestion will find your approval.	*Wir hoffen, dass dieser Vorschlag Ihre Zustimmung finden wird.*
We look forward to doing further business with you in the future.	*Wir freuen uns darauf, zukünftig wieder mit Ihnen ins Geschäft zu kommen.*

Writing a reminder

I am writing in connection with the attached unpaid invoice for work done at your premises.	*Ich schreibe im Zusammenhang mit der angefügten unbezahlten Rechnung für Arbeit auf Ihrem Firmengelände.*
I would like to draw your attention to invoice no. …	*Ich möchte Ihre Aufmerksamkeit auf Mahnung Nr. … lenken.*
Would you please settle your account by the end of the month at the latest.	*Bitte bezahlen Sie die Rechnung bis spätestens Ende des Monats.*
We insist on payment within the next five working days.	*Wir bestehen auf die Zahlung innerhalb der nächsten fünf Arbeitstage.*
If we have not received your payment within the next seven days, we will have to instruct our solicitors to take legal action.	*Wenn wir Ihre Zahlung nicht innerhalb der nächsten sieben Tage erhalten, werden wir unseren Anwalt hinzuziehen, um rechtliche Schritte einzuleiten.*

Writing a cover letter

Unit 10

Showing interest and suitability	Interesse und Eignung zeigen
I was extremely interested to read your advertisement for the post of …	*Ich habe Ihre Anzeige für die Stelle des/der … mit großem Interesse gelesen.*
I wish to gain experience in …	*Ich möchte gerne Erfahrungen in … sammeln.*
I would like to make use of my foreign language skills.	*Ich möchte gerne meine Fremdsprachenkompetenzen einsetzen.*
I feel sure that your company has the post I am looking for.	*Ich bin sicher, dass Ihr Unternehmen die Stelle hat, die ich suche.*
I believe I am particularly suited for the post advertised because …	*Ich glaube, dass ich besonders für die annoncierte Stelle geeignet bin, weil …*
Describing your skills	**Die eigenen Fertigkeiten beschreiben**
As a native speaker of …	*Als … Muttersprachler/in …*
I am fluent in spoken and written …	*Ich beherrsche … fließend in gesprochener und geschriebener Sprache.*
I have a good knowledge of …	*Ich habe gute Kenntnisse in …*

Useful phrases

Talking about previous experience	Über vorherige Erfahrungen sprechen
▪ Before my traineeship, I completed a work placement at … in the … department.	▪ *Vor meiner Ausbildung habe ich ein Praktikum bei … in der …-abteilung absolviert.*
▪ My traineeship at … has confirmed my interest in …	▪ *Meine Ausbildung bei … hat mein Interesse an … bestärkt.*
▪ … has enabled me to develop my skills in …	▪ *… hat mir ermöglicht, meine Fähigkeiten in … auszubauen.*
Expressing availability for an interview / the job	**Verfügbarkeit für ein Vorstellungsgespräch / die Stelle ausdrücken**
▪ I am available for an interview immediately.	▪ *Ich stehe ab sofort für ein Vorstellungsgespräch zur Verfügung.*
▪ I would be able to start work any time after …	▪ *Ich könnte jederzeit nach dem … anfangen zu arbeiten.*
▪ I very much look forward to hearing from you at your earliest convenience.	▪ *Ich freue mich darauf, möglichst bald von Ihnen zu hören.*

Basic word list

Diese Liste enthält ca. 700 Grundwörter, die in *Trade Matters – 3rd Edition* als bekannt vorausgesetzt werden. Nicht aufgeführt, jedoch vorausgesetzt, sind einige elementare Wörter, wie Pronomen, Zahlen, Wochentage sowie Wörter, die im Englischen und Deutschen die gleiche Bedeutung haben, wie z. B. *monitor*, *restaurant* und *hotel*.

A

able, to be ~ können, in der Lage sein
about über, etwa
above über, oben(stehend), oben genannt
absolutely absolut, völlig
accept annehmen, akzeptieren
across (quer) über
active aktiv(iert)
activity Tätigkeit, Aktivität
actor Schauspieler
add zusammenzählen, hinzufügen
address Adresse; adressieren
advert(isement) Werbung, Anzeige
afraid, I'm ~ leider
after nach
afternoon Nachmittag
again wieder
age Alter
agree zustimmen, vereinbaren, sich einigen
air Luft
airport Flughafen
all alle(s)
allow erlauben, gestatten, (zu) lassen
almost fast, beinahe
alone allein(e)
along entlang
already schon, bereits
also auch, außerdem
although obwohl
altogether insgesamt
always immer
a.m. vormittags, morgens (vor 12 Uhr)
among zwischen, unter
amount Menge, Betrag
angry wütend, verärgert
another noch eine/r/s
answer Antwort, Lösung; (be)antworten
anybody/anyone jemand, jede/r
anything etwas, alles
anyway jedenfalls, sowieso
anywhere irgendwo(hin)
apart from abgesehen von, außer
area Gebiet, Bereich
arrange arrangieren, vereinbaren, ausmachen
arrive ankommen
ask fragen, bitten
away weg, entfernt

B

back Rückseite, Rücken; zurück
bad schlecht, schlimm
bag Tasche, Tüte, Beutel
basic grundsätzlich, einfach
basically grundsätzlich, im Grunde
because weil
become werden
before vor(her)
begin anfangen, beginnen
beginning Anfang
behind hinter, hinten
believe glauben
belong gehören
below unter, unten(stehend)
best beste, am besten
better besser
between zwischen
big groß
biscuit Keks, Plätzchen
board Brett, Tafel
body Körper
book Buch; buchen, reservieren
boring langweilig
bored gelangweilt
born geboren
both beide
bottle Flasche
bottom Unterseite, Unterteil, Boden, Ende
box Kasten, Kästchen, Schachtel, Kiste
boy Junge
bracket Klammer
break Pause; (zer)brechen, kaputtmachen
breakfast Frühstück
bring bringen, holen
broken kaputt
brother Bruder
build bauen, aufbauen, erbauen
building Gebäude
busy beschäftigt, besetzt
buy kaufen
bye tschüs

C

call Anruf; (an)rufen, nennen
caller Anrufer/in
camera Fotoapparat, Kamera
car Auto
care, take ~ of sich kümmern um
careful(ly) vorsichtig, sorgfältig
case Fall
cash Bargeld
certain(ly) sicher(lich), gewiss, bestimmt
chair Stuhl, Sessel
change (Ver-)Änderung; (aus) wechseln, (sich) ändern
cheap billig, günstig
check überprüfen, kontrollieren
cheque Scheck
child Kind
choice Wahl, Auswahl
choose (aus)wählen
cinema Kino
city (Groß-)Stadt
class Klasse
classmate Klassenkamerad/in
clean sauber; reinigen, säubern
clear klar, deutlich
clever klug, intelligent
clock Uhr
close schließen, zumachen
close (to) nahe (bei)
clothes Kleidung, Kleider
clue Hinweis, Tip
coffee Kaffee
colour Farbe
come kommen, geliefert werden
complete vollständig; vervollständigen
completely völlig
contact Kontakt, Verbindung
control Kontrolle; kontrollieren, regeln, steuern, überwachen
copy Exemplar, Kopie; abschreiben, kopieren
corner Ecke
correct richtig, genau; korrigieren
cost Kosten; kosten
count zählen
country Land, Staat
couple Paar
create (er)schaffen, erstellen, gestalten
creative kreativ, schöpferisch
cross (an)kreuzen
culture Kultur
cup Tasse

D
damage Schaden, Beschädigung; beschädigen
danger Gefahr
dangerous gefährlich
dark Dunkelheit; dunkel
data Daten
date Datum, Termin
date of birth Geburtsdatum
day Tag
dear liebe/r
decide entscheiden, beschließen
definite(ly) (ganz) sicher, bestimmt, eindeutig
describe beschreiben
description Beschreibung, Schilderung
desk (Schreib-)Tisch, Schalter, Arbeitsplatz
details Einzelheiten, Angaben
dialogue Gespräch, Dialog
dictionary Wörterbuch
die sterben
difference Unterschied
different unterschiedlich, verschieden
difficult schwer, schwierig
dinner (Abend-)Essen
direct direkt, gerade
dirty schmutzig
dislike nicht mögen
display Bildschirm, Anzeige
door Tür
drink Getränk; trinken
drive fahren
during während

E
each jede/r/s
early früh
east (nach) Osten, Ost-
easy, easily leicht, einfach
education Erziehung, (Aus-, Schul-)Bildung
either entweder
empty leer
end Ende, Schluss; (be)enden
ending Ende
energy Energie
enjoy genießen, gefallen, gern tun
enough ausreichend, genug
enter eintreten, betreten, eingeben
entrance Eingang, Einfahrt
especially besonders
even sogar (noch)
evening Abend
ever je(mals)
every jede/r/s
everybody jede/r
everyone jede/r/s, alle
everything alles
exactly exakt, genau
example Beispiel
excellent hervorragend, ausgezeichnet
excited aufgeregt, begeistert
exciting aufregend, spannend
excuse Ausrede, Entschuldigung; entschuldigen
exercise Übung
exercise book (Schul-)Heft
expect erwarten, annehmen
expensive teuer
experience Erfahrung; erfahren, erleben
expert Fachmann/frau
extra zusätzlich
extreme äußerst
eye Auge

F
fact Tatsache
factory Fabrik
false falsch
family Familie
far weit (entfernt)
fast schnell
feel (sich) fühlen, meinen, glauben
feeling Gefühl, Meinung, Ansicht
(a) few ein paar, wenig/e
fight Kampf; (be)kämpfen
final letzte/r/s, endgültig
finally schließlich, endlich
financial finanziell
find finden, suchen
find out herausfinden
fine gut, schön, in Ordnung
finish (be)enden, abschließen, fertig werden
firm Firma
first erste/r/s; zuerst
flight Flug
floor Etage, Stockwerk; (Fuß-)Boden
fly fliegen
follow (be)folgen
(the) following der/die/das Folgende
food Essen, Nahrung
foreign ausländisch, Auslands-, fremd
forget vergessen
form Form, Formular; bilden, formen
forward nach vorne
free frei; gratis, kostenlos
friend Freund/in
friendly freund(schaft)lich
friendship Freundschaft
front Vorderseite
front, in ~ of vor
full voll
fully völlig
funny komisch, merkwürdig
further weitere/r/s
future Zukunft; (zu)künftig

G
gap Lücke
general allgemein, generell, normal
generally im Allgemeinen, normalerweise
get holen, bekommen, werden, gelangen
girl Mädchen
give geben
go gehen, fahren
go on weitermachen, fortfahren
go out ausgehen
good gut
goodbye auf Wiedersehen
great groß(artig)
greatly in hohem Maße
greet (be)grüßen
greeting Gruß(formel), Begrüßung
ground Boden, Grund
group Gruppe; gruppieren
grow wachsen, werden, zunehmen
guess Annahme; raten, schätzen
guest Gast

H
half Hälfte; halb
hall Diele, Saal, Halle
handle umgehen mit, bearbeiten, erledigen, fertigwerden mit
happen passieren, geschehen
happy glücklich, zufrieden
health Gesundheit
hear hören
heart Herz
heavy schwer
height Höhe, Größe
help Hilfe; helfen
helpful hilfreich, nützlich
here hier
high; highly hoch; äußerst
history Geschichte
holiday Ferien, Urlaub, Feiertag
home Zuhause, Heim; nach Hause
hope Hoffnung; hoffen
hopefully hoffentlich
horrible furchtbar, schrecklich
hot heiß, scharf
hour Stunde
house Haus
how wie
however doch, jedoch, allerdings
huge riesig
human menschlich
husband (Ehe-)Mann

I

idea Vorstellung, Idee
if wenn, falls, ob
ill krank
illness Krankheit
image Bild
important wichtig
impossible unmöglich
individual einzeln, individuell; Einzelperson
industry Branche, Industrie
inform informieren, unterrichten
information Auskunft, Information(en), Angaben
inside innerhalb, drinnen
instead stattdessen
instead of statt
interest Interesse; interessieren
interested interessiert
interesting interessant

J

job Arbeit(sstelle), Aufgabe
join beitreten, verbinden
just einfach, nur, genau

K

keep (be)halten, weiterhin tun
key Schlüssel, Taste; Haupt-
kind freundlich; Art, Sorte
kitchen Küche
knife Messer
know kennen, wissen

L

language Sprache
large groß
last dauern; letzte/r/s
late spät
later später
latest neueste/r/s
lead führen
learn lernen, erfahren
least, at ~ wenigstens
leave lassen, verlassen, hinterlassen, ab-/wegfahren
left links; übrig
length Länge
less weniger, abzüglich
let erlauben, (zu)lassen
letter Buchstabe, Brief
level Ebene, Niveau
lie Lüge; (be)lügen
life Leben
lift Fahrstuhl, Aufzug
light Licht, Leuchte; hell, leicht
like mögen; (ähnlich) wie
line Linie, Leitung, Zeile
list Liste; auflisten, notieren
listen zuhören
little klein, wenig
live wohnen, leben
local örtlich, lokal
log in/on einloggen
log off/out ausloggen
long lang
look Blick, Aussehen; (aus)sehen, blicken
look after sich kümmern um
look for suchen nach
look forward to sth sich auf etw freuen
lose verlieren
lots of / a lot of viel, viele
love Liebe; lieben, sehr gern mögen
lovely schön, hübsch, reizend
low niedrig
lunch Mittagessen

M

machine Gerät, Maschine
magazine Zeitschrift
main Haupt-, wichtigste/r/s
make machen
manage leiten, verwalten, regeln, (es) schaffen
many viele
market Markt
match zuordnen, passen (zu)
maximum Maximum; maximal
may dürfen, können, mögen
maybe vielleicht
meal Essen, Mahlzeit
mean bedeuten, meinen, heißen
medium mittlere; Medium, Mittel
meet (zusammen)treffen, begegnen, sich (mit jdm) treffen
meeting Sitzung, Besprechung, Treffen
memory Gedächtnis, Erinnerung, Speicher
message Meldung, Nachricht, Mitteilung, Botschaft
metal Metall
middle Mitte
might könnte(n) (vielleicht)
milk Milch
minimum Minimum; minimal
miss verpassen, vermissen
missing fehlende/r/s
mistake Fehler, Irrtum
mobile (phone) Mobiltelefon, Handy
money Geld
month Monat
more mehr
morning Morgen
most der/die/das meiste, die meisten
mountain Berg
mouse Maus
move (sich) bewegen, umziehen
movement Bewegung
much viel

N

name Name; nennen, benennen
national national, staatlich
near in der Nähe von
nearly beinahe, fast
necessary nötig, notwendig, erforderlich
need Bedarf, Bedürfnis; brauchen, benötigen
negative verneinend, negativ
neither ... nor weder ... noch
never nie(mals)
new neu
news Neuigkeit(en); Nachricht(en)
next nächste/r/s; danach
night Nacht
normal(ly) normal(erweise)
north (nach) Norden, Nord-
note Notiz, Anmerkung; beachten, notieren, bemerken, feststellen
nothing nichts
now nun, jetzt
nowadays heutzutage
number Nummer, Zahl, Anzahl

O

object Gegenstand
of course natürlich, selbstverständlich
offer Angebot; anbieten, bieten
office Büro
often oft, häufig
oil Öl
old alt
once einmal, einst; sobald
only nur, einzig
open öffnen, eröffnen; offen, geöffnet
opposite Gegenteil; gegensätzlich, gegenüber
option Möglichkeit, Option
or oder
order Bestellung, Auftrag, Reihenfolge; bestellen, ordern
organization Organisation
organize organisieren
original original, ursprünglich, Original(-)
other andere/r/s
ought to sollen
outside außerhalb (von)
own eigene/r/s; besitzen

P

page Seite
pain Schmerz
pair Paar
paper Papier, Zeitung
part Teil, Bauteil
pay Lohn, Bezahlung; zahlen, bezahlen

per cent Prozent
perfect vollkommen, perfekt
perfectly völlig
perhaps vielleicht, eventuell
period Zeit(raum)
personal persönlich
phone Telefon; anrufen
photo(graphy) Foto(grafie)
phrase Redewendung, Satz(teil)
picture Bild
piece Stück, Teil
place Stelle, Platz; setzen, stellen
plan Plan; planen
plane Flugzeug
plastic Plastik, Kunststoff
plenty viel, reichlich
p.m. nachmittags, abends (nach 12 Uhr)
point Punkt; Komma
poor arm, schlecht, mangelhaft
popular beliebt, populär
position Stellung, Lage, Position
positive positiv, bejahend
possibility Möglichkeit
possible möglich
possibly möglicherweise
power Kraft, Strom; antreiben
powerful mächtig, stark
practical praktisch
practice Praxis, Training
practise (ein)üben, trainieren
prefer vorziehen, bevorzugen, lieber mögen
prepare (sich) vorbereiten, zubereiten, erstellen
present Gegenwart; Geschenk; aktuell, gegenwärtig; vorstellen, präsentieren
press drücken
price Preis
print Druck; drucken, ausdrucken
printer Drucker/in
private privat, persönlich
probably wahrscheinlich
produce produzieren, herstellen
product Produkt, Erzeugnis
program(me) Programm, Sendung
promise Versprechen; versprechen
provide liefern, (an)bieten, zur Verfügung stellen
public öffentlich; Öffentlichkeit
push schieben, drücken
put setzen, stellen, legen

Q

quality Eigenschaft, Qualität
(a) quarter past/to Viertel nach/vor
question Frage
quick(ly) schnell
quiet ruhig
quite ziemlich, ganz

R

rather ziemlich, lieber
reach erreichen, greifen
read lesen
reader Leser/in, Lektüre
ready bereit, fertig
real echt, wirklich
really wirklich, eigentlich, tatsächlich
reason Vernunft, Grund
receive erhalten, empfangen, bekommen
recent aktuell, neu, jüngst
recently neulich, vor kurzem, in letzter Zeit
recommend empfehlen
regular(ly) regelmäßig
relative Verwandte/r; relativ
remain (ver)bleiben
remember sich erinnern, daran denken
repeat wiederholen
report Bericht; berichten
reservation Reservierung, Buchung
reserve reservieren
respect Respekt, Achtung; (be)achten, respektieren
result Resultat, Ergebnis; folgen, resultieren
return zurückkehren, zurückgeben
rich reich
right rechts, richtig
risk Risiko; riskieren
road (Land-)Straße
role-play Rollenspiel
room Zimmer, Raum
round Runde; rund
rule Regel, Vorschrift
run laufen (lassen); betreiben, leiten

S

sad traurig
safe(ly) sicher
same gleiche/r/s, der-, die-, dasselbe
save retten, sparen
say sagen
school Schule
score Ergebnis, Punkt(estand)
screen Bildschirm, Leinwand
search Suche; (durch)suchen
second zweite/r/s, Sekunde
secretary Sekretär/in
see sehen, besuchen, verstehen
seem (er)scheinen
sell (sich) verkaufen
send senden, schicken
sentence Satz
serious ernst, ernsthaft
service Dienst, Dienstleistung, Service
set setzen, stellen
several etliche, einige, mehrere
shall sollen, werden
shelf Regal
shop Laden, Geschäft; einkaufen
short kurz, klein, knapp
should solle/n, sollte/n
shoulder Schulter
show zeigen
shut schließen
side Seite
sightseeing Besichtigen von Sehenswürdigkeiten
sign Zeichen, Anzeichen, Schild
simple einfach
since da, weil, seit
single einzig, einzeln
sit sitzen, sich hinsetzen
site Website
size Größe
slow langsam
small klein
smile Lächeln; lächeln
someone jemand
something etwas
sometimes manchmal
somewhere irgendwo(hin)
soon bald
sorry traurig; Verzeihung
sound Klang, Geräusch; klingen, sich anhören
south (nach) Süden, Süd-
space Raum, Platz, Abstand
speak sprechen, reden
special besondere/r/s
specially speziell, extra, besonders
speed Geschwindigkeit
spell buchstabieren, schreiben
spelling Rechtschreibung, Schreibweise
spend (Geld) ausgeben, (Zeit) verbringen
stand stehen, aushalten
start Beginn; anfangen, starten
statement Aussage, Feststellung, Erklärung
stay Aufenthalt; bleiben
step Schritt, Stufe
still still, trotzdem, (immer) noch
stop (an)halten, aufhören (mit)
street Straße
strong stark, heftig
student Student/in, Lernende/r
study lernen, studieren, untersuchen, betrachten
stuff Material, Stoff, Zeug
subject (Schul-)Fach, Thema
success Erfolg
successful erfolgreich
sugar Zucker
suggest vorschlagen, andeuten
suggestion Vorschlag
sun Sonne

sure sicher
surname Nachname, Familienname
surprise Überraschung; überraschen

T

table Tisch, Tabelle
take nehmen, bringen, dauern
take off ausziehen, abnehmen, abheben
take part teilnehmen, mitmachen
talk Gespräch, Vortrag; sprechen, reden
tall groß, hoch
task Aufgabe
tea Tee
teach unterrichten, lehren
teacher Lehrer/in
team Mannschaft
technology Technik, Technologie
telephone (call) Telefon(anruf)
television Fernsehen, Fernseher
tell sagen, erzählen
test untersuchen, prüfen
than als
thank danken
thank you danke
thanks Dank; danke
then dann
thin dünn
thing Sache, Ding, Gegenstand
think denken, meinen, finden, glauben
though obwohl, allerdings, aber
through durch
throw werfen
tick (off) mit einem Häkchen versehen, abhaken
ticket Karte, Fahrschein
time Zeit; Mal
tip Hinweis, Tipp
today heute
together zusammen
tomorrow morgen
tonight heute Abend/Nacht
too zu, auch
top Spitze, Gipfel; Spitzen-
topic Thema
total (Gesamt-)Summe; gesamte/r/s, Gesamt-
touch anfassen, berühren
town Stadt
traffic Verkehr
train Zug
translate übersetzen
translation Übersetzung
travel Reisen; reisen, fahren
trip Ausflug, Reise, Besuch
trouble Mühe, Umstände, Problem(e), Ärger
true wahr, richtig
try versuchen, probieren
turn (sich) drehen, wenden, werden
twice zweimal
type Art, Sorte, Typ; tippen, Schreibmaschine schreiben
typical typisch

U

unable unfähig, nicht in der Lage
under unter
understand verstehen, begreifen
university Universität
unless es sei denn, außer wenn
unlike anders als, im Gegensatz zu
until bis
use Gebrauch; gebrauchen, benutzen, verwenden
useful nützlich
user Anwender/in, Benutzer/in
usual gewöhnlich, normal, üblich
usually gewöhnlich, normalerweise, meistens

V

verb Verb
visit Besuch; besuchen, besichtigen
visitor Besucher/in, Gast

W

wait warten
wall Wand, Mauer
want wollen
wash waschen
watch Armbanduhr
water Wasser
way Weg, Methode, Art (und Weise)
weather Wetter
week Woche
weekend Wochenende
weekly wöchentlich
welcome Willkommen; willkommen heißen
well gesund, gut; also
west (nach) Westen, West-
whatever was auch immer
when wenn, als, wann
whenever immer wenn
where wo(hin)
whether ob
which welche
while während
whole ganz
why warum
wide breit, weit
wife (Ehe-)Frau
will Wille; werde(n), wollen
window Fenster
wine Wein
wish Wunsch; wünschen
with mit, bei
within innerhalb (von), in
without ohne
woman Frau
wonderful wunderbar
wood Holz
word Wort
work Arbeit; funktionieren, arbeiten
worker Arbeiter/in
world Welt
worldwide weltweit
worried besorgt, beunruhigt
worse schlechter, schlimmer
worst schlechteste/r/s, schlimmste/r/s
would würde/n
write schreiben
wrong falsch

Y

year Jahr
yesterday gestern
young jung

Chronological word list

Dieses Wörterverzeichnis enthält alle neuen Wörter aus *Trade Matters – 3rd Edition* in der Reihenfolge ihres Erscheinens (Seitenzahlen sind angegeben). Nicht aufgeführt sind die Wörter aus dem Grundwortschatz (vgl. *Basic word list*). Wörter aus den Hörverständnisübungen sind mit einem T *(Transkript)* und Wörter aus den *Partner files* mit einem P gekennzeichnet. Die Zahl am linken Rand gibt die Seitenzahl an.

Abkürzungen			
	AE = amerikanisches Englisch	*jdm* = jemandem	*pl* = plural noun
	BE = britisches Englisch	*jdn* = jemanden	*sb* = somebody
	etw = etwas	*jds* = jemandes	*sth* = something

Unit 1

6	**company** ['kʌmpəni]	Unternehmen, Firma, Gesellschaft
	to **be based in …** [bi 'beɪst ɪn]	in … ansässig sein, seinen/ihren Sitz in … haben
	to **be located in …** [bi ləʊ'keɪtɪd ɪn]	in … ansässig sein, seinen/ihren Sitz in … haben
	to **import** [ɪm'pɔːt]	importieren, einführen
	to **export** [ɪk'spɔːt]	exportieren, ausführen
	to **specialize in sth** ['speʃəlaɪz ɪn]	sich auf etw spezialisieren
	customer ['kʌstəmə]	Kunde/Kundin
	mainly ['meɪnli]	hauptsächlich
	commercial [kə'mɜːʃl]	Geschäfts-
	industrial [ɪn'dʌstriəl]	Industrie-
	staff [stɑːf]	Mitarbeiter, Belegschaft, Personal
	administrative [əd'mɪnɪstrətɪv]	Verwaltungs-
	warehouse ['weəhaʊs]	Lager
7	**wholesaler** ['həʊlseɪlə]	Großhändler, Händler
	various ['veəriəs]	verschieden
	receptionist [rɪ'sepʃənɪst]	Empfangsmitarbeiter/in
	appointment [ə'pɔɪntmənt]	Termin
	to **let sb know** [ˌlet 'nəʊ]	Bescheid sagen
	unfortunately [ʌn'fɔːtʃənətli]	leider, unglücklicherweise
	to **delay sb** [dɪ'leɪ]	jdn aufhalten
	assistant [ə'sɪstənt]	Assistent/in
	department [dɪ'pɑːtmənt]	Abteilung
	Pleased to meet you. [ˌpliːzd tə 'miːt ju]	Nett, Sie kennen zu lernen.
	You're welcome. [ˌjɔː 'welkəm]	Bitte (sehr). Gern geschehen.
	accident ['æksɪdənt]	Unfall
	motorway ['məʊtəweɪ]	Autobahn
	traffic jam ['træfɪk dʒæm]	Stau
	this way ['ðɪs weɪ]	hier entlang
	apprenticeship [ə'prentɪsʃɪp]	Ausbildung, Lehre
	wholesale ['həʊlseɪl]	Großhandel
	export ['ekspɔːt]	Export
	official(ly) [ə'fɪʃl]	offiziell
	to **take sb on** [ˌteɪk 'ɒn]	jdn einstellen, anstellen
	full-time [ˌfʊl 'taɪm]	Vollzeit-, auf Vollzeitbasis
8	**expression** [ɪk'spreʃn]	Ausdruck
	to **transport** [træn'spɔːt]	befördern, transportieren
	goods *(pl)* [gʊdz]	Ware(n)
	business ['bɪznəs]	Unternehmen, Firma, Geschäft
	end customer [ˌend 'kʌstəmə]	Endkunde/-kundin
	traineeship [treɪ'niːʃɪp]	Ausbildung, Lehre
	specific [spə'sɪfɪk]	bestimmt, speziell
	section ['sekʃn]	Teil, Abteilung, Abschnitt
	responsible [rɪ'spɒnsəbl]	verantwortlich, zuständig
	function ['fʌŋkʃn]	Funktion, Aufgabe
	sales [seɪlz]	Vertrieb, Verkauf
	previously ['priːviəsli]	zuvor, vorher
	similar ['sɪmələ]	ähnlich
	meaning ['miːnɪŋ]	Bedeutung
	assistance [ə'sɪstəns]	Hilfe, Unterstützung
	to **introduce** [ˌɪntrə'djuːs]	vorstellen, einführen
	pleasure ['pleʒə]	Vergnügen
	refreshment [rɪ'freʃmənt]	Erfrischung
	intercultural [ˌɪntə'kʌltʃərəl]	kulturübergreifend, interkulturell
	awareness [ə'weənəs]	Wissen, Bewusstsein
	polite [pə'laɪt]	höflich
	social(ly) ['səʊʃl]	sozial, gesellschaftlich
	acceptable [ək'septəbl]	akzeptabel
	to **vary** ['veəri]	schwanken, unterschiedlich sein
	widely ['waɪdli]	*hier:* stark
	to **do business** [du 'bɪznəs]	Geschäfte machen

	to **check sth out** [ˌtʃek ˈaʊt]	sich etw ansehen
	major [ˈmeɪdʒə]	größte/r/s, bedeutend(ste/r/s), Haupt-
	cultural [ˈkʌltʃərəl]	kulturell, Kultur-
	to **look sth up** [ˌlʊk ˈʌp]	etw nachschlagen, nachschauen
	increasing [ɪnˈkriːsɪŋ]	zunehmend, steigend
	to **observe** [əbˈsɜːv]	beobachten
	colleague [ˈkɒliːg]	Kollege/-in
	client [ˈklaɪənt]	Kunde/-in
9	to **accept** [əkˈsept]	annehmen, akzeptieren
	to **carry out** [ˌkæri ˈaʊt]	ausführen, durchführen
10	**profile** [ˈprəʊfaɪl]	Porträt, Profil
	importer [ɪmˈpɔːtə]	Importeur
	exporter [ekˈspɔːtə]	Exporteur
	premises *(pl)* [ˈpremɪsɪz]	(Betriebs-)Gelände, Räumlichkeiten
	to **service** [ˈsɜːvɪs]	bearbeiten, bedienen
	to **fulfil (an order)** [fʊlˈfɪl]	(einen Auftrag) bearbeiten, abwickeln, erfüllen
	to **found** [faʊnd]	gründen
	domestic [dəˈmestɪk]	Inlands-, inländisch
	overseas [ˌəʊvəˈsiːz]	in/aus/nach Übersee, in/aus dem/ins Ausland
	customer base [ˈkʌstəmə beɪs]	Kundenstamm
	retailer [ˈriːteɪlə]	Einzelhändler
	continually [kənˈtɪnjuəli]	kontinuierlich, stetig
	to **generate** [ˈdʒenəreɪt]	*(Gewinn, Umsatz etc.)* erzielen, erwirtschaften
	turnover [ˈtɜːnəʊvə]	Umsatz
	to **employ sb** [ɪmˈplɔɪ]	jdn beschäftigen, anstellen, einstellen
	administration [ədˌmɪnɪˈstreɪʃn]	Verwaltung
	headquarters *(pl)* [ˌhedˈkwɔːtəz]	Zentrale, Firmensitz
	remaining [rɪˈmeɪnɪŋ]	übrige/r/s, restliche/r/s
	employee [ɪmˈplɔɪiː]	Angestellte/r, Beschäftigte/r
	facilities *(pl)* [fəˈsɪlətiz]	Einrichtungen, Anlagen, Gebäude
	litre [ˈliːtə]	Liter
	per annum [pər ˈænəm]	pro Jahr
	to **source** [sɔːs]	beschaffen, beziehen
	beverage [ˈbevərɪdʒ]	Getränk
	manufacturer [ˌmænjuˈfæktʃərə]	Hersteller
	to **be on the lookout for sth** [bi ɒn ðə ˈlʊkaʊt fə]	nach etw Ausschau halten
	fresh [freʃ]	neu, frisch
	to **supply** [səˈplaɪ]	liefern, versorgen, (an)bieten
	to **be delighted to do sth** [bi dɪˈlaɪtɪd tə]	etw gern tun, sich freuen, etw zu tun
	range [reɪndʒ]	(Produkt-)Palette, Sortiment, Auswahl, Angebot
	tab [tæb]	*(Karteikarte etc.:)* Reiter
	heading [ˈhedɪŋ]	Überschrift
	statistics *(pl)* [stəˈtɪstɪks]	Statistik(en)
	shipper [ˈʃɪpə]	Versender
	situated [ˈsɪtʃueɪtɪd]	gelegen
	site [saɪt]	Gelände
	distribution centre [ˌdɪstrɪˈbjuːʃn sentə]	Versandzentrum
	to **establish** [ɪˈstæblɪʃ]	gründen
	store [stɔː]	Laden, Geschäft
	revenue [ˈrevənjuː]	Einkünfte
	selection [sɪˈlekʃn]	Auswahl
11	**tour** [tʊə]	Rundgang, Führung
	staff café [ˌstɑːf ˈkæfeɪ]	Cafeteria
	floor plan [ˈflɔː plæn]	Grundriss
	distribution area [ˌdɪstrɪˈbjuːʃn eəriə]	Versandbereich
	finance department [ˈfaɪnæns dɪpɑːtmənt]	Finanzabteilung
	senior management [ˌsiːniə ˈmænɪdʒmənt]	Geschäftsleitung
	reception [rɪˈsepʃn]	Empfang
T	**at all** [ət ˈɔːl]	überhaupt
	in a little while [ɪn ə ˌlɪtl ˈwaɪl]	gleich
	corridor [ˈkɒrɪdɔː]	Flur, Korridor, Gang
	to **turn right/left** [tɜːn ˈraɪt/ˈleft]	rechts/links abbiegen
	human resources (HR) [ˌhjuːmən rɪˈsɔːsɪz]	Personalabteilung
	suite [swiːt]	(Büro-)Räume
	managing director [ˌmænɪdʒɪŋ dəˈrektə]	Geschäftsführer/in
	in charge of [ɪn ˈtʃɑːdʒ əv]	zuständig für, verantwortlich für
	finances [ˈfaɪnænsɪz]	Finanzen
	to **chat** [tʃæt]	sich unterhalten
	to **get on with sth** [ˌget ˈɒn wɪð]	(mit etw) weitermachen
	to **affect** [əˈfekt]	betreffen, beeinträchtigen
	global [ˈgləʊbl]	weltweit, global
	recession [rɪˈseʃn]	Rezession, Konjunkturrückgang
	lucky [ˈlʌki]	glücklich
	slight [slaɪt]	leicht, klein
	dip [dɪp]	Rückgang
	growth [grəʊθ]	Wachstum
	to **lift** [lɪft]	sich auflösen, allmählich verschwinden
	shelf, shelves [ʃelf, ʃelvz]	Regal, Regale

	to **hold** [həʊld]	fassen, Platz haben/ bieten für
	pallet ['pælət]	Palette
	square metre [ˌskweə 'mi:tə]	Quadratmeter
	floor space ['flɔ: speɪs]	Grundfläche
	to **store** [stɔ:]	lagern
	bound for [ˌbaʊnd tə]	bestimmt für, unterwegs nach
	to **account for sth** [ə'kaʊnt fə]	etw ausmachen
	care [keə]	Sorgfalt
	to **package** ['pækɪdʒ]	verpacken
	to **ship** [ʃɪp]	versenden, verschicken
	condition [kən'dɪʃn]	Zustand
12	to **show sb around** [ˌʃəʊ ə'raʊnd]	jdn herumführen
	hall [hɔ:l]	Flur
	straight on/ahead [ˌstreɪt 'ɒn/e'hed]	geradeaus
	graph [grɑ:f]	Diagramm
	pattern ['pætn]	Muster
13	**structure** ['strʌktʃə]	Struktur
	relationship [rɪ'leɪʃnʃɪp]	Verhältnis, Beziehung
	alongside [ə'lɒŋsaɪd]	neben, mit
	to **head sb/sth up** [ˌhed 'ʌp]	jdm vorgesetzt sein, etw leiten
	to **report to sb** [rɪ'pɔ:t tə]	jdm unterstehen
	responsibility [rɪˌspɒnsə'bɪləti]	Verantwortung, Zuständigkeit, Aufgabenbereich
	staff member ['stɑ:f membə]	Mitarbeiter/in
	organization chart [ˌɔ:gənaɪ'zeɪʃn tʃɑ:t]	Organigramm
	operations director [ˌɒpə'reɪʃnz dərektə]	Betriebs-/Produktions-leiter/in
	purchasing manager ['pɜ:tʃəsɪŋ mænɪdʒə]	Einkaufsleiter/in, Leiter/ in Beschaffung
	purchasing assistant ['pɜ:tʃəsɪŋ əsɪstənt]	Einkaufsassistent/in
	shipping manager ['ʃɪpɪŋ mænɪdʒə]	Versandleiter/in
	shipping assistant ['ʃɪpɪŋ əsɪstənt]	Versandassistent/in
	accounts assistant [ə'kaʊnts əsɪstənt]	Buchhaltungsassistent/ in
	to **recruit sb** [rɪ'kru:t]	jdn einstellen, anwerben
	to **train sb** [treɪn]	jdn ausbilden, schulen
	payment ['peɪmənt]	Zahlung, Auszahlung
	salary ['sæləri]	Lohn, Gehalt
	to **deal with sth** ['di:l wɪð]	etw bearbeiten, erledigen, sich um etw kümmern
	taxation [tæk'seɪʃn]	Steuern, Besteuerung
	investment [ɪn'vestmənt]	Geldanlage, Investitionen
	cash management ['kæʃ mænɪdʒmənt]	Kassenführung, Gelddisposition, Finanzmittelverwaltung
	invoice ['ɪnvɔɪs]	Rechnung
	paperwork ['peɪpəwɜ:k]	Formalitäten, Unter-lagen, Schriftverkehr
	after-sales service ['ɑ:ftəseɪlz sɜ:vɪs]	Kundendienst
	query ['kwɪəri]	Frage, Anfrage
	to **make sure** [ˌmeɪk 'ʃʊə]	sicherstellen, gewährleisten, sich vergewissern
	proper(ly) ['prɒpəli]	richtig, korrekt, ordentlich
	undamaged [ˌʌn'dæmɪdʒd]	unbeschädigt, unbeschadet
14	**port** [pɔ:t]	Hafen
	to **develop** [dɪ'veləp]	entwickeln
	to **concentrate on sth** ['kɒnsntreɪt ɒn]	sich auf etw konzentrieren
	current(ly) ['kʌrəntli]	aktuell, momentan
15 T	to **encourage** [ɪn'kʌrɪdʒ]	ermutigen, motivieren
	economy [ɪ'kɒnəmi]	Wirtschaft
	to **profit** ['prɒfɪt]	profitieren
	to **join sb** [dʒɔɪn]	bei jdm sein
	machine tool [mə'ʃi:n tu:l]	Werkzeugmaschine
	to **hit** [hɪt]	treffen
	downturn ['daʊntɜ:n]	Rückgang, Abschwung, Rezession
	to **express** [ɪk'spres]	ausdrücken, zum Ausdruck bringen
	term [tɜ:m]	Begriff
	to **imagine sth** [ɪ'mægɪn]	sich etw vorstellen
	terrific [tə'rɪfɪk]	fantastisch, toll
	opportunity [ˌɒpə'tju:nəti]	Chance, Gelegenheit
	challenge ['tʃælɪndʒ]	schwierige Aufgabe, Herausforderung
	largely ['lɑ:dʒli]	größtenteils, weitgehend
	automobile ['ɔ:təməbi:l]	Automobil-, Auto-
	obviously ['ɒbviəsli]	natürlich, selbstverständlich
	to **undergo** [ˌʌndə'gəʊ]	durchmachen, sich unterziehen
	dramatic [drə'mætɪk]	dramatisch, drastisch
	restructuring [ˌri:'strʌktʃərɪŋ]	Umstrukturierung
	conscious ['kɒnʃəs]	bewusst
	increasingly [ɪn'kri:sɪŋli]	zunehmend, immer *(+ Komparativ)*
	sophisticated [sə'fɪstɪkeɪtɪd]	hoch entwickelt, raffi-niert, fortschrittlich

	technological [ˌteknə'lɒdʒɪkl]	technologisch, technisch
	solution [sə'lu:ʃn]	Lösung
	to **improve** [ɪm'pru:v]	verbessern
	to **put sth in a nutshell** [ˌpʊt ɪn ə 'nʌtʃel]	etw kurz sagen
	to **overcome sth** [ˌəʊvə'kʌm]	etw überwinden
	figure ['fɪgə]	Zahl
	to **invest** [ɪn'vest]	investieren
	research [rɪsɜ:tʃ]	Forschung
	development [dɪ'veləpmənt]	Entwicklung
	research and development (R&D) [rɪˌsɜ:tʃ ən dɪ'veləpmənt]	Forschung(s-) und Entwicklung(sabteilung)
	to **impress** [ɪm'pres]	beeindrucken
	sort [sɔ:t]	Art
	specific [spə'sɪfɪk]	genau
	in advance of [ɪn əd'vɑ:ns əv]	vor
	product launch ['prɒdʌkt lɔ:ntʃ]	Produkteinführung
	to **mention** ['menʃn]	erwähnen, sagen
	engineering [ˌendʒɪ'nɪərɪŋ]	Maschinenbau
	reputation [ˌrepju'teɪʃn]	Ruf
	to **cut costs** [ˌkʌt 'kɒsts]	Kosten senken
	realistic [ˌri:ə'lɪstɪk]	realistisch
	to **compete** [kəm'pi:t]	konkurrieren, im Wettbewerb stehen
	fraction ['frækʃn]	Bruchteil
	to **catch up** [ˌkætʃ 'ʌp]	aufholen, einholen
	in terms of [ɪn 'tɜ:mz əv]	was … angeht
	competitive [kəm'petətɪv]	wettbewerbsfähig, konkurrenzfähig
	course [kɔ:s]	Verlauf, Lauf
	attempt [ə'temt]	Versuch
	to **boost** [bu:st]	steigern, stärken
16	**pretty** ['prɪti]	ziemlich
	obvious ['ɒbviəs]	offensichtlich
	impression [ɪm'preʃn]	Eindruck
	role [rəʊl]	Rolle
	body language ['bɒdi læŋgwɪdʒ]	Körpersprache
	amazed [ə'meɪzd]	verblüfft, erstaunt
	to **benefit** ['benɪfɪt]	profitieren
	for goodness' sake [fə ˌgʊdnəs 'seɪk]	um Himmels willen
	to **stand up** [ˌstænd 'ʌp]	aufstehen
	to **engage sb** [ɪn'geɪdʒ]	*hier:* jdm begegnen
	equal (to) ['i:kwəl]	gleich, gleichwertig
	to **remain seated** [rɪˌmeɪn 'si:tɪd]	sitzen bleiben
	all-important [ˌɔ:l ɪm'pɔ:tnt]	äußerst wichtig
	handshake ['hændʃeɪk]	Handschlag, Händeschütteln
	firm [fɜ:m]	fest
	to **crush** [krʌʃ]	zerquetschen
	to **shake hands** [ˌʃeɪk 'hændz]	die Hände schütteln, die Hand geben
	eye contact ['aɪ kɒntækt]	Blickkontakt
	to **demonstrate** ['demənstreɪt]	vorführen, zeigen
	introduction [ˌɪntrə'dʌkʃn]	Bekanntmachen, Vorstellen
	stage [steɪdʒ]	Phase, Stadium, Etappe
	to **continue to do sth** [kən'tɪnju:]	etw weiterhin tun
	to **cross your arms** [ˌkrɒs jɔ:r 'ɑ:mz]	die Arme verschränken
	relaxed [rɪ'lækst]	locker
	to **illustrate** ['ɪləstreɪt]	veranschaulichen, darstellen
	to **wave sth about** [ˌweɪv ə'baʊt]	mit etw herumfuchteln
	frantically ['fræntɪkli]	wie verrückt
	to **appear** [ə'pɪə]	scheinen, erscheinen, auftreten
	nervous ['nɜ:vəs]	nervös
	off-putting ['ɒf pʊtɪŋ]	abstoßend, unangemehm
	nerve wracking ['nɜ:v rekɪŋ]	nervenaufreiben
	headline ['hedlaɪn]	Überschrift
	to **summarize** ['sʌməraɪz]	zusammenfassen
	to **brainstorm** ['breɪnstɔ:m]	Ideen sammeln

Unit 2

17	**(piece of) advice** [əd'vaɪs]	Rat, Ratschlag, Tipp
	breath [breθ]	Atem, Luft
	to **take a deep breath** [teɪk ə ˌdi:p 'breθ]	tief einatmen, durchatmen
18	**clothing** ['kləʊðɪŋ]	Bekleidung, Kleidung
	chain [tʃeɪn]	Kette
	wear [weə]	Bekleidung, Kleidung
	to **stock sth** [stɒk]	etw *(Ware)* führen, ins Sortiment nehmen
	to **put sb through** [ˌpʊt 'θru:]	*(Telefon:)* jdn durchstellen, verbinden
	to **hold (the line)** [həʊld]	*(Telefon:)* am Apparat bleiben
	to **take a message** [ˌteɪk ə 'mesɪdʒ]	*(Telefon:)* etw ausrichten
	to **dial** ['daɪəl]	*(Telefon:)* wählen
	extension [ɪk'stenʃn]	Durchwahl
	to **catch sth** [kætʃ]	etw verstehen
	to **reach** [ri:tʃ]	erreichen

	secretary ['sekrətri]	Sekretär/in
	engaged [ɪn'geɪdʒd]	*(Telefon:)* besetzt
	to **return sb's call** [rɪˌtɜːn sʌmbədiz 'kɔːl]	jdn zurückrufen
	urgent ['ɜːdʒənt]	dringend, eilig
	to **put sb on hold** [pʊt ɒn 'həʊld]	*(Telefon:)* jdn in die Warteschleife stellen/legen
	Hold on. [ˌhəʊld 'ɒn]	Einen Moment.
	production line [prə'dʌkʃn laɪn]	Fertigungsstraße
	to **step** [step]	treten, gehen
19	**boss** [bɒs]	Chef/in
	to **address sb** [ə'dres]	jdn anreden, ansprechen
	first name ['fɜːst neɪm]	Vorname
	to **invite sb to do sth** [ɪn'vaɪt]	jdn dazu auffordern, etw zu tun
	business contact ['bɪznəs kɒntækt]	Geschäftspartner/in
	approach [ə'prəʊtʃ]	Vorgehen(sweise), Ansatz, Herangehensweise
	old-fashioned [ˌəʊld'fæʃənd]	veraltet, altmodisch
	equivalent [ɪ'kwɪvələnt]	Entsprechung
	to **get back to sb** [ˌget 'bæk tə]	jdn zurückrufen, sich bei jdm melden
	connection [kə'nekʃn]	Verbindung
	to **connect** [kə'nekt]	verbinden
	busy ['bɪzi]	*(Telefon:)* besetzt
20	**digit** ['dɪdʒɪt]	Ziffer
	separate(ly) ['seprət]	einzeln, getrennt
	except for [ɪk'sept fə]	außer
	country code ['kʌntri kəʊd]	Ländervorwahl
	landline ['lændlaɪn]	Festnetz
	to **act out** [ˌækt 'aʊt]	spielen, vor-/durchspielen
21	to **transfer** ['trænsfɜː]	weiterleiten, weitergeben
	to **apologize** [ə'pɒlədʒaɪz]	sich entschuldigen, um Entschuldigung bitten
	to **be available** [bi ə'veɪləbl]	*(Telefon:)* zu sprechen sein
	to **spell** [spel]	buchstabieren
T	to **cut off** [ˌkʌt 'ɒf]	trennen
	Never mind. [ˌnevə 'maɪnd]	Das macht nichts.
	publicity [pʌb'lɪsəti]	Werbung, Werbe-
	straight (away) [ˌstreɪt ə'weɪ]	sofort, gleich
	first thing ['fɜːst θɪŋ]	gleich, als erstes
22	to **note down** [ˌnəʊt 'daʊn]	notieren, aufschreiben
	dot [dɒt]	Punkt
	hyphen ['haɪfn]	Bindestrich
	forward slash ['fɔːwəd slæʃ]	Schrägstrich
	underscore [ˌʌndə'skɔː]	Unterstrich
	answerphone ['ɑːnsəfəʊn]	Anrufbeantworter
	to **leave a message** [liːv ə 'mesɪdʒ]	eine Nachricht hinterlassen
23 T	to **bother sb** ['bɒðə]	jdm Umstände bereiten, jdn belästigen
	to **confirm** [kən'fɜːm]	bestätigen
	presentation [ˌprezn'teɪʃn]	Präsentation, Vorstellung
	brand [brænd]	Marke
	fashion ['fæʃn]	Mode
	to **take place** [teɪk 'pleɪs]	stattfinden
	alternatively [ɔːl'tɜːnətɪvli]	alternativ, oder, auch
	cheers [tʃɪəz]	danke
	tone [təʊn]	Ton, Tonfall
	to **record** ['rekɔːd]	aufnehmen, aufzeichnen
	politeness [pə'laɪtnəs]	Höflichkeit
	frequent(ly) ['friːkwənt]	häufig
	helpful ['helpfl]	hilfsbereit
	rude [ruːd]	unhöflich, unverschämt
	to **mind** [maɪnd]	etw dagegen haben
	Would you mind … [ˌwʊd juː 'maɪnd]	Könnten Sie bitte …
	to **soften** ['sɒfn]	abmildern, mildern
	to **avoid** [ə'vɔɪd]	vermeiden
24	to **slow down** [ˌsləʊ 'daʊn]	langsamer werden/sprechen
	unclear(ly) [ˌʌn'klɪə]	undeutlich, unklar
	clear(ly) ['klɪəli]	deutlich, klar
	to **speak up** [ˌspiːk 'ʌp]	lauter sprechen
	to **put sth into action** [ˌpʊt ɪntu 'ækʃn]	etw in die Tat umsetzen
	to **rephrase** [ˌriː'freɪz]	neu formulieren, umformulieren
25	**cap** [kæp]	Mütze, Kappe
	series ['sɪəriːz]	Reihe, Serie
P	**reference** ['refərəns]	Bezug, Referenz
	availability [əˌveɪlə'bɪləti]	Verfügbarkeit, Lieferbarkeit
	quantity ['kwɒntəti]	Menge
	to **specify** ['spesɪfaɪ]	(genau) angeben, bestimmen
	to **compromise** ['kɒmprəmaɪz]	sich einigen, einen Kompromiss eingehen
	consignment [kən'saɪnmənt]	Sendung, Lieferung
	to **deliver** [dɪ'lɪvər]	liefern, anliefern, zustellen
	appropriate [ə'prəʊpriət]	passend, angemessen
	despite [dɪ'spaɪt]	trotz

	on time [ɒn 'taɪm]	pünktlich
	lunchtime ['lʌntʃtaɪm]	Mittag(szeit)
26	**greeting** ['gri:tɪŋ]	Begrüßung, Grußformel
	complicated ['kɒmplɪkeɪtɪd]	kompliziert
	power ['paʊə]	Macht, Stärke, Kraft
	honest ['ɒnɪst]	ehrlich
	pleasant ['pleznt]	angenehm
	essential [ɪ'senʃl]	wesentlich, unerlässlich
	emotional [ɪ'məʊʃənl]	Gefühls-, Gemüts, gefühlsmäßig, emotional
	listener ['lɪsnə]	Zuhörer/in
	to **tend to do sth** ['tend tə]	dazu neigen, etw zu tun
	to **mirror** ['mɪrə]	spiegeln, widerspiegeln
	state [steɪt]	Zustand
	to **respond** [rɪ'spɒnd]	reagieren
	chances are [ˌtʃɑ:nsɪz 'ɑ:]	es ist wahrscheinlich, dass
	edge [edʒ]	Kante
	sincerity [sɪn'serəti]	Aufrichtigkeit
	sincere [sɪn'sɪə]	aufrichtig
	glad [glæd]	froh
	sentiment ['sentɪmənt]	Gefühl, Sentimentalität
	brevity ['brevəti]	Kürze
	to **fear** [fɪə]	befürchten
	to **run out of sth** [ˌrʌn 'aʊt əv]	ausgehen, wegbleiben
	excessive(ly) [ɪk'sesɪv]	übertrieben, übermäßig
	to **execute** ['eksɪkju:t]	ausführen
	to **waste** [weɪst]	verschwenden, vergeuden
	fortunately ['fɔ:tʃənətli]	glücklicherweise
	guideline ['gaɪdlaɪn]	Richtlinie
	to **assure** [ə'ʃʊə]	sicherstellen
27	**brick** [brɪk]	Backstein, Ziegel
	to **weigh** [weɪ]	wiegen
	to **recharge** [ˌri:'tʃɑ:dʒ]	*(Akku)* aufladen
	battery ['bætəri]	Akku
	power ['paʊə]	Strom
	at a time [ət ə 'taɪm]	auf einmal, jeweils
	neat(ly) [ni:t]	schlank, formschön, elegant
	computing power [kəm'pju:tɪŋ paʊə]	Rechenleistung
	moon [mu:n]	Mond
	to **access sth** ['ækses]	auf etw zugreifen
	database ['deɪtəbeɪs]	Datenbank
	demonstration [ˌdemən'streɪʃn]	Vorführung
	incredible [ɪn'kredəbl]	unglaublich
	device [dɪ'vaɪs]	Gerät
	to **argue** ['ɑ:gju:]	argumentieren
	tool [tu:l]	Werkeug, Hilfsmittel
	obsolete ['ɒbsəli:t]	veraltet, überholt
	globalized ['gləʊbəlaɪzd]	globalisiert
	increasingly [ɪn'kri:sɪŋli]	in zunehmendem Maße
	context ['kɒntekst]	Zusammenhang
	to **give up on sth** [ˌgɪv 'ʌp ɒn]	etw aufgeben, auf etw verzichen
	pain [peɪn]	Schmerz(en)
	shoulder ['ʃəʊldə]	Schulter
	to **fit** [fɪt]	passen
	jacket ['dʒækɪt]	Jacke, Sakko
	pocket ['pɒkɪt]	Tasche
	disadvantage [ˌdɪsəd'vɑ:ntɪdʒ]	Nachteil
	frustrating [frʌ'streɪtɪŋ]	frustrierend
	compared to [kəm'peəd tə]	im Vergleich zu
	saving ['seɪvɪŋ]	Einsparung, Ersparnis
	to **switch to** ['swɪtʃ tə]	wechseln zu
	reality [ri'æləti]	Wirklichkeit
	to **equip** [ɪ'kwɪp]	ausstatten, ausrüsten
	infrastructure ['ɪnfrəstrʌktʃə]	Infrastruktur
	impressive [ɪm'presɪv]	beeindruckend
	functionality [ˌfʌŋkʃə'næləti]	Funktionalität
	to **convince** [kən'vɪns]	überzeugen
	to **replace** [rɪ'pleɪs]	ersetzen
	to **outsmart** [ˌaʊt'smɑ:t]	überlisten
	advantage [əd'vɑ:ntɪdʒ]	Vorteil
	to **make sense** [meɪk 'sens]	sinnvoll sein

Unit 3

28	**equipment** [ɪ'kwɪpmənt]	Geräte, Ausrüstung, Ausstattung
	enquiry [ɪn'kwaɪəri]	Anfrage
	supplier [sə'plaɪə]	Lieferant/in, Zulieferer, Anbieter
	suitable ['su:təbl]	geeignet
	event [ɪ'vent]	Veranstaltung
	contract ['kɒntrækt]	Vertrag
	temporary ['temprəri]	vorübergehend, provisorisch
	village ['vɪlɪdʒ]	Dorf
	to **house sb** [haʊs]	jdn unterbringen, beherbergen
	organizer ['ɔ:gənaɪzə]	Organisator/in
	artist ['ɑ:tɪst]	Künstler/in
	competitor [kəm'petɪtə]	(Wettbewerbs-) Teilnehmer/in
	purchasing director ['pɜ:tʃəsɪŋ dərektə]	Einkaufsleiter/in, Leiter/in Beschaffung
	modular building [ˌmɒdjələ 'bɪldɪŋ]	Haus in Modularbauweise, Fertighaus
	source [sɔ:s]	Quelle

	requirement [rɪ'kwaɪəmənt]	Anforderung, Wunsch
29	**Attn. (= attention)** [ə'tenʃn]	zu Händen
	leading ['li:dɪŋ]	führend
	beyond [bɪ'jɒnd]	darüber hinaus
	to **hold sth** [həʊld]	etw *(Veranstaltung etc.)* abhalten
	entire [ɪn'taɪə]	ganze/r/s, gesamte/r/s
	including [ɪn'klu:dɪŋ]	einschließlich
	discount ['dɪskaʊnt]	Rabatt
	terms [tɜ:mz]	Konditionen, Bedingungen
	delivery [dɪ'lɪvəri]	Lieferung
	terms of delivery [ˌtɜ:mz əv dɪ'lɪvəri]	Lieferbedingungen
	terms of payment [ˌtɜ:mz əv 'peɪmənt]	Zahlungsbedingungen
	to **appreciate** [ə'pri:ʃieɪt]	schätzen, zu schätzen wissen
	by (+ date) [baɪ]	bis (+ Datum)
	at the latest [ət ðə 'leɪtɪst]	spätestens
	to **enclose** [ɪn'kləʊz]	beifügen, beilegen
	to **require** [rɪ'kwaɪə]	benötigen, wünschen
	to **refer to sth** [rɪ'fɜ: tə]	in etw nachschauen
	satisfied ['sætɪsfaɪd]	zufrieden
	Yours sincerely [jɔ:z sɪn'sɪəli]	Hochachtungsvoll, Mit freundlichen Grüßen
	Enc (= enclosure[s]) [ɪn'kləʊʒə]	*(Brief:)* Anlage(n), Anhang
	body ['bɒdi]	*(Brief:)* Haupttext
	complimentary close [ˌkɒmplɪˌmentri 'kləʊz]	*(Brief:)* Schlußformel
	letterhead ['letəhed]	Briefkopf
	reference initials ['refərəns ɪnɪʃlz]	Zeichen, Referenz
	salutation [ˌsælju'teɪʃn]	Anrede
	signatory ['sɪgnətri]	Unterzeichner/in
	signature ['sɪgnətʃə]	Unterschrift
	subject line ['sʌbdʒɪkt laɪn]	Betreffzeile
30 T	to **call (by)** [ˌkɔ:l 'baɪ]	vorbeischauen, vorbeikommen
	diary ['daɪəri]	Terminkalender
	to **suit** [su:t]	passen
	return flight [rɪˌtɜ:n 'flaɪt]	Rückflug
	preferably ['prefərəbli]	am besten, am liebsten
	booked up [ˌbʊkt 'ʌp]	ausgebucht
	to **get in touch with sb** [ˌget ɪn 'tʌtʃ wɪð]	sich bei jdm melden
	alternative [ɔ:l'tɜ:nətɪv]	Alternative, *hier:* Ausweichtermin
31	**quotation** [kwəʊ'teɪʃn]	Angebot, Preisangebot, Kostenvoranschlag
	reply [rɪ'plaɪ]	Antwort
	to **manufacture** [ˌmænju'fæktʃə]	herstellen, fertigen
	throughout ... [θru:'aʊt]	in ganz ...
	to **judge** [dʒʌdʒ]	urteilen, beurteilen
	to **point out** [ˌpɔɪnt 'aʊt]	darauf hinweisen
	to **dismantle** [dɪs'mæntl]	abbauen, demontieren
	value ['vælju:]	Wert
	re-sale value [ˌri: seɪl 'vælju:]	Wiederverkaufswert
	as regards [əz rɪ'gɑ:dz]	bezüglich, was ... anbelangt
	unit ['ju:nɪt]	Einheit, Gebäude
	to **be pleased to do sth** [bi 'pli:zd tə]	etw gern tun
	to **submit** [səb'mɪt]	einreichen
	article ['ɑ:tɪkl]	Artikel
	disabled toilet [dɪs'eɪbld tɔɪlət]	Behindertentoilette
	shower ['ʃaʊə]	Dusche
	dormitory ['dɔ:mətri]	Schlafsaal
	attachment [ə'tætʃmənt]	*(Brief etc.:)* Anhang, Anlage
	to **quote** [kwəʊt]	*(Preis)* angeben, nennen
	CPT (carriage paid to) [ˌsi: pi: 'ti:/ˌkærɪdʒ 'peɪd tə]	frachtfrei
	carriage ['kærɪdʒ]	Beförderung, Transport
	receipt of order [rɪˌsi:t əv 'ɔ:də]	Auftragseingang
	cash with order [ˌkæʃ wɪð 'ɔ:də]	Vorauszahlung, Vorkasse, Zahlung bei Auftragserteilung
	to **be to sb's liking** [bi tə sʌmbədɪz 'laɪkɪŋ]	jds Vorstellungen entsprechen, Zustimmung finden
32	to **take sth into account** [ˌteɪk ɪntu ə'kaʊnt]	etw berücksichtigen
	purchasing department ['pɜ:tʃəsɪŋ dɪpɑ:tmənt]	Einkaufs-, Beschaffungsabteilung
	catalogue ['kætəlɒg]	Katalog
	to **attach** [ə'tætʃ]	beifügen, beilegen
	insurance [ɪn'ʃʊərəns]	Versicherung
	CIP (cost and insurance paid) [ˌsi: aɪ 'pi: / ˌkɒst ənd ɪnˌʃʊərəns 'peɪd]	frachtfrei versichert
	finish ['fɪnɪʃ]	Schluss, Ende
	trade [treɪd]	Handel, Handelsverkehr
	contract of sale [ˌkɒntrækt əv 'seɪl]	Kaufvertrag
	to **define** [dɪ'faɪn]	definieren
	right [raɪt]	Recht
	obligation [ˌɒblɪ'geɪʃn]	Pflicht, Verpflichtung

	buyer ['baɪə]	Käufer
	seller ['selə]	Verkäufer
	packing ['pækɪŋ]	Verpackung
	customs duty [ˌkʌstəmz 'dju:ti]	Zollgebühr(en)
	documentation [ˌdɒkjumen'teɪʃn]	Dokumente, Dokumentation, Unterlagen
	to **evaluate** [ɪ'væljueɪt]	bewerten, auswerten, einschätzen
	destination [ˌdestɪ'neɪʃn]	Bestimmungsort, Zielort
	multimodal transport [mʌltiˌməʊdl 'trænspɔ:t]	kombinierte Beförderung, multimodaler Transport
	customary ['kʌstəməri]	handelsüblich
	to **clear for export** [ˌklɪə fər 'ekspɔ:t]	Ausfuhrformalitäten erledigen
	cleared for export [ˌklɪəd fər 'ekspɔ:t]	zur Ausfuhr freigemacht/verzollt
	carrier ['kæriə]	Frachtführer
	to **nominate** ['nɒmɪneɪt]	benennen
	to **bear** [beə]	tragen
	custody ['kʌstədi]	Obhut
	excluding [ɪk'sklu:dɪŋ]	ausgenommen
	import duty ['ɪmpɔ:t dju:ti]	Einfuhrzoll
	tax [tæks]	Steuer
	to **unload** [ˌʌn'ləʊd]	entladen
33	**freight forwarder** ['freɪt fɔ:wədə]	Spediteur, Spedition
	to **pass (from sb to sb)** ['pɑ:s]	(von jdm auf jdn) übergehen
	to **load** [ləʊd]	verladen
	expense [ɪk'spens]	Kosten
	to **cover** ['kʌvə]	*(Kosten)* decken, aufkommen für
	to **negotiate** [nɪ'gəʊʃieɪt]	verhandeln, aushandeln
	to **grumble** [grʌmbl]	meckern, klagen, sich beschweren
	windy ['wɪndi]	windig
	load [ləʊd]	Ladung
	to **insure** [ɪn'ʃʊə]	versichern
	to **collect** [kə'lekt]	abholen
	compensation [ˌkɒmpən'seɪʃn]	Schadenersatz, Entschädigung
	insurer [ɪn'ʃʊərə]	Versicherer
	to **quote sb** [kwəʊt]	jdm ein Angebot machen
	up to now [ʌp tə 'naʊ]	bislang, bis jetzt
	rate [reɪt]	Gebühr, Satz
	deal [di:l]	Geschäft
	delivery period [dɪ'lɪvəri pɪəriəd]	Lieferfrist
	documents against payment (D/P) [ˌdɒkjumənts əgenst 'peɪmənt]	Dokumente gegen Zahlung, Kasse gegen Dokumente
35	**spring** [sprɪŋ]	Frühling, Frühjahr
	lorry ['lɒri]	Lastwagen
	to **break down** [ˌbreɪk 'daʊn]	kaputtgehen, eine Panne haben
	car crash ['kɑ: kræʃ]	Autounfall
	to **crash** [kræʃ]	einen Unfall haben
	to **place an order** [ˌpleɪs ən 'ɔ:də]	einen Auftrag erteilen
	to **calculate** ['kælkjuleɪt]	berechnen, ausrechnen, ermitteln
	increase ['ɪŋkri:s]	Steigerung
	percentage [pə'sentɪdʒ]	Anteil, Prozentsatz, prozentual
	as compared to [əz kəm'peəd tə]	im Vergleich zu
	once [wʌns]	sobald
	dated … ['deɪtɪd]	vom …
	unit price [ˌju:nɪt 'praɪs]	Einzelpreis, Preis pro Stück
	documentary credit [dɒkjuˌməntri 'kredɪt]	Dokumentenakkreditiv
	in sb's favour [ɪn ˌsʌmbədiz 'feɪvə]	zu jds Gunsten
	confirmation [ˌkɒnfə'meɪʃn]	Bestätigung
	confirmation of order [kɒnfəˌmeɪʃn əv 'ɔ:də]	Auftragsbestätigung
36	**right away** [ˌraɪt ə'weɪ]	sofort
	to **impact** ['ɪmpækt]	sich auswirken auf
	cash flow ['kæʃ fləʊ]	Geldumlauf, Kapitalfluss
	to **deal with sth** ['di:l wɪð]	mit etw zurechtkommen, mit etw fertig werden
	to **advance sth** [əd'vɑ:ns]	etw vorschießen
	to **invoice sb** ['ɪnvɔɪs]	jdm eine Rechnung stellen
	immediate [ɪ'mi:diət]	sofortig, unmittelbar
	cash [kæʃ]	Bargeld, Geldmittel
	face value [ˌfeɪs 'vælju:]	Nennwert
	due [dju:]	fällig
	to **transfer** ['trænsfɜ:]	*(Geld)* überweisen
	to **deduct** [dɪ'dʌkt]	abziehen
	fee [fi:]	Honorar, Gebühr
	interest ['ɪntrəst]	Zins(en)
	interest charge ['ɪntrəst tʃɑ:dʒ]	Zinsgebühr, -forderung
	to **charge** [tʃɑ:dʒ]	*(Preis, Gebühren etc.)* verlangen, fordern, berechnen
	to **depend on sth** [dɪ'pend ɒn]	von etw abhängen
	creditworthiness ['kredɪwɜ:ðinəs]	Kreditwürdigkeit
	to **qualify for sth** ['kwɒlɪfaɪ]	für etw in Frage kommen

	to engage in sth [ɪn'geɪdʒ]	an etw teilnehmen, in etw aktiv sein
	commerce ['kɒmɜːs]	Handel
	downside ['daʊnsaɪd]	Nachteil, Kehrseite
	matter ['mætə]	Angelegenheit, Sache
	due to ['djuː tə]	aufgrund
	bankruptcy ['bæŋkrʌptsi]	Bankrott, Pleite
37	**certificate** [sə'tɪfɪkət]	Bescheinigung, Zertifikat
	compulsory [kəm'pʌlsəri]	obligatorisch, verpflichtend, Pflicht-
	to obtain [əb'teɪn]	erhalten, bekommen
	safety mark ['seɪfti mɑːk]	Sicherheits(kenn)-zeichen, Prüfsiegel
	scope [skəʊp]	Geltungsbereich
	certification [ˌsɜːtɪfɪ'keɪʃn]	Zulassung
	applicant ['æplɪkənt]	Antragsteller/in
	disconnector [dɪskə'nektə]	Trennschalter
	isolator ['aɪsəleɪtə]	Isolator
	working principle ['wɜːkɪŋ prɪnsəpl]	Funktionsweise, Funktionsprizip
	switch [swɪtʃ]	Schalter
	high current [ˌhaɪ 'kʌrənt]	Starkstrom
	application [ˌæplɪ'keɪʃn]	Anwendung
	electrolysis [ɪˌlek'trɒləsɪs]	Elektrolyse
	process ['prəʊses]	Verfahren
	cell [sel]	Zelle
	voltage ['vəʊltɪdʒ]	Spannung
	short circuit [ˌsɔːt 'sɜːkɪt]	Kurzschluss
	supply voltage [sə'plaɪ vəʊltɪdʒ]	Betriebsspannung, Netzspannung
	to switch sth on [ˌswɪtʃ 'ɒn]	etw einschalten
	current ['kʌrənt]	Strom
	to flow [fləʊ]	fließen
	operation voltage [ˌɒpə'reɪʃn vəʊltɪdʒ]	Betriebspannung
	rated current [ˌreɪtɪd 'kʌrənt]	Nennstrom
	protection [prə'tekʃn]	Schutz
	weight [weɪt]	Gewicht
	dimensions [daɪ'menʃnz]	Abmessungen
	data sheet ['deɪtə ʃiːt]	Datenblatt
	site of use [ˌsaɪt əv 'juːs]	Einsatzort
	metal ['metl]	Metall
	copper ['kɒpə]	Kupfer
	zinc ['zɪŋk]	Zink
	series number ['sɪəriːz nʌmbə]	Seriennummer
	to enter sth ['entə]	nach/in *(ein Land)* kommen, gelangen
	to assist sb [ə'sɪst]	jdm helfen, jdn unterstützen
	customs clearance ['kʌstəmz klɪərəns]	(Erledigung der) Zollformalitäten
	common ['kɒmən]	häufig, gewöhnlich

Unit 4

38	**trade fair** ['treɪd feə]	Handelsmesse, Fachmesse
	travel arrangements *(pl)* ['trævl əreɪndʒmənts]	Reisevorbereitungen
	item ['aɪtəm]	Gegenstand, Artikel, Sache
	abroad [ə'brɔːd]	im/ins Ausland
	credit card ['kredɪt kɑːd]	Kreditkarte
	passport ['pɑːspɔːt]	Reisepass
	boarding card ['bɔːdɪŋ kɑːd]	Bordkarte
39	**business development** ['bɪznəs dɪveləpmənt]	Geschäftsentwicklung
	to attend sth [ə'tend]	an etw teilnehmen, etw besuchen
	to take care of sth [ˌteɪk ˌkeər əv]	sich um etw kümmern
	to return [rɪ'tɜːn]	zurückfahren, -fliegen, -kommen, -kehren
	rental car [ˌrentl 'kɑː]	Mietwagen
	to depart [dɪ'pɑːt]	abfahren, -fliegen, -reisen
	to catch sth [kætʃ]	etw bekommen, erreichen, erwischen
	accommodation [əˌkɒmə'deɪʃn]	Unterkunft
	exhibition [eksɪ'bɪʃn]	Ausstellung
	conference ['kɒnfərəns]	Konferenz
	exhibition and conference centre [eksɪˌbɪʃn ənd 'kɒnfərəns sentə]	Ausstellungs- und Konferenzzentrum
	smoker ['sməʊkə]	Raucher/in
	to smoke [sməʊk]	rauchen
	to keep sth in mind [ˌkiːp ɪn 'maɪnd]	an etw denken
	gym [dʒɪm]	Fitnessstudio
	sauna ['sɔːnə]	Sauna
	to pick sb/sth up [ˌpɪk 'ʌp]	jdn/etw abholen
41 P	**destination** [ˌdestɪ'neɪʃn]	Reiseziel, Zielort
	departure [dɪ'pɑːtʃə]	Abreise, Abfahrt, Abflug
	arrival [ə'raɪvl]	Ankunft
	to note sth [nəʊt]	etw beachten

	confusion [kən'fju:ʒn]	Verwirrung, Verwechslung
	to **be worth** [bi 'wɜ:θ]	sich lohnen
42	to **search** [sɜ:tʃ]	suchen
	passenger ['pæsɪndʒə]	Passagier/in
	surname ['sɜ:neɪm]	Nachname
	baggage ['bægɪdʒ]	Gepäck
	charge [tʃɑ:dʒ]	Gebühr
	excess baggage [ˌekses 'bægɪdʒ]	Übergepäck
	method ['meθəd]	Art, Weise, Methode
	to **cancel** ['kænsl]	stornieren
	terms and conditions [ˌtɜ:mz ənd kən'dɪʃnz]	Konditionen, (Allgemeine) Geschäftsbedingungen
	to **be in a hurry** [bi ɪn ə 'hʌri]	in Eile sein, es eilig haben
	speedy ['spi:di]	schnell
	boarding ['bɔ:dɪŋ]	An-Bord-Gehen
	frequent ['fri:kwənt]	häufig
	benefit ['benɪfɪt]	Vorteil, Nutzen
	expiry [ɪk'spaɪəri]	Ablauf
	customer loyalty [ˌkʌstəmə 'lɔɪəlti]	Kundentreue, Kundenbindung
	scheme [ski:m]	Programm
	luggage ['lʌgɪdʒ]	Gepäck
	to **check in** [ˌtʃek 'ɪn]	einchecken
	to **enter sth** ['entə]	etw *(Text etc.)* eingeben
43	**flyer** ['flaɪə]	Werbezettel, Prospekt
	within walking distance [wɪðɪn 'wɔ:kɪŋ dɪstəns]	in Laufweite
	to **comprise** [kəm'praɪz]	umfassen, bestehen aus
	suite [swi:t]	Suite
	single room [ˌsɪŋgl 'ru:m]	Einzelzimmer
	double room [ˌdʌbl 'ru:m]	Doppelzimmer
	fully-equipped [ˌfʊli ɪ'kwɪpt]	voll ausgestattet
	en-suite bathroom [ɒ ˌswi:t 'bɑ:θru:m]	eigenes Badezimmer
	to **accommodate** [ə'kɒmədeɪt]	unterbringen, Platz bieten für
	participant [pɑ:'tɪsɪpənt]	Teilnehmer/in
	latest ['leɪtɪst]	neueste/r/s
	digital projector [ˌdɪdʒɪtl prə'dʒektə]	Beamer
	cordless ['kɔ:dləs]	schnurlos
	microphone ['maɪkrəfəʊn]	Mikrofon
	to **complement** ['kɒmplɪmənt]	ergänzen
	to **photocopy** ['fəʊtəʊkɒpi]	fotokopieren
	wireless ['waɪələs]	drahtlos
	access ['ækses]	Zugang, Zugriff
	leisure ['leʒə]	Freizeit
	to **unwind** [ˌʌn'waɪnd]	sich entspannen, abschalten
	to **dine** [daɪn]	speisen
	to **be spoilt for choice** [bi ˌspɔɪlt fə 'tʃɔɪs]	die Qual der Wahl haben
	eatery ['i:təri]	Restaurant, Speiselokal
	snack [snæk]	Imbiss
	course [kɔ:s]	*(Menü:)* Gang
	peace and quiet [ˌpi:s ənd 'kwaɪət]	Ruhe und Frieden
	comfort ['kʌmfət]	Komfort, Annehmlichkeit
	to **operate sth** ['ɒpəreɪt]	betreiben, *hier:* vertreten, umsetzen
	policy ['pɒləsi]	Politik, Vorgehensweise, Linie
	on business [ɒn 'bɪznəs]	geschäftlich
	to **relax** [rɪ'læks]	sich ausruhen, sich entspannen
	confidential [ˌkɒnfɪ'denʃl]	vertraulich
	secretarial [ˌsekrə'teəriəl]	Sekretariats-
	in addition (to) [ɪn ə'dɪʃn]	zusätzlich (zu)
	up-to-date [ˌʌp tə 'deɪt]	auf dem neuesten Stand
	available [ə'veɪləbl]	verfügbar, erhältlich
44	**aspect** ['æspekt]	Aspekt, Seite
	unsuitable [ˌʌn'su:təbl]	ungeeignet
T	**limited** ['lɪmɪtɪd]	begrenzt, beschränkt
	conservatory [kən'sɜ:vətri]	Wintergarten, Gewächshaus
	worried ['wʌrid]	besorgt
	to **vacate** [və'keɪt]	räumen
	to **drop sth off** [ˌdrɒp 'ɒf]	etw abgeben, dalassen
45	**twin room** [ˌtwɪn 'ru:m]	Zweibettzimmer
P	**closed** [kləʊzd]	geschlossen
	additional [ə'dɪʃənəl]	zusätzlich, Zusatz-
	to **exceed** [ɪk'si:d]	überschreiten, übertreffen
	mileage allowance [ˌmaɪlɪdʒ ə'laʊəns]	Freikilometer (*bzw.* -meilen)
	rental ['rentl]	Miete
	rental period [ˌrentl 'pɪəriəd]	Mietzeitraum
	tank [tæŋk]	Tank
	fuel ['fju:əl]	Treibstoff, Benzin
	vehicle ['vi:əkl]	Fahrzeug
	delighted [dɪ'laɪtɪd]	erfreut
	to **bill sb sth** [bɪl]	jdm etw in Rechnung stellen
	mile [maɪl]	Meile

	additionally [ə'dɪʃənəli]	außerdem
	return [rɪ'tɜ:n]	Rückgabe
	to **charge sb sth** [tʃɑ:dʒ]	jdm etw in Rechnung stellen
	to **refill** [ˌri:'fɪl]	auffüllen
	Best regards [best rɪ'gɑ:dz]	Mit freundlichen Grüßen
	to **include** [ɪn'klu:d]	einschließen, beinhalten
	VAT (value added tax) [ˌvælju: 'ædɪd tæks]	Mehrwertsteuer
46	**hire** ['haɪə]	Miete
	to **incur** [ɪn'kɜ:]	*(Kosten:)* anfallen
	opening ['əʊpənɪŋ]	Eröffnungs-
	importance [ɪm'pɔ:tns]	Bedeutung, Wichtigkeit
47	**board** [bɔ:d]	Kommission
	booth ['bu:ð]	Messestand
	eco- ['i:kəʊ]	Öko-
	wall [wɔ:l]	Wand
	spotlight ['spɒtlaɪt]	Scheinwerfer
	ID sign [ˌaɪ 'di: saɪn]	Namensschild
	counter ['kaʊntə]	Tresen, Theke
	stool [stu:l]	Hocker
	carpet ['kɑ:pɪt]	Teppich
	straight [streɪt]	gerade
	socket ['sɒkɪt]	Steckdose
	inclined [ɪn'klaɪnd]	schräg, geneigt
	in advance [ɪn əd'vɑ:ns]	im Voraus
48	**rapid(ly)** ['ræpɪdli]	rasch, schnell
	to **showcase** ['ʃəʊkeɪs]	ausstellen, zur Schau stellen
	to **prove sth** [pru:v]	sich als etw erweisen
	considerable [kən'sɪdərəbl]	beträchtlich
	exhibitor [ɪg'zɪbɪtə]	Aussteller
	enhanced [ɪn'hɑ:nst]	verbessert
	to **establish** [ɪ'stæblɪʃ]	herstellen
	target group ['tɑ:gɪt gru:p]	Zielgruppe
	trade [treɪd]	Branche
	representative [reprɪ'zentətɪv]	Vertreter/in
	admission [əd'mɪʃn]	Eintritt
	free of charge [ˌfri: əf 'tʃɑ:dʒ]	kostenlos
	to **be involved in sth** [bi ɪn'vɒlvd ɪn]	mit etw zu tun haben
	fence [fens]	Zaun
	to **be eager to do sth** [bi 'i:gə tə]	etw (unbedingt) tun wollen
	distributor [dɪ'strɪbjətə]	Vertrieb, Händler
	to **place** [pleɪs]	platzieren
	to **approach sb** [ə'prəʊtʃ]	sich an jdn wenden, jdn ansprechen
	to **represent** [ˌreprɪ'zent]	vertreten, repräsentieren
	show [ʃəʊ]	Austellung
	guide [gaɪd]	Führer
	entry ['entri]	Eintrag, Aufnahme
	badge [bædʒ]	(Namens-)Schild
	custom-made ['kʌstəm meɪd]	maßgefertigt
	to **apply** [ə'plaɪ]	gelten
	shell [sel]	Hülle, *hier:* Außenwände
	package ['pækɪdʒ]	Paket
	to **turn up** [ˌtɜ:n 'ʌp]	auftauchen, ankommen
	standardized ['stændədaɪzd]	genormt
	feature ['fi:tʃə]	Merkmal, Eigenschaft
	fascia panel ['feɪʃə pænl]	Blendentafel
	ceiling ['si:lɪŋ]	Decke
	grid [grɪd]	Gitter
	overhead ['əʊvəhed]	von oben, obenliegend
	lighting ['laɪtɪŋ]	Beleuchtung
	to **customize** ['kʌstəmaɪz]	individuell anpassen
	to **pick sth (out)** [ˌpɪk 'aʊt]	sich etw aussuchen

Unit 5

49	to **label** ['leɪbl]	etikettieren, beschriften, benennen
	conference call ['kɒnfərəns kɔ:l]	Konferenzschaltung
	face-to-face [ˌfeɪs tə 'feɪs]	persönlich
	extreme [ɪk'stri:m]	extrem
	condition [kən'dɪʃn]	Bedingung
	to **fire sb** ['faɪə]	jdn entlassen
	job interview ['dʒɒb ɪntəvju:]	Vorstellungsgespräch
	weekly ['wi:kli]	wöchentlich
	to **draw** [drɔ:]	zeichnen
	to **rank** [ræŋk]	einstufen
50	**circle** ['sɜ:kl]	Kreis
	branch [brɑ:ntʃ]	Ast
	to **radiate** ['reɪdieɪt]	sternförmig ausgehen
	thin [θɪn]	dünn
	screen [skrin]	Bildschirm
	brewery ['bru:əri]	Brauerei
	to **brew** [bru:]	brauen
	draft [drɑ:ft]	Entwurf
	agenda [ə'dʒendə]	Tagesordnung, Programm
	doubt [daʊt]	Zweifel
	no doubt [ˌnəʊ 'daʊt]	zweifellos, bestimmt
	to **postpone** [pə'spəʊn]	verschieben
	to **consult sb** [kən'sʌlt]	jdn fragen, sich mit jdm beraten

	to schedule ['ʃedju:l]	*(Besprechung etc.)* ansetzen
	order situation ['ɔ:də sɪtʒueɪʃn]	Auftragslage
	to install [ɪn'stɔ:l]	installieren
	to operate sth ['ɒpəreɪt]	etw bedienen, betreiben
	any other business (AOB) [ˌeni ˌʌðə 'bɪznəs]	Sonstiges
	suggestion [sə'dʒestʃən]	Vorschlag
	addition [ə'dɪʃn]	Zusatz, Ergänzung
	to circulate sth ['sɜ:kjəleɪt]	etw verteilen, verschicken
	minutes ['mɪnɪts]	Protokoll
51	**record** ['rekɔ:d]	Aufzeichnung, Unterlage
	to finalize ['faɪnəlaɪz]	festlegen, beschließen, abschließen
	to reply [rɪ'plaɪ]	antworten
	to suggest [sə'dʒest]	vorschlagen
	issue ['ɪʃu:]	Frage, Thema, Problem
	complaint [kəm'pleɪnt]	Reklamation, Beschwerde
	punctual ['pʌŋktʃuəl]	pünktlich
	second-hand [ˌsekənd'hænd]	gebraucht
	repair [rɪ'peə]	Reparatur
	to be in agreement with sth [bi ɪn ə'gri:mənt wɪð]	einer Sache zustimmen
	travel expenses *(pl)* ['trævl ɪkspensɪz]	Reisekosten, Reisespesen
52	**recipient** [rɪ'sɪpiənt]	Empfänger/in
	to sign off [ˌsaɪn 'ɒf]	einen Brief beenden, unterschreiben
	otherwise ['ʌðəwaɪz]	ansonsten, sonst, auch
	capital letter ['kæpɪtl letə]	Großbuchstabe
	reference ['refərəns]	Erwähnung
	previous ['pri:viəs]	vorherig/r/s, frühere/r/s
	to split [splɪt]	teilen, aufteilen
	paragraph ['pærəgrɑ:f]	*(Text:)* Absatz
	to separate ['sepəreɪt]	trennen
	free line [ˌfri: 'laɪn]	Leerzeile
	to refer to sth [rɪ'fɜ: tə]	auf etw verweisen, etw erwähnen
	convention [kən'venʃn]	Versammlung
	theme [θi:m]	Motto, Thema
	passionate(ly) ['pæʃənət]	leidenschaftlich
	to support [sə'pɔ:t]	unterstützen
	charity ['tʃærəti]	Wohltätigkeit-(sorganisation), Initiative, guter Zweck
	Chief Executive Officer (CEO) [ˌtʃi:f ɪg'zekjətɪv ɒfɪsə]	Vorstandsvorsitzende/r, Geschäftsführer/in
53	**to forward sth** ['fɔ:wəd]	etw weiterleiten
	to get to the point [get tə ðə 'pɔɪnt]	zum Thema kommen
	request [rɪ'kwest]	Bitte, Wunsch
	closing sentence ['kləʊzɪŋ sentəns]	Schlussatz
	to come on board [ˌkʌm ɒn 'bɔ:d]	an Bord kommen, dabei sein
	to act [ækt]	handeln, fungieren
	agent ['eɪdʒənt]	Agent/in
	on behalf of sb [ɒn bɪ'hɑ:f əv]	für jdn
	to go ahead [ˌgəʊ ə'hed]	anfangen
	upward ['ʌpwəd]	aufwärts
	to conclude [kən'klu:d]	abschließend
	to be well received [bi ˌwel rɪ'si:vd]	gut *(beim Publikum etc.)* ankommen
54	**to comment** ['kɒment]	sich äußern, etw dazu sagen
	to move on [ˌmu:v 'ɒn]	weitergehen, übergehen (zu)
	brief [bri:f]	kurz, knapp
	thoroughly ['θʌrəli]	völlig
	to pass sth on [ˌpɑ:s 'ɒn]	etw weitergeben, -leiten, -reichen
	to cover sth ['kʌvə]	*(Thema)* behandeln
	to wrap sth up [ˌræp 'ʌp]	etw abschließen
55	**to interrupt** [ˌɪntə'rʌpt]	unterbrechen
	to disagree [ˌdɪsə'gri:]	nicht zustimmen, anderer Meinung sein
	to rise [raɪz]	steigen
	to increase ['ɪŋkri:s]	zunehmen, steigen
	stable ['steɪbl]	stabil
	to remain [rɪ'meɪn]	bleiben
	to even out [ˌi:vn 'aʊt]	sich einpendeln
	downward ['daʊnwəd]	abwärts
	to drop [drɒp]	fallen, sinken
	to decrease ['di:kri:s]	abnehmen, sinken
	to indicate ['ɪndɪkeɪt]	anzeigen
	degree [dɪ'gri:]	Ausmaß, Grad
	negligibly ['neglɪdʒəbli]	vernachlässigbar
	slightly ['slaɪtli]	geringfügig
	significantly [sɪg'nɪfɪkəntli]	erheblich
	considerably [kən'sɪdərəbli]	erheblich
	sharply ['ʃɑ:pli]	drastisch, rapide
	dramatically [drə'mætɪkli]	dramatisch
	line graph [laɪn grɑ:f]	Liniendiagramm
	chart [tʃɑ:t]	Diagramm
	hectolitre [ˌhektə'li:tə]	Hektoliter

56	**formation** [fɔː'meɪʃn]	Bildung
	press officer ['pres ɒfɪsə]	Pressereferent/in
	brochure ['brəʊʃə]	Prospekt, Werbebroschüre
	trainee [treɪ'niː]	Auszubildende/r
	training officer ['treɪnɪŋ ɒfɪsə]	Ausbildungsleiter/in
	to **structure** ['strʌktʃə]	strukturieren
T	**(suit)case** ['suːtkeɪs]	Koffer
	to **suppose** [sə'pəʊz]	annehmen, glauben
	inquisitive [ɪn'kwɪzətɪv]	neugierig
	sight [saɪt]	Sehenswürdigkeit
	aeroplane ['eərəpleɪn]	Flugzeug
	meat [miːt]	Fleisch
	dish [dɪʃ]	Gericht, Speise
	cow [kaʊ]	Kuh
	beef [biːf]	Rindfleisch
	sausage ['sɒsɪdʒ]	Wurst, Würstchen
	shopping mall ['ʃɒpɪŋ mɔːl]	Einkaufspassage, -zentrum
	celebrity [sə'lebrəti]	Prominente/r
57	**native speaker** [ˌneɪtɪv 'spiːkə]	Muttersprachler/in
	to **be considered sth** [bi kən'sɪdəd]	als etw gelten
	impolite [ˌɪmpə'laɪt]	unhöflich
	atmosphere ['ætməsfɪə]	Atmosphäre
	politics *(pl)* ['pɒlətɪks]	Politik
	heat [hiːt]	Hitze
	to **shadow sb** ['ʃædəʊ]	bei jdm hospitieren
	return visit [rɪ'tɜːn vɪsɪt]	Gegenbesuch
P	**homestay accommodation** ['həʊmsteɪ əkɒmədeɪʃn]	Unterbringung bei Gastfamilien
	exam [ɪg'zæm]	Prüfung
	flat [flæt]	Wohnung
	workmate ['wɜːkmeɪt]	Arbeitskollege/-in
	Easter ['iːstə]	Ostern
58	to **take the minutes** [ˌteɪk ðə 'mɪnɪts]	Protokoll führen
	to **review sth** [rɪ'vjuː]	etw Revue passieren lassen
T	**review** [rɪ'vjuː]	Rückschau
	especially [ɪ'speʃəli]	besonders, insbesondere
	to **come in on sth** [ˌkʌm 'ɪn ɒn]	etw zu etw sagen, sich einschalten
	to **enrol for sth** [ɪn'rəʊl fə]	sich für etw anmelden
	vocational college [vəʊˌkeɪʃənl 'kɒlɪdʒ]	Berufsfachschule
	time difference ['taɪm dɪfrəns]	Zeitverschiebung
	to **collect** [kə'lekt]	sammeln
	a good cause [ə ˌgʊd 'kɔːz]	ein guter Zweck, eine gute Sache
	disability [ˌdɪsə'bɪləti]	Behinderung
	Count me in. [ˌkaʊnt miː 'ɪn]	Ich bin dabei.
	helper ['helpə]	Helfer/in
	to **be involved in sth** [bi ɪn'vɒlvd ɪn]	an etw beteiligt sein, bei etw mitmachen
	guest house ['gesthaʊs]	Pension
	freedom ['friːdəm]	Freiheit
	I suppose so. [aɪ sə'pəʊz səʊ]	Mag sein. Kann schon sein.
	internal(ly) [ɪn'tɜːnəli]	intern
	to **sum up** [ˌsʌm 'ʌp]	zusammenfassen
	attendee [əˌten'diː]	Anwesende/r
	charitable ['tʃærətəbl]	Wohltätigkeits-
	community [kə'mjuːnəti]	Gemeinde, Gemeinschaft
59	**beer** [bɪə]	Bier
	to **greet sb** [griːt]	jdn begrüßen
	chat [tʃæt]	Unterhaltung, Schwätzchen
	to **invent** [ɪn'vent]	erfinden
	opening hours ['əʊpənɪŋ aʊəz]	Öffnungszeiten
	gallery ['gæləri]	Galerie
60	to **stink** [stɪŋk]	stinken
	extract ['ekstrækt]	Auszug
	tense [tens]	angespannt
	sociology [ˌsəʊsi'ɒlədʒi]	Soziologie
	to **sense** [sens]	spüren, erspüren
	to **seek** [siːk]	suchen
	goggles *(pl)* ['gɒglz]	(Schutz-)Brille
	to **glow** [gləʊ]	leuchten
	human ['hjuːmən]	Mensch
	vibes [vaɪbz]	Schwingungen, Atmosphäre
	particularly [pə'tɪkjələli]	insbesondere, ganz besonders
	averse [ə'vɜːs]	abgeneigt
	to **assert** [ə'sɜːt]	behaupten
	explanation [ˌeksplə'neɪʃn]	Erklärung, Erläuterung
	definite(ly) ['defɪnətli]	bestimmt
	crazy ['kreɪzi]	verrückt
	to **roll eyeballs** [ˌrəʊl 'aɪbɔːlz]	mit den Augen rollen
	blank stare [ˌblæŋk 'steə]	starrer Gesichtsausdruck
	silence ['saɪləns]	Schweigen
	to **gang up on sb** [ˌgæŋ 'ʌp ɒn]	sich gegen jdn zusammenschließen
	to **laugh at sb/sth** ['lɑːf ət]	jdn auslachen, über etw lachen
	to **slouch** [slaʊtʃ]	sich lümmeln
	to **entertain** [ˌentə'teɪn]	unterhalten

	to **get along** [ˌget əˈlɒŋ]	gut miteinander auskommen, sich gut verstehen
	decent [ˈdiːsnt]	anständig
	joke [dʒəʊk]	Witz, Scherz
	gossip [ˈgɒsɪp]	Klatsch, Tratsch
	educational [ˌedʒuˈkeɪʃənl]	lehrreich
	seriously [ˈsɪəriəsli]	im Ernst
	to **get into full swing** [get ɪntə ˌfʊl ˈswɪŋ]	richtig ins Rollen kommen
	to **degenerate** [dɪˈdʒenəreɪt]	ausarten
	particular [pəˈtɪkjələ]	bestimmt
	agency [ˈeɪdʒənsi]	Agentur
	dozen [ˈdʌzn]	Dutzend
	government [ˈgʌvənmənt]	Regierung, öffentliche Verwaltung
	to **whip sth out** [ˌwɪp ˈaʊt]	etw zücken
	leather portfolio [ˌleðə pɔːtˈfəʊliəʊ]	lederne Aktenmappe
	group dynamics *(pl)* [ˌgruːp daɪˈnæmɪks]	Gruppendynamik
	to **go into motion** [ˌgəʊ ɪntə ˈməʊʃn]	in Bewegung geraten
	behaviour [bɪˈheɪvjə]	Verhalten, Benehmen
	boring [ˈbɔːrɪŋ]	langweilig

Unit 6

61	**cycle** [ˈsaɪkl]	Fahrrad
	to **market** [ˈmɑːkɪt]	vermarkten
	advertising [ˈædvətaɪzɪŋ]	Werbung
	to **analyse** [ˈænəlaɪz]	analysieren
	potential [pəˈtenʃl]	potenziell
	advertising campaign [ˈædvətaɪzɪŋ kæmpeɪn]	Werbekampagne
	to **launch** [lɔːntʃ]	(in den Markt) einführen
	bicycle [ˈbaɪsɪkl]	Fahrrad
	progress report [ˈprəʊgres rɪpɔːt]	Zwischenbericht
	to **turn to sth** [ˈtɜːn tə]	sich einer Sache zuwenden
	fascinating [ˈfæsɪneɪtɪŋ]	hochinteressant, faszinierend
62	**cult** [kʌlt]	Kult
	enormous [ɪˈnɔːməs]	gewaltig, enorm
	to **be up to sth** [bi ˈʌp tə]	etw vorhaben, etw machen
	promotion [prəˈməʊʃn]	Werbung
	progress [ˈprəʊgres]	Fortschritt(e)
	in effect [ɪn ɪˈfekt]	eigentlich, tatsächlich
	bright [braɪt]	*(Farbe:)* hell, leuchtend
	market research [ˌmɑːkɪt rɪˈsɜːtʃ]	Marktforschung
	speed [spiːd]	Gang
	single speed (bicycle) [ˈsɪŋgl spiːd]	Eingangrad
	strategy [ˈstrætədʒi]	Strategie
	to **make sth up** [ˌmeɪk ˈʌp]	etw ausmachen, bilden
	segment [ˈsegmənt]	Segment
	competition [ˌkɒmpəˈtɪʃn]	Konkurrenz
	competitor [kəmˈpetɪtə]	Konkurrent/in
	consultant [kənˈsʌltənt]	Berater/in
	channel [ˌtʃænl]	Kanal
	distribution channel [ˌdɪstrɪˈbjuːʃn tʃænl]	Vertriebskanal
	advertising agency [ˈædvətaɪzɪŋ eɪdʒənsi]	Werbeagentur
	recommendation [ˌrekəmenˈdeɪʃn]	Empfehlung
	regarding [rɪˈgɑːdɪŋ]	betreffend, bezüglich
	comparison [kəmˈpærɪsn]	Vergleich
	to **contain** [kənˈteɪn]	enthalten, beinhalten
	to **aim at sth** [ˈeɪm ət]	auf etw abzielen, (etw/sich) an etw richten
	to **uncover** [ʌnˈkʌvə]	enthüllen, aufdecken, *hier: (Daten)* erheben
	to **hire sb** [ˈhaɪə]	jdn beauftragen
63	**independent** [ˌɪndɪˈpendənt]	unabhängig
	advisor [ədˈvaɪzə]	Berater/in
	portion [ˈpɔːʃn]	Teil, Anteil
	to **lay sth out** [ˌlaɪ ˈaʊt]	etw gestalten, anlegen, niederlegen
	There's little point in … [ðeəz ˌlɪtl ˈpɔɪnt ɪn]	Es hat wenig Sinn, …
	to **pitch** [pɪtʃ]	anbieten
	to **establish** [ɪˈstæblɪʃ]	feststellen
	for instance [fəˈrɪnstəns]	zum Beispiel
	to **consider sth sth** [kənˈsɪdə]	etw für etw halten
	effort [ˈefət]	Bemühungen, Anstrengungen
	to **engage in sth** [ɪnˈgeɪdʒ ɪn]	sich mit etw beschäftigen
	retail [ˈriːteɪl]	Einzelhandel
	by means of [baɪ ˈmiːnz əv]	mittels
	to **feature sth** [ˈfiːtʃə]	etw aufweisen
	characteristic [ˌkærəktəˈrɪstɪk]	Merkmal, Eigenschaft
	unique selling point [juˌniːk ˈselɪŋ pɔɪnt]	Alleinstellungsmerkmal
	to **distinguish** [dɪˈstɪŋgwɪʃ]	unterscheiden
64	**inexpensive** [ˌɪnɪkˈspensɪv]	preiswert
	in total [ɪn ˈtəʊtl]	insgesamt

	purchase ['pɜ:tʃəs]	Kauf
	consumer [kən'sju:mə]	Verbraucher/in
	perception [pə'sepʃn]	Wahrnehmung
	summary report ['sməri rɪpɔ:t]	zusammenfassender Bericht
	overview ['əʊvəvju:]	Überblick
	findings *(pl)* ['faɪndɪŋz]	Ergebnisse
	at the outset [ət ði 'aʊtset]	zu Beginn
	in question [ɪn 'kwestʃən]	fraglich
	to **rely on sth** [rɪ'laɪ ɒn]	sich auf etw verlassen, sich auf etw stützen
	established [ɪ'stæblɪʃt]	etabliert, herkömmlich
	concerning [kən'sɜ:nɪŋ]	betreffend, bezüglich
	buying patterns *(pl)* ['baɪɪŋ pætnz]	Kaufverhalten
	survey ['sɜ:veɪ]	Umfrage, Studie
	to **collect** [kə'lekt]	zusammentragen
	cyclist ['saɪklɪst]	Radfahrer/in
	to **ride (a bike)** [raɪd]	(Fahrrad) fahren
	unsurprisingly [ˌʌnsə'praɪzɪŋli]	erwartungsgemäß
	interviewee [ˌɪntəvju:'i:]	Befragte/r
	as opposed to [əz ə'pəʊzd tə]	im Gegensatz zu
	to **admit** [əd'mɪt]	zugeben, gestehen, eingestehen
	response [rɪ'spɒns]	Reaktion
	sticker ['stɪkə]	Aufkleber
	environmentally conscious [ɪnˌvaɪrən'mentli kɒnʃəs]	umweltbewusst
	sporty ['spɔ:ti]	sportlich
	fashionable ['fæʃnəbl]	modebewusst
	militant ['mɪlɪtənt]	*jd, der entschieden für etw eintritt*
65	**bulk** [bʌlk]	Großteil, Löwenanteil
	budget ['bʌdʒɪt]	Budget, Haushalt, Etat
	to **identify** [aɪ'dentɪfaɪ]	identifizieren, feststellen, herausfinden
	primary ['praɪməri]	Haupt-, hauptsächlich
	to **regard sb/sth as sth** [rɪ'gɑ:d əz]	jdn/etw für etw halten
	to **target sth at sb/sth** ['tɑ:gɪt ət]	etw an jdn/etw richten
	to **associate sth with sth** [ə'səʊʃieɪt wɪð]	etw mit etw in Verbindung bringen, assoziieren
	to **design** [dɪ'zaɪn]	gestalten, entwerfen
	balance ['bæləns]	Gleichgewicht
66	**audio-visual** [ˌɔ:diəʊ'vɪʒuəl]	audiovisuell
T	to **link sth up to sth** [ˌlɪŋk 'ʌp]	etw mit etw verbinden
	OHP [ˌəʊ eɪtʃ 'pi:]	Overheadprojektor
	marker ['mɑ:kə]	(Filz-)Stift
	animated ['ænɪmeɪtɪd]	bewegt
	to **be softly spoken** [bi ˌsɒftli 'spəʊkən]	leise sprechen
	design [dɪ'zaɪn]	Entwurf, Gestaltung
	folder ['fəʊldə]	Mappe
	to **consist of sth** [kən'sɪst əv]	aus etw bestehen
	to **gather** ['gæðə]	sammeln
	character [ˌkærəktə]	*(Roman, Film etc.:)* Figur
	to **recognize** ['rekəgnaɪz]	erkennen, wiedererkennen
	rough(ly) [rʌf]	grob
	to **unfold** [ˌʌn'fəʊld]	sich entwickeln
	to **advise** [əd'vaɪz]	raten
	excitement [ɪk'saɪtmənt]	Spannung, Aufregung
	to **capture sb's attention** [ˌkæptʃə sʌmbədiz ə'tenʃn]	jds Aufmerksamkeit fesseln
	to **look out for sth** [ˌlʊk 'aʊt fə]	nach etw Ausschau halten
	to **urge sb to do sth** [ɜ:dʒ]	jdm dringend empfehlen, etw zu tun
	clue [klu:]	Hinweis
	to **register** ['redʒɪstə]	anmelden, registrieren
	beauty ['bju:ti]	Schönheit, *hier:* das Gute (an etw)
	to **stretch to sth** [stretʃ]	*(Geld:)* für etwas reichen
	to **give away** [ˌgɪv ə'weɪ]	verschenken
67	**audience** ['ɔ:diəns]	Publikum, Zuhörer(schaft), Zuschauer
	visuals ['vɪʒuəlz]	visuelle Hilfsmittel
	conclusion [kən'klu:ʒn]	Schluss
	purpose ['pɜ:pəs]	Zweck
	aim [eɪm]	Ziel
	objective [əb'dʒektɪv]	Ziel
	on the whole [ɒn ðə 'həʊl]	im Großen und Ganzen
	visual aids *(pl)* ['vɪʒuəl eɪdz]	visuelle Hilfsmittel
	criticism ['krɪtɪsɪzm]	Kritik
	intonation [ˌɪntə'neɪʃn]	Tonfall, Betonung
	to **vary** ['veəri]	variieren
	speech [spi:tʃ]	Sprechweise
	stress [stres]	Betonung
	minor ['maɪnə]	unbedeutend, kleinere/r/s
68	**thoroughly** ['θʌrəli]	gründlich
	introduction [ˌɪntrə'dʌkʃn]	Einleitung, Einführung
	flow chart ['fləʊ tʃɑ:t]	Flussdiagramm
	to **persuade** [pə'sweɪd]	überzeugen, überreden

	overloaded [ˌəʊvəˈləʊdɪd]	überfrachtet, überladen
	volume [ˈvɒljuːm]	Lautstärke
	pitch [pɪtʃ]	Tonhöhe
	lively [ˈlaɪvli]	lebendig
	to **steal** [stiːl]	stehlen
	principle [ˈprɪnsəpl]	Prinzip
	to **take account of sth** [ˌteɪk əˈkaʊnt əv]	etw berücksichtigen
	to **fail** [feɪl]	scheitern, nicht funktionieren
	prompt card [ˈprɒmpt kɑːd]	Moderationskarte
	confidence [ˈkɒnfɪdəns]	Selbstvertrauen
69	to **monitor** [ˈmɒnɪtə]	kontrollieren, überwachen
	to **measure** [ˈmeʒə]	messen
	demand [dɪˈmɑːnd]	Nachfrage, Bedarf
	to **meet demand** [ˌmiːt dɪˈmɑːnd]	die Nachfrage befriedigen, den Bedarf decken
	to **assume** [əˈsjuːm]	annehmen, vermuten
	to **increase** [ˈɪŋkriːs]	erhöhen
	to **keep up with sb** [ˌkiːp ˈʌp wɪð]	mit jdm Schritt halten
70	to **head (for)** [ˈhed fə]	hinführen zu, zulaufen auf
	straightforward [ˌstreɪtˈfɔːwəd]	einfach, unkompliziert
	to **sit back** [ˌsɪt ˈbæk]	sich zurücklehnen
	to **get up to speed** [get ˌʌp tə ˈspiːd]	sich auf den neuesten Stand bringen
	marketeer [ˌmɑːkɪˈtɪə]	Vermarkter/in, *(im Plural:)* Marketingleute
	willingness [ˈwɪlɪŋnəs]	Bereitschaft
	providing [prəˈvaɪdɪŋ]	vorausgesetzt
	surprised [səˈpraɪzd]	erstaunt, überrascht
	nevertheless [ˌnevəðəˈles]	trotzdem, dennoch, nichtsdestotrotz
	to **guarantee** [ˌgærənˈtiː]	garantieren
	buzz [bʌz]	Aufmerksamkeit (durch Mundpropaganda)
	conventional [kənˈvenʃənl]	herkömmlich, konventionell
	technique [tekˈniːk]	Methode, Technik
	crude(ly) [kruːd]	primitiv, simpel
	to **convey** [kənˈveɪ]	vermitteln
	unconventional [ˌʌnkənˈvenʃənl]	unkonventionell
	significant [sɪgˈnɪfɪkənt]	erheblich
71	**executive** [ɪgˈzekjətɪv]	Manager/in
	glamorous [ˈglæmərəs]	glanzvoll, glamourös
	lot [lɒt]	*etwa:* Haufen
	to **toast sth** [təʊst]	auf etw anstoßen
	undoubtedly [ʌnˈdaʊtɪdli]	zweifellos
	creator [kriˈeɪtə]	Schöpfer/in
	stupid [ˈstjuːpɪd]	dumm, doof
	obedient [əˈbiːdiənt]	gehorsam, folgsam
	to **ignore** [ɪgˈnɔː]	nicht beachten, ignorieren
	the latter [ðe ˈlætə]	letztere/r/s, der/die/das Letztgenannte
	savvy [ˈsævi]	gewieft, schlau, ausgebufft
	to **give sb credit for sth** [ˌgɪv ˈkredɪt fə]	jdm etw zutrauen, jdm etw zuschreiben
	to **realize sth** [ˈrɪəlaɪz]	etw erkennen
	glance [glɑːns]	Blick
	instantly [ˈɪnstəntli]	augenblicklich, sofort
	literalness [ˈlɪtərəlnəs]	Wörtlichkeit
	back then [ˌbæk ˈðen]	damals
	to **spell sth out** [ˌspel ˈaʊt]	etw einfach darlegen
	confidence [ˈkɒnfɪdəns]	Vertrauen, Zutrauen
	to **sway sb** [sweɪ]	jdn beeinflussen
	to **engage with sb** [ɪnˈgeɪdʒ wɪð]	sich mit jdm auseinandersetzen
	category [ˈkætəgəri]	Kategorie, Klasse
	proof [pruːf]	Beweis(e), Nachweis(e)
	to **display sth** [dɪsˈpleɪ]	etw zur Schau stellen
	affinity [əˈfɪnəti]	Verbundenheit, Affinität
	choosing [ˈtʃuːzɪŋ]	Wahl
	to **promote sth** [prəˈməʊt]	etw bewerben, für etw Werbung machen
	to **contribute** [kənˈtrɪbjuːt]	beitragen
	realization [ˌrɪəlaɪˈzeɪʃn]	Erkenntnis
	to **view** [vjuː]	betrachten, sehen

Unit 7

72	**negotiation** [nɪˌgəʊʃiˈeɪʃn]	Verhandlung
	to **assess** [əˈses]	einschätzen
	authority [ɔːˈθɒrəti]	Befugnis
	to **sign sth off** [ˌsaɪn ˈɒf]	etw abzeichnen
	fall-back position [ˌfɔːl ˈbæk pəzɪʃn]	Rückzugsposition
	prepared [prɪˈpeəd]	bereit
	flexible [ˈfleksəbl]	flexibel
73	to **enquire about sth** [ɪnˈkwaɪə əbaʊt]	sich nach etw erkundigen
	on behalf of sb [ɒn bɪˈhɑːf əv]	in jds Auftrag
	initial [ɪˈnɪʃəl]	erste/r/s, Erst-, anfänglich, *hier:* vorläufig
	sales potential [ˈseɪlz pətenʃl]	Absatzpotenzial
	to **tolerate** [ˈtɒləreɪt]	tolerieren

	unknown [ˌʌn'nəʊn]	unbekannt
	to **compete with sb/ sth** [kəm'piːt wɪð]	mit jdm/etw konkurrieren
	shipment ['ʃɪpmənt]	Versand, Lieferung
	grateful ['greɪtfl]	dankbar
74	to **be keen to do sth** [bi 'kiːn]	etw unbedingt tun wollen
	to **explore** [ɪk'splɔː]	erkunden, *hier:* ausführlich besprechen
	to **raise sth** [reɪz]	*(Thema etc.)* ansprechen
	considering [kən'sɪdərɪŋ]	angesichts
	to **come up with sth** [ˌkʌm 'ʌp wɪð]	sich etw einfallen lassen, sich etw ausdenken
	to **be honest** [tə bi 'ɒnɪst]	ehrlich gesagt
	to **miss the point** [ˌmɪs ðə 'pɔɪnt]	nicht verstehen, worum es geht
75	to **hard sell sb** [ˌhɑːd 'sel]	jdn zum Kauf drängen/ zwingen
	to **stampede sb into doing sth** [stæm'piːd]	jdn dazu drängen, etw zu tun
	to **rethink** [ˌriː'θɪŋk]	überdenken
	to **consider sth** [kən'sɪdə]	etw in Erwägung ziehen
	exception [ɪk'sepʃn]	Ausnahme
	order size ['ɔːdə saɪz]	Bestellmenge, Auftragsvolumen
	ballpark figure ['bɔːlpɑːk fɪgə]	ungefähre Zahl, Anhaltswert
	generous ['dʒenərəs]	großzügig
	court [kɔːt]	(Tennis-)Platz
	firm [fɜːm]	konkret
	to **panic sb** ['pænɪk]	jdn in Panik versetzen
	estimate ['estɪmət]	Schätzung
	to **investigate** [ɪn'vestɪgeɪt]	sich erkundigen, untersuchen
	to **force** [fɔːs]	zwingen, drängen
	to **be up to sb** [bi 'ʌp tə]	an jdm liegen
76	**robust** [rəʊ'bʌst]	robust, mit harten Bandagen
	to **reflect** [rɪ'flekt]	(sich) widerspiegeln
	hostile ['hɒstaɪl]	feindselig
	provided [prə'vaɪdɪd]	vorausgesetzt
	to **upset sb** [ˌʌp'set]	jdn verärgern
	to **reject** [rɪ'dʒekt]	ablehnen
	to **come across** [ˌkʌm ə'krɒs]	wirken
	firm [fɜːm]	entschlossen, fest
	to **pressure sb into sth** ['preʃə]	jdn zu etw drängen
P	**initial order** [ɪˌnɪʃl 'ɔːdə]	Erstauftrag, Erstbestellung
77	to **set sth out** [ˌset 'aʊt]	etw darlegen
	to **get down to business** [ˌget 'daʊn tə 'bɪznəs]	zur Sache kommen
	stock [stɒk]	Lager(bestand)
	comma ['kɒmə]	Komma
T	**initially** [ɪ'nɪʃəli]	anfänglich, zunächst
	to **run sth past sb** ['rʌn pɑːst]	jdm etw (zur Genehmigung) vorlegen
	cash in advance [ˌkæʃ ɪn əd'vɑːns]	Vorkasse
	remainder [rɪ'meɪndə]	Rest
	doable ['duːəbl]	machbar
	credit check ['kredɪt tʃek]	Bonitätsprüfung, Kreditprüfung
	up front [ˌʌp 'frʌnt]	im Voraus
	to **back sth up** [ˌbæk 'ʌp]	etw absichern
	support [sə'pɔːt]	Unterstützung
78	to **formulate** ['fɔːmjuleɪt]	formulieren, ausarbeiten
	cash on delivery [ˌkæʃ ɒn dɪ'lɪvəri]	(per) Nachnahme, zahlbar bei Lieferung
79	to **settle** [setl]	klären, regeln, zu einer Einigung kommen
	warranty ['wɒrənti]	Garantie, Gewährleistung
	legally binding [ˌliːgəli 'baɪndɪŋ]	rechtsverbindlich
	agreement [ə'griːmənt]	Vereinbarung, Abmachung
	party ['pɑːti]	(Vertrags-)Partei
	said [sed]	genannte/r/s
	sum [sʌm]	Summe, Betrag
	lock [lɒk]	Schloss
	fastener ['fɑːsnə]	Verschluss
	to **prevent** [prɪ'vent]	verhindern
	accidental [ˌæksɪ'dentl]	unbeabsichtigt, versehentlich, zufällig
	theft [θeft]	Diebstahl
	contents *(pl)* [kən'tents]	Inhalt
	to **cover sth** ['kʌvə]	decken, abdecken
	to **result from sth** [rɪ'zʌlt frəm]	aus etw resultieren
	misuse [mɪs'juːs]	Missbrauch, Zweckentfremdung
	abuse [ə'bjuːs]	unsachgemäßger Gebrauch, Missbrauch
	wear and tear [ˌweər ən 'teə]	Verschleiß, Abnutzung
	to **cause** [kɔːz]	verursachen
	hereafter [ˌhɪər'ɑːftə]	im Folgenden, nachfolgend
	binding ['baɪndɪŋ]	verbindlich
	defect ['diːfekt]	Fehler
	workmanship ['wɜːkmənʃɪp]	Verarbeitung(squalität)
	shipment ['ʃɪpmənt]	Sendung, Lieferung

80	to **raise sth** [reɪz]	etw anheben, erhöhen
	Ex Works (EXW) [ˌeks 'wɜ:ks]	ab Werk
	to **insist on sth** [ɪn'sɪst ɒn]	auf etw bestehen
81	**flexibility** [ˌfleksə'bɪləti]	Flexibilität
	secure [sɪ'kjuə]	sicher
	bill [bɪl]	Rechnung
	payable ['peɪəbl]	zahlbar
	to **detail** ['di:teɪl]	(im einzelnen) aufführen
	to **settle** ['setl]	bezahlen, begleichen
	ideally [aɪ'di:əli]	im Idealfall
82	**environment** [ɪn'vaɪrənmənt]	*hier:* Umfeld
	negotiator [nɪ'gəʊʃieɪtə]	Unterhändler/in
	logistics *(pl)* [lə'dʒɪstɪks]	Logistik
	experienced [ɪks'pɪəriənst]	erfahren
	distribution [ˌdɪstrɪ'bju:ʃn]	Versand, Auslieferung
	to **minimize** ['mɪnɪmaɪz]	minimieren
	disruption [dɪs'rʌpʃn]	Störung, Unterbrechung
	extent [ɪk'stent]	Umfang, Ausmaß
	operations *(pl)* [ˌɒpə'reɪʃnz]	Geschäftstätigkeit(en)
	expertise [ˌekspɜ:'ti:z]	Sachkenntnis
	hard-nosed [ˌhɑ:d 'nəʊzd]	abgebrüht
	mode [məʊd]	Modus
	to **bargain** ['bɑ:gɪn]	verhandeln, handeln
	neighbouring ['neɪbərɪŋ]	benachbart
	to **progress** [prə'gres]	weitergehen, fortschreiten
	aggressive [ə'gresɪv]	aggressiv
	attitude ['ætɪtju:d]	Haltung, Einstellung
	to **put sb off sth** [ˌpʊt 'ɒf]	jdn von etw abschre-cken
	rice wine ['raɪs waɪn]	Reiswein
	satisfaction [ˌsætɪs'fækʃn]	Zufriedenheit
	to **concede** [kən'si:d]	zugestehen
	dealings *(pl)* ['di:lɪŋz]	Geschäftsgebaren, Geschäfte

Unit 8

83	**regulations** *(pl)* [ˌregju'leɪʃnz]	Bestimmungen, Vorschriften
	means of transport [ˌmi:nz əv 'trænspɔ:t]	Transportmittel
	mode of transport [ˌməʊd əv 'trænspɔ:t]	Transportart
	pollution [pə'lu:ʃn]	Umweltverschmutzung
	carbon ['kɑ:bən]	Kohlenstoff, Kohlendioxid
	footprint ['fʊtprɪnt]	Fußabdruck
84	**word spider** [ˌwɜ:d 'spaɪdə]	Wortnetz
	barge [bɑ:dʒ]	(Last-)Kahn
	bulky ['bʌlki]	sperrig
	cable car ['keɪblkɑ:]	Seilbahn
	chemicals *(pl)* ['kemɪklz]	Chemikalien
	gas [gæs]	Gas, Benzin
	livestock ['laɪvstɒk]	Vieh
	raw material [ˌrɔ: mə'tɪəriəl]	Rohstoff
	bale [beɪl]	Ballen
	barrel ['bærəl]	Fass, Tonne
	cask [kɑ:sk]	Fass, Tonne
	chest [tʃest]	(Metall-)Kiste
	drum [drʌm]	Trommel
	plastic wrap [ˌplæstɪk 'ræp]	Plastikfolie
	canister ['kænɪstə]	Kanister
	purchase order ['pɜ:tʃəs ɔ:də]	Bestellung
	production facilities *(pl)* [prə'dʌkʃn fəsɪlətiz]	Produktionsanlagen, Werk
	steel [sti:l]	Stahl
	steel mill ['sti:l mɪl]	Stahlwerk, Walzwerk
	third party order [ˌθɜ:d pɑ:ti 'ɔ:də]	Streckenauftrag, -bestellung
85	to **take a close look at sth** [teɪk ə ˌkləʊs 'lʊk ət]	sich etw genau ansehen
	Free Carrier (FCA) [ˌfri: 'kæriə]	frei Frachtführer
	guarantee [ˌgærən'ti:]	Garantie
	punishment ['pʌnɪʃmənt]	Strafe
86	**currency** ['kʌrənsi]	Währung
	country of origin [ˌkʌntri əv 'ɒrɪdʒɪn]	Ursprungsland, Herkunftsland
	dispatch [dɪs'pætʃ]	Versand, Lieferung
	instruction [ɪn'strʌkʃn]	Anweisung
	customs duties *(pl)* [ˌkʌstəmz 'dju:tiz]	Zollgebühren
	as per [əz pə]	gemäß, wie
	contractual [kən'træktʃuəl]	vertraglich
	forwarding ['fɔ:wədɪŋ]	Spedition, Versand
	freight [freɪt]	Fracht
	to **communicate** [kə'mju:nɪkeɪt]	mitteilen
	commissioning [kə'mɪʃənɪŋ]	Auftragserteilung
	inspection [ɪn'spekʃn]	Prüfung, Kontrolle, Inspection

	applicable [ə'plɪkəbl]	zutreffend
	approval [ə'pru:vl]	Genehmigung, Zustimmung
	prior to ['praɪə tə]	vor
	penalty ['penəlti]	Strafe
	receipt [rɪ'si:t]	Erhalt, Empfang
	forwarder's certificate of receipt [ˌfɔ:wədəz səˌtɪfɪkət əv rɪ'si:t]	Spediteur-Übernahme-bescheinigung
	packing list ['pækɪŋ lɪst]	Packliste, Versandliste
	certificate of origin [səˌtɪfɪkət əv 'ɒrɪdʒɪn]	Ursprungszeugnis
	order acknowledgement [ˌɔ:dər ək'nɒlɪdʒmənt]	Auftragsbestätigung
	bundling ['bʌndlɪŋ]	Bündelung
	air waybill [ˌeə 'weɪbɪl]	Luftfrachtbrief
	industrial estate [ɪnˌdʌstriəl ɪ'steɪt]	Industriegebiet
87	**airworthy** ['eəwɜ:ði]	flugtüchtig
	consignee [ˌkɒnsaɪ'ni:]	Adressat, Empfänger
	gross [grəʊs]	brutto
	net [net]	netto
	tare weight [ˌteə 'weɪt]	Leergewicht, Tara
	volume ['vɒlju:m]	Volumen
	width [wɪdθ]	Breite
	to **stand in for sb** [ˌstænd 'ɪn fə]	jdn vertreten
	consignor [kən'saɪnə]	Versender
	nought [nɔ:t]	null
	cubic metre [ˌkju:bɪk 'mi:tə]	Kubikmeter
	in writing [ɪn 'raɪtɪŋ]	schriftlich, in Schriftform
88	**internal** [ɪn'tɜ:nl]	Innen-
	external [ɪk'stɜ:nl]	Außen-
	measurement ['meʒəmənt]	Maß
	payload ['peɪləʊd]	Zuladung
	bill of lading (B/L) [ˌbɪl əv 'leɪdɪŋ]	Konnossement
	apparent [ə'pærənt]	offensichtlich, augenscheinlich
	foul [faʊl]	faul
	negotiable [nɪ'gəʊʃiəbl]	*(Konnossement:)* begebbar
	document of title [ˌdɒkjument əv 'taɪtl]	Traditionspapier
	to **accompany** [ə'kʌmpəni]	begleiten
	consignment note [kən'saɪnmənt nəʊt]	Frachtbrief
	to **issue** ['ɪʃu:]	*(Dokument)* ausstellen
	chamber of commerce [ˌtʃeɪmbər əv 'kɒmɜ:s]	Handelskammer
	commercial invoice [kəˌmɜ:ʃl 'ɪnvɔɪs]	Handelsrechnung
89	**ownership** ['əʊnəʃɪp]	Eigentumsrecht
	transferable [træns'fɜ:rəbl]	übertragbar
	insurance certificate [ɪn'ʃʊərəns sətɪfɪkət]	Versicherungsschein
	forklift ['fɔ:klɪft]	Gabelstapler
	to **stack** [stæk]	stapeln
	flammable ['flæməbl]	brennbar, leicht entzündbar
	fragile ['frædʒaɪl]	zerbrechlich
	dry [draɪ]	trocken
	This way up [ˌðɪs weɪ 'ʌp]	Hier oben
	toxic ['tɒksɪk]	giftig
	hook [hʊk]	Haken
90	**at sb's expense** [ət ˌsʌmbədiz ɪk'spens]	auf jds Kosten
	thereafter [ˌðeər'ɑ:ftə]	danach
91	**terminology** [ˌtɜ:mɪ'nɒlədʒi]	Terminologie
	broker ['brəʊkə]	Makler/in
	insurance claim [ɪn'ʃʊərəns kleɪm]	Schadenmeldung
	insurance cover [ɪn'ʃʊərəns kʌvə]	Versicherungssumme
	insurance policy [ɪn'ʃʊərəns pɒləsi]	Versicherungspolice/-schein
	insurance premium [ɪn'ʃʊərəns pri:miəm]	Versicherungsprämie
	irrevocable [ɪ'revəkəbl]	unwiderruflich
	agreement [ə'gri:mənt]	Zustimmung
	to **stipulate** ['stɪpjuleɪt]	festlegen
T	**air cargo** ['eə kɑ:gəʊ]	Luftfracht
	to **hand over** [ˌhænd 'əʊvə]	übergeben
	stipulation [ˌstɪpju'leɪʃn]	Festlegung
	letter of credit (L/C) [ˌletər əf 'kredɪt]	Akkreditiv
	export licence ['ekspɔ:t laɪsns]	Ausfuhrgenehmigung
	draft [drɑ:ft]	Wechsel
	bill of exchange (B/E) [ˌbɪl əv ɪks'tʃeɪndʒ]	Wechsel
92	to **ensure** [ɪn'ʃʊə]	sich vergewissern
	survey report ['sɜ:veɪ rɪpɔ:t]	Schadensbericht, Gutachten
	thief, thieves [θi:f, 'θi:vz]	Dieb, Diebe
	security guards *(pl)* [sɪ'kjʊərəti gɑ:dz]	Wachpersonal
	prison ['prɪzn]	Gefängnis
	to **publish** ['pʌblɪʃ]	veröffentlichen
94	**specialty** ['speʃəlti]	Spezialgebiet, Spezial-
	food critic ['fu:d krɪtɪk]	Restaurantkritiker/in
	taste bud ['teɪst bʌd]	Geschmacksknospen

	earthquake ['ɜ:θkweɪk]	Erdbeben
	humble [hʌmbl]	bescheiden, einfach, klein
	merchant ['mɜ:tʃənt]	Kaufmann
	vessel ['vesl]	Schiff
	unique(ly) [ju'ni:k]	einzigartig
	corporation [ˌkɔ:pə'reɪʃn]	Kapitalgesellschaft, Unternehmen
	syndicate ['sɪndɪkət]	Konsortium
	event [ɪ'vent]	Ereignis
	shipwreck ['ʃɪprek]	Schiffbruch
	plane crash ['pleɪn kræʃ]	Flugzeugabsturz
	oil rig ['ɔɪl rɪg]	Bohrinsel
	marine [mə'ri:n]	See-
	aviation [ˌeɪvi'eɪʃn]	Luftfahrt
	motor ['məʊtə]	Auto-
	unlimited [ˌʌn'lɪmɪtɪd]	unbegrenzt, unbeschränkt
	liability [ˌlaɪə'bɪləti]	Haftung
	to **underwrite** [ʌndə'raɪt]	versichern
	to **possess** [pə'zes]	besitzen
	insurance claim [ɪn'ʃʊərəns kleɪm]	Versicherungsanspruch, -forderung
	string [strɪŋ]	Reihe
	massive ['mæsɪv]	massiv
	loss [lɒs]	Verlust
	to **amount to** [ə'maʊnt tə]	sich belaufen auf
	to **go bankrupt** [ˌgəʊ 'bæŋkrʌpt]	Pleite gehen
	to **admit** [əd'mɪt]	zulassen
	misprint ['mɪsprɪnt]	Druckfehler
	proportion [prə'pɔ:ʃn]	Anteil, Teil
	wealth [welθ]	Vermögen
	to **refuse** [rɪ'fju:z]	sich weigern

Unit 9

95	to **take action** [teɪk 'ækʃn]	Maßnahmen ergreifen
	to **complain** [kəm'pleɪn]	sich beschweren, reklamieren
	handling ['hændlɪŋ]	Handhabung, Umschlag, Beförderung
	delayed [dɪ'leɪd]	verspätet
	deadline ['dedlaɪn]	Frist, Termin
96	**delay** [dɪ'leɪ]	Verspätung, Verzögerung
	above-mentioned [əˌbʌv 'menʃnd]	oben genannt
	overdue [ˌəʊvə'dju:]	überfällig
	to **threaten** ['θretn]	drohen
	elsewhere [els'weə]	anderswo
	to **trust** [trʌst]	vertrauen, hoffen
	prompt ['prɒmpt]	prompt, unverzüglich
	to **reassure** [ˌri:ə'ʃʊə]	beruhigen
	rush [rʌʃ]	Ansturm
	to **assure** [ə'ʃʊə]	zusichern, versichern
	apology [ə'pɒlədʒi]	Entschuldigung
	inconvenience [ˌɪnkən'vi:niəns]	Unannehmlichkeiten
	to **hesitate** ['hezɪteɪt]	zögern
97	**sudden** ['sʌdn]	plötzlich
	dissatisfied [dɪs'sætɪsfaɪd]	unzufrieden
98	**trial order** ['traɪəl ɔ:də]	Probebestellung, Probeauftrag
	dissatisfactory [dɪssætɪs'fæktəri]	unzulänglich, nicht zufriedenstellend
	sample [sɑ:mpl]	Muster
	poorly finished [ˌpɔ:li 'fɪnɪʃt]	schlecht verarbeitet
	inferior [ɪn'fɪəriə]	minderwertig, schlecht
	to **be up to sth** [bi 'ʌp tə]	einer Sache entsprechen, genügen
	sub-standard [ˌsʌb'stændəd]	minderwertig
	replacement [rɪ'pleɪsmənt]	Ersatz
99	**businessman** ['bɪznəsmən]	Geschäftsmann
	back [bæk]	Rücken
	noisy ['nɔɪsi]	laut, lärmend
	to **catch fire** [ˌkætʃ 'faɪə]	in Brand geraten
	to **evacuate** [ɪ'vækjueɪt]	evakuieren
	to **burn** [bɜ:n]	brennen
	mechanic [mɪ'kænɪk]	Mechaniker/in
	careless ['keələs]	nachlässig, unvorsichtig, leichtsinnig
	a lit cigarette [ə ˌlɪt sɪgə'ret]	eine brennende Zigarette
	(job) interview ['dʒɒb ɪntəvju:]	Vorstellungsgespräch
100	**dismayed** [dɪs'meɪd]	bestürzt
	in the meantime [ɪn ðə 'mi:ntaɪm]	in der Zwischenzeit
	by return [baɪ rɪ'tɜ:n]	umgehend, postwendend
101	**shark** [ʃɑ:k]	Hai
	prevention [prɪ'venʃn]	Schutz
	net [net]	Netz
	maintenance ['meɪntənəns]	Wartung, Instandhaltung
	unfortunate [ʌn'fɔ:tʃənət]	unglücklich, bedauerlich
	for ages [fər 'eɪdʒɪz]	eine/seit einer Ewigkeit
	guilty ['gɪlti]	schuldig
	admission [əd'mɪʃn]	Eingeständnis
	guilt [gɪlt]	Schuld
	to **regret** [rɪ'gret]	bedauern

	to be at fault [bi ət 'fɔ:lt]	Schuld sein
	faulty ['fɔ:lti]	fehlerhaft, defekt, schadhaft
	regret [rɪ'gret]	Bedauern
103	**idiomatic** [ˌɪdiə'mætɪk]	idiomatisch
	accent ['æksent]	Akzent
	expediency [ɪk'spi:diənsi]	Zweckdienlichkeit
	criterion [kraɪ'tɪəriən]	Kriterium
	the powers that be [ðə 'paʊəz ðət 'bi]	die da oben, die maßgeblichen Stellen
	routinely [ru:'ti:nli]	routinemäßig
	to maximize ['mæksɪmaɪz]	maximieren
	clarification [ˌklærɪfɪ'keɪʃn]	Erläuterung, Erklärung
	to be afraid to do sth [bi ə'freɪd tə]	Angst haben, etw zu tun
104 T	**exercise bike** ['eksəsaɪz baɪk]	Heimtrainer
	to unpack [ʌn'pæk]	auspacken
	escalator ['eskəleɪtə]	Rolltreppe
	capacity [kə'pæsəti]	Auslastung, Kapazität
	spare part [ˌspeə 'pɑ:t]	Ersatzteil
	improvement [ɪm'pru:vmənt]	Verbesserung
	misunderstanding [ˌmɪsʌndə'stændɪŋ]	Missverständnis
	marvellous ['mɑ:vələs]	wunderbar
105	**contrast** ['kɒntrɑ:st]	Gegensatz
	punctuality [ˌpʌŋktʃu'æləti]	Pünktlichkeit
	anger ['æŋgə]	Wut, Ärger
	to solve [sɒlv]	lösen
	to approach sth [ə'prəʊtʃ]	*(Problem, Sache etc.:)* etw angehen

Unit 10

106	**job centre** *(BE)* ['dʒɒb sentə]	Arbeitsamt
	employment center *(AE)* [ɪm'plɔɪmənt sentə]	Arbeitsamt
	recruitment agency [rɪ'kru:tmənt eɪdʒənsi]	Personalagentur, Arbeitsvermittlung
	curriculum vitae (CV) *(BE)* [kəˌrɪkjələm 'vi:teɪ]	Lebenslauf
	résumé *(AE)* ['rezjumeɪ]	Lebenslauf
	certificate [sə'tɪfɪkət]	Zeugnis
	application [ˌæplɪ'keɪʃn]	Bewerbung
	applicant ['æplɪkənt]	Bewerber/in
	post [pəʊst]	Stelle, Posten
	work placement ['wɜ:k pleɪsmənt]	Praktikum
	internship *(AE)* ['ɪntɜ:nʃɪp]	Praktikum
107	**job hunting** ['dʒɒb hʌntɪŋ]	Stellensuche
	stressed (out) [strest]	gestresst, fix und fertig
	to be short-listed [bi 'ʃɔ:tlɪstɪd]	in die engere Auswahl kommen
	to select [sɪ'lekt]	auswählen
	short-list ['ʃɔ:tlɪst]	engere Auswahl
	careers advisor [kə'rɪəz ədvaɪzə]	Berufsberater/in, Laufbahnberater/in
	to tailor sth to sth ['teɪlə tə]	etw auf etw zuschneiden
	to register with sb/sth ['redʒɪstə wɪð]	sich bei jdm/etw anmelden
	to bin [bɪn]	wegwerfen
	to prejudice ['predʒudɪs]	beeinflussen
108	**permanent** ['pɜ:mənənt]	unbefristet
	duty ['dju:ti]	Pflicht, Aufgabe
	to ensure [ɪn'ʃʊə]	sicherstellen, gewährleisten
	accurate ['ækjərət]	korrekt, genau
	to resolve [rɪ'zɒlv]	*(Problem)* lösen, klären
	fluent ['flu:ənt]	fließend
	confident ['kɒnfɪdənt]	selbstbewusst, selbstsicher
	calm [kɑ:m]	ruhig
	pressure ['preʃə]	Druck
	to adapt [ə'dæpt]	sich anpassen
	rapport [ræ'pɔ:]	gutes Verhältnis, gute Beziehung(en)
	pay [peɪ]	Bezahlung, Lohn, Gehalt
	stressful ['stresfl]	anstrengend, stressig
109	**working hours** *(pl)* [ˌwɜ:kɪŋ 'aʊəz]	Arbeitszeit(en)
	content [kən'tent]	Inhalt
	hourly rate [ˌaʊəli 'reɪt]	Stundenlohn
	overtime ['əʊvətaɪm]	Überstunden
	time off [ˌtaɪm 'ɒf]	Freizeit
	lunch break ['lʌntʃ breɪk]	Mittagspause
	whereas [ˌweər'æz]	während, dagegen
110	**to model sth on sth** ['mɒdl ɒn]	etw für etw als Muster nehmen
	qualification [ˌkwɒlɪfɪ'keɪʃn]	Abschluss, Qualifikation
	accomplishment [ə'kʌmplɪʃmənt]	Errungenschaft, Erfolg
	competition [ˌkɒmpə'tɪʃn]	Wettbewerb
	to optimize ['ɒptɪmaɪz]	optimieren
	accountancy [ə'kaʊntənsi]	Buchführung
	business studies *(pl)* ['bɪznəs stʌdiz]	Betriebswirtschaft(slehre)
	economics [ˌi:kə'nɒmɪks]	Wirtschaftswissenschaft(en)
	command [kə'mɑ:nd]	Beherrschung

	dual system [ˌdjuːəl ˈsɪstəm]	duales Ausbildungssystem
	block release [ˌblɒk rɪliːs]	Blockunterricht
	attendance [əˈtendəns]	Teilnahme
	grade [ɡreɪd]	Note
	final grade [ˌfaɪnl ˈɡreɪd]	Abschlussnote
	merit [ˈmerɪt]	Verdienst, *(als Schulnote:)* gut
	minor [ˈmaɪnə]	Neben-
	history [ˈhɪstri]	Geschichte
	biology [baɪˈɒlədʒi]	Biologie
	to **be awarded sth** [bi əˈwɔːdɪd]	etw *(Preis etc.)* bekommen
	prize [praɪz]	Preis, Auszeichnung
111	**work experience** [ˈwɜːk ɪkspɪəriəns]	Berufserfahrung
	to **gain** [ɡeɪn]	gewinnen, erwerben
	insight [ˈɪnsaɪt]	Einblick
	climbing [ˈklaɪmɪŋ]	Klettern
	skiing [ˈskiːɪŋ]	Skifahren
	nationality [ˌnæʃəˈnæləti]	Staatsangehörigkeit
	marital status [ˌmærɪtl ˈsteɪtəs]	Familienstand
	driving licence [ˈdraɪvɪŋlaɪsns]	Führerschein
	to **boost** [buːst]	stärken, untermauern
	price tag [ˈpraɪs tæɡ]	Preisschild
	to **sell** [sel]	sich verkaufen
	field [fiːld]	Feld
	to **set sth up** [ˌset ˈʌp]	etw einrichten, aufbauen
	procedure [prəˈsiːdʒə]	Verfahren, Ablauf
	efficiency [ɪˈfɪʃnsi]	Effizienz
	temporary [ˈtemprəri]	befristet
	ability [əˈbɪləti]	Fähigkeit
112	**cover letter** [ˈkʌvə letə]	Anschreiben, Begleitschreiben
	to **be proficient in sth** [bi prəˈfɪʃnt ɪn]	*(Sprache etc.)* beherrschen
	vacancy [ˈveɪkənsi]	offene Stelle, Stellenangebot, -ausschreibung
	recruitment manager [rɪˈkruːtmənt mænɪdʒə]	Leiter/in Personalbeschaffung
	precise(ly) [prɪˈsaɪs]	genau
	vacation *(AE)* [vəˈkeɪʃn]	Ferien
	hands-on [ˌhændz ˈɒn]	praxisorientiert
	working environment [ˌwɜːkɪŋ ɪnˈvaɪrənmənt]	Arbeitsumfeld
	immense(ly) [ɪˈmens]	enorm
	to **enable** [ɪˈneɪbl]	befähigen, (es) ermöglichen

	service provider [ˈsɜːvɪs prəvaɪdə]	Dienstleister
	customer-focused [ˈkʌstəmə fəʊkəst]	kundenorientiert
	tight [taɪt]	engere Auswahl
	time frame [ˈtaɪm freɪm]	Zeitrahmen
	linguistic [lɪnˈɡwɪstɪk]	sprachlich, Sprach-
	final examination [ˌfaɪnl ɪɡˌzæmɪˈneɪʃn]	Abschlussprüfung
	consideration [kənˌsɪdəˈreɪʃn]	Überlegung, Erwägung
	at your earliest convenience [ət jɔːr ˌɜːliɪst kənˈviːniəns]	sobald es Ihnen möglich ist
113	**suitability** [ˌsuːtəˈbɪləti]	Eignung
	to **advertise** [ˈædvətaɪz]	*(Stelle)* ausschreiben
	notice [ˈnəʊtɪs]	Bescheid, Ankündigung
	at short notice [ət ˌʃɔːt ˈnəʊtɪs]	kurzfristig
	at a week's notice [ət ə ˌwiːks ˈnəʊtɪs]	eine Woche im voraus
	credit controller [ˈkredɪt kəntrəʊlə]	Sachbearbeiter/in Kreditcontrolling
	to **join** [dʒɔɪn]	beitreten, mitmachen
	to **chase sb** [tʃeɪs]	jdn verfolgen, hinter jdm her sein
	branch [brɑːntʃ]	Abteilung
	candidate [ˈkændɪdət]	Kandidat/in, Bewerber/in
114	**strength** [streŋθ]	Stärke
	weakness [ˈwiːknəs]	Schwäche
	hard-working [ˌhɑːd ˈwɜːkɪŋ]	fleißig
	lack of sth [ˈlæk əv]	Mangel an etw
	link [lɪŋk]	Verbindung
T	**permission** [pəˈmɪʃn]	Genehmigung, Erlaubnis
	qualified [ˈkwɒlɪfaɪd]	qualifiziert
	in a nutshell [ɪn ə ˈnʌtʃel]	kurz gesagt
	to **take the initiative** [ˌteɪk ði ɪˈnɪʃətɪv]	die Initiative ergreifen
	contribution [ˌkɒntrɪˈbjuːʃn]	Beitrag
	to **make a contribution** [ˌmeɪk ə kɒntrɪˈbjuːʃn]	etw beitragen
	to **post sb** [pəʊst]	jdn versetzen
115	to **train as** [ˈtreɪn əz]	eine Ausbildung zum/zur … machen
	expectation [ˌekspekˈteɪʃn]	Erwartung
	point of view [ˌpɔɪnt əv ˈvjuː]	Standpunkt, Gesichtspunkt
	to **justify** [ˈdʒʌstɪfaɪ]	rechtfertigen, begründen
116	**virtual** [ˈvɜːtʃuəl]	virtuell

vacant ['veɪkənt]	frei
close-up ['kləʊs ʌp]	Nahaufnahme
to **transform** [træns'fɔːm]	(grundlegend) verändern
familiar [fə'mɪliə]	vertraut, bekannt
to **scan** [skæn]	*(Text etc.)* überfliegen, durchsuchen
to **despatch** [dɪ'spætʃ]	verschicken, absenden
direction [də'rekʃn]	Richtung
to **stand out** [ˌstænd 'aʊt]	herausragen
crowded ['kraʊdɪd]	übervölkert, überfüllt
to **resort to sth** [rɪ'zɔːt tə]	auf etw zurückgreifen
to **throw sth up** [ˌθrəʊ 'ʌp]	etw zutage fördern
breed [briːd]	Menschenschlag, Sorte
job-seeker ['dʒɒbsiːkə]	Stellensuchende/r
offering ['ɒfərɪŋ]	Darbietung, Angebot
to **be among** [bi ə'mʌŋ]	dazu gehören
to **bring sb to life** [ˌbrɪŋ tə 'laɪf]	jdn zum Leben erwecken, lebendig machen
to **show sth off** [ˌʃəʊ 'ɒf]	etw zur Geltung bringen
to **amaze** [ə'meɪz]	verblüffen, erstaunen
guy [gaɪ]	Typ, Kerl
to **outline** ['aʊtlaɪn]	skizzieren

Alphabetical word list

Dieses Wörterverzeichnis enthält alle neuen Wörter aus *Trade Matters – 3rd Edition* in alphabetischer Reihenfolge. Nicht aufgeführt sind Wörter, die zum Grundwortschatz *(Basic word list)* gehören. Die Zahl nach dem Stichwort bezieht sich auf die Seite, auf der das Wort zum ersten Mal erscheint. Wörter aus den Hörverständnisübungen sind zusätzlich mit einem T *(Transkript)* und Wörter aus den *Partner files* mit einem P gekennzeichnet.

A

ability *111* Fähigkeit
above-mentioned *96* oben genannt
abroad *38* im/ins Ausland
abuse *79* unsachgemäßger Gebrauch, Missbrauch
accent *103* Akzent
to **accept** *9* annehmen, akzeptieren
acceptable *8* akzeptabel
access *43* Zugang, Zugriff
to **access sth** *27* auf etw zugreifen
accident *7* Unfall
accidental *79* unbeabsichtigt, versehentlich, zufällig
to **accommodate** *43* unterbringen, Platz bieten für
accommodation *39* Unterkunft; *homestay ~* *57F* Unterbringung bei Gastfamilien
to **accompany** *88* begleiten
accomplishment *110* Errungenschaft, Erfolg
to **account for sth** *11T* etw ausmachen
account, to take ~ of sth *68* etw berücksichtigen; *to take sth into ~* *32* etw berücksichtigen
accountancy *110* Buchführung
accounts assistant *13* Buchhaltungsassistent/in
accurate *108* korrekt, genau
to **act** *53* handeln, fungieren
to **act out** *20* spielen, vor-/durchspielen
action, to put sth into ~ *24* etw in die Tat umsetzen; *to take ~* *95* Maßnahmen ergreifen
to **adapt** *108* sich anpassen
addition *50* Zusatz, Ergänzung; *in ~ (to)* *43* zusätzlich (zu)
additional *45* zusätzlich, Zusatz-
additionally *45* außerdem
to **address sb** *19* jdn anreden, ansprechen
administration *10* Verwaltung
administrative *6* Verwaltungs-
admission *48* Eintritt; *101* Eingeständnis
to **admit** *64* zugeben, gestehen, eingestehen; *94* zulassen
to **advance sth** *36* etw vorschießen
advance, cash in ~ *77T* Vorkasse; *in ~* *47* im Voraus; *15T* vor
advantage *27* Vorteil
to **advertise** *113* *(Stelle)* ausschreiben
advertising *61* Werbung
advertising agency *62* Werbeagentur
advertising campaign *61* Werbekampagne
(piece of) advice *17* Rat, Ratschlag, Tipp
to **advise** *66T* raten
advisor *63* Berater/in
aeroplane *56T* Flugzeug
to **affect** *11T* betreffen, beeinträchtigen
affinity *71* Verbundenheit, Affinität
afraid, to be ~ to do sth *103* Angst haben, etw zu tun
after-sales service *13* Kundendienst
age, for ~s *101* eine/seit einer Ewigkeit
agency *60* Agentur
agenda *50* Tagesordnung, Programm
agent *53* Agent/in
aggressive *82* aggressiv
agreement *79* Vereinbarung, Abmachung; *91* Zustimmung; *to be in ~ with sth* *51* einer Sache zustimmen
aim *67* Ziel
to **aim at sth** *62* auf etw abzielen, (etw/sich) an etw richten
air cargo *91T* Luftfracht
air waybill *86* Luftfrachtbrief
airworthy *87* flugtüchtig
all, at ~ *11T* überhaupt
all-important *16* äußerst wichtig
alongside *13* neben, mit
alternative *30* Alternative, *hier:* Ausweichtermin
alternatively *23T* alternativ, oder, auch
to **amaze** *116* verblüffen, erstaunen
amazed *16* verblüfft, erstaunt
among, to be ~ *116* dazu gehören
to **amount to** *94* sich belaufen auf
to **analyse** *61* analysieren
anger *105* Wut, Ärger
animated *66T* bewegt
annum, per ~ *10* pro Jahr
answerphone *22* Anrufbeantworter
any other business (AOB) *50* Sonstiges
to **apologize** *21* sich entschuldigen, um Entschuldigung bitten
apology *96* Entschuldigung
apparent *88* offensichtlich, augenscheinlich
to **appear** *16* scheinen, erscheinen, auftreten
applicable *86* zutreffend
applicant *37* Antragsteller/in; *106* Bewerber/in
application *37* Anwendung; *106* Bewerbung
to **apply** *48* gelten
appointment *7* Termin
to **appreciate** *29* schätzen, zu schätzen wissen
apprenticeship *7* Ausbildung, Lehre
approach *19* Vorgehen(sweise), Ansatz, Herangehensweise
to **approach sb** *48* sich an jdn wenden, jdn ansprechen; *~ sth* *105* *(Problem, Sache etc.:)* etw angehen
appropriate *25* passend, angemessen
approval *86* Genehmigung, Zustimmung
to **argue** *27* argumentieren
arrival *41* Ankunft
article *31* Artikel
artist *28* Künstler/in
as per *86* gemäß, wie
as regards *31* bezüglich, was … anbelangt
aspect *44* Aspekt, Seite
to **assert** *60* behaupten
to **assess** *72* einschätzen
to **assist sb** *37* jdm helfen, jdn unterstützen
assistance *8* Hilfe, Unterstützung
assistant *7* Assistent/in
to **associate sth with sth** *65* etw mit etw in Verbindung bringen, assoziieren
to **assume** *69* annehmen, vermuten
to **assure** *26* sicherstellen; *96* zusichern, versichern
at all *11T* überhaupt

atmosphere *57* Atmosphäre
to **attach** *32* beifügen, beilegen
attachment *31* *(Brief etc.:)* Anhang, Anlage
attempt *15T* Versuch
to **attend sth** *39* an etw teilnehmen, etw besuchen
attendance *110* Teilnahme
attendee *58* Anwesende/r
attention, to capture sb's ~ *66T* jds Aufmerksamkeit fesseln
attitude *82* Haltung, Einstellung
Attn. (= attention) *29* zu Händen
audience *67* Publikum, Zuhörer(schaft), Zuschauer
audio-visual *66* audiovisuell
authority *72* Befugnis
automobile *15T* Automobil-, Auto-
availability *25F* Verfügbarkeit, Lieferbarkeit
available *43* verfügbar, erhältlich; *to be ~* *21* *(Telefon:)* zu sprechen sein
averse *60* abgeneigt
aviation *94* Luftfahrt
to **avoid** *23* vermeiden
award, to be ~ed sth *110* etw *(Preis etc.)* bekommen
awareness *8* Wissen, Bewusstsein

B

back *99* Rücken
back then *71* damals
to **back sth up** *77T* etw absichern
badge *48* (Namens-)Schild
baggage *42* Gepäck
balance *65* Gleichgewicht
bale *84* Ballen
ballpark figure *75* ungefähre Zahl, Anhaltswert
bankrupt, to go ~ *94* Pleite gehen
bankruptcy *36* Bankrott, Pleite
to **bargain** *82* verhandeln, handeln
barge *84* (Last-)Kahn
barrel *84* Fass, Tonne
based in ..., to be ~ *6* in ... ansässig sein, seinen/ihren Sitz in ... haben
battery *27* Akku
to **bear** *32* tragen
beauty *66T* Schönheit, *hier:* das Gute (an etw)
beef *56T* Rindfleisch
beer *59* Bier
behalf, on ~ of sb *53* für jdn; *73* in jds Auftrag
behaviour *60* Verhalten, Benehmen
benefit *42* Vorteil, Nutzen
to **benefit** *16* profitieren
Best regards *45* Mit freundlichen Grüßen
beverage *10* Getränk
beyond *29* darüber hinaus
bicycle *61* Fahrrad
to **bill sb sth** *45* jdm etw in Rechnung stellen
bill *81* Rechnung
bill of exchange (B/E) *91T* Wechsel
bill of lading (B/L) *88* Konnossement
to **bin** *107* wegwerfen
binding *79* verbindlich
biology *110* Biologie
blank stare *60* starrer Gesichtsausdruck
block release *110* Blockunterricht
board *47* Kommission
board, to come on ~ *53* an Bord kommen, dabei sein
boarding *42* An-Bord-Gehen
boarding card *38* Bordkarte
body *29* *(Brief:)* Haupttext
body language *16* Körpersprache
booked up *30T* ausgebucht
to **boost** *15T* steigern, stärken; *111* untermauern
booth *47* Messestand
boring *60* langweilig
boss *19* Chef/in
to **bother sb** *22T* jdm Umstände bereiten, jdn belästigen
bound for *11T* bestimmt für, unterwegs nach
to **brainstorm** *16* Ideen sammeln
branch *50* Ast; *113* Abteilung
brand *23T* Marke
to **break down** *35* kaputtgehen, eine Panne haben
breath *17* Atem, Luft; *to take a deep ~* *17* tief einatmen, durchatmen
breed *116* Menschenschlag, Sorte
brevity *26* Kürze
to **brew** *50* brauen
brewery *50* Brauerei
brick *27* Backstein, Ziegel
brief *54* kurz, knapp
bright *62* *(Farbe:)* hell, leuchtend
to **bring sb to life** *116* jdn zum Leben erwecken, lebendig machen
brochure *56* Prospekt, Werbebroschüre
broker *91* Makler/in
budget *65* Budget, Haushalt, Etat
bulk *65* Großteil, Löwenanteil
bulky *84* sperrig
bundling *86* Bündelung
to **burn** *99* brennen
business *8* Unternehmen, Firma, Geschäft; *on ~* *43* geschäftlich; *to do ~* *8* Geschäfte machen; *to get down to ~* *77* zur Sache kommen
business contact *19* Geschäftspartner/in
business development *39* Geschäftsentwicklung
business studies *(pl)* *110* Betriebswirtschaft(slehre)
businessman *99* Geschäftsmann
busy *19* *(Telefon:)* besetzt
buyer *32* Käufer
buying patterns *(pl)* *64* Kaufverhalten
buzz *70* Aufmerksamkeit (durch Mundpropaganda)
by (+ date) *29* bis (+ Datum)

C

cable car *84* Seilbahn
to **calculate** *35* berechnen, ausrechnen, ermitteln
to **call (by)** *30T* vorbeischauen, vorbeikommen
call, to return sb's ~ *18* jdn zurückrufen
calm *108* ruhig
to **cancel** *42* stornieren
candidate *113* Kandidat/in, Bewerber/in
canister *84* Kanister
cap *25* Mütze, Kappe
capacity *104T* Auslastung, Kapazität
capital letter *52* Großbuchstabe
to **capture sb's attention** *66T* jds Aufmerksamkeit fesseln
car crash *35* Autounfall
carbon *83* Kohlenstoff, Kohlendioxid
care *11T* Sorgfalt
careers advisor *107* Berufsberater/in, Laufbahnberater/in
careless *99* nachlässig, unvorsichtig, leichtsinnig
carpet *47* Teppich
carriage *31* Beförderung, Transport
Carriage Paid to (CPT) *31* frachtfrei
carrier *32* Frachtführer
to **carry out** *9* ausführen, durchführen
case *56T* Koffer
cash *36* Bargeld, Geldmittel
cash flow *36* Geldumlauf, Kapitalfluss
cash management *13* Kassenführung, Gelddisposition, Finanzmittelverwaltung
cash in advance *77T* Vorkasse

cash on delivery 78 (per) Nachnahme, zahlbar bei Lieferung
cash with order 31 Vorauszahlung, Vorkasse, Zahlung bei Auftragserteilung
cask 84 Fass, Tonne
catalogue 32 Katalog
to **catch sth** 18 etw verstehen; 39 etw bekommen, erreichen, erwischen
to **catch up** *15T* aufholen, einholen
to **catch fire** 99 in Brand geraten
category 71 Kategorie, Klasse
cause, a good ~ *58T* ein guter Zweck, eine gute Sache
to **cause** 79 verursachen
ceiling 48 Decke
celebrity 56 Prominente/r
cell 37 Zelle
certificate 37 Bescheinigung, Zertifikat; 106 Zeugnis; *forwarder's ~ of receipt* 86 Spediteur-Übernahmebescheinigung
certificate of origin 86 Ursprungszeugnis
certification 37 Zulassung
chain 18 Kette
challenge *15T* schwierige Aufgabe, Herausforderung
chamber of commerce 88 Handelskammer
chances are 26 es ist wahrscheinlich, dass
channel 62 Kanal
character *66T* *(Roman, Film etc.:)* Figur
characteristic 63 Merkmal, Eigenschaft
charge 42 Gebühr; *free of ~* 48 kostenlos
charge, in ~ of *11T* zuständig für, verantwortlich für
to **charge** 36 *(Preis, Gebühren etc.)* verlangen, fordern, berechnen; *~ sb sth* 45 jdm etw in Rechnung stellen
charitable 58 Wohltätigkeits-
charity 52 Wohltätigkeit(sorganisation), Initiative, guter Zweck
chart 55 Diagramm; flow ~ 68 Flussdiagramm
to **chase sb** 113 jdn verfolgen, hinter jdm her sein
chat 59 Unterhaltung, Schwätzchen
to **chat** *11T* sich unterhalten
to **check in** 42 einchecken
to **check sth out** 8 sich etw ansehen
cheers *23T* danke
chemicals *(pl)* 84 Chemikalien
chest 84 (Metall-)Kiste
Chief Executive Officer (CEO) 52 Vorstandsvorsitzende/r, Geschäftsführer/in
choice, to be spoilt for ~ 43 die Qual der Wahl haben
choosing 71 Wahl
circle 50 Kreis
to **circulate sth** 50 etw verteilen, verschicken
clarification 103 Erläuterung, Erklärung
clear(ly) 24 deutlich, klar
to **clear for export** 32 Ausfuhrformalitäten erledigen
clearance, customs ~ 37 (Erledigung der) Zollformalitäten
cleared for export 32 zur Ausfuhr freigemacht/verzollt
client 8 Kunde/-in
climbing 111 Klettern
close, to take a ~ look at sth 85 sich etw genau ansehen
close-up 116 Nahaufnahme
closed *45F* geschlossen
closing sentence 53 Schlussatz
clothing 18 Bekleidung, Kleidung
clue *66T* Hinweis
colleague 8 Kollege/-in
to **collect** 33 abholen; *58T* sammeln; 64 zusammentragen
to **come across** 76 wirken
to **come in on sth** *58T* etw zu etw sagen, sich einschalten
to **come up with sth** 74 sich etw einfallen lassen, sich etw ausdenken
to **come on board** 53 an Bord kommen, dabei sein
comfort 43 Komfort, Annehmlichkeit
comma 77 Komma
command 110 Beherrschung
to **comment** 54 sich äußern, etw dazu sagen
commerce 36 Handel
commercial 6 Geschäfts-
commercial invoice 88 Handelsrechnung
commissioning 86 Auftragserteilung
common 37 häufig, gewöhnlich
to **communicate** 86 mitteilen
community 58 Gemeinde, Gemeinschaft
company 6 Unternehmen, Firma, Gesellschaft
compared, ~ to 27 im Vergleich zu; *as ~ to* 35 im Vergleich zu
comparison 62 Vergleich
compensation 33 Schadenersatz, Entschädigung
to **compete** *15T* konkurrieren, im Wettbewerb stehen
competition 62 Konkurrenz; 110 Wettbewerb
competitive *15T* wettbewerbsfähig, konkurrenzfähig
competitor 28 (Wettbewerbs-) Teilnehmer/in; 62 Konkurrent/in
to **complain** 95 sich beschweren, reklamieren
complaint 51 Reklamation, Beschwerde
to **complement** 43 ergänzen
complicated 26 kompliziert
complimentary close 29 *(Brief:)* Schlußformel
to **comprise** 43 umfassen, bestehen aus
to **compromise** *25F* sich einigen, einen Kompromiss eingehen
compulsory 37 obligatorisch, verpflichtend, Pflicht-
computing power 27 Rechenleistung
to **concede** 82 zugestehen
to **concentrate on sth** 14 sich auf etw konzentrieren
concerning 64 betreffend, bezüglich
conclude, to ~ 53 abschließend
conclusion 67 Schluss
condition *11T* Zustand; 49 Bedingung; *terms and ~s* 42 Konditionen, (Allgemeine) Geschäftsbedingungen
conference 39 Konferenz
conference call 49 Konferenzschaltung
confidence 68 Selbstvertrauen; 71 Vertrauen, Zutrauen
confident 108 selbstbewusst, selbstsicher
confidential 43 vertraulich
to **confirm** *22T* bestätigen
confirmation 35 Bestätigung
confirmation of order 35 Auftragsbestätigung
confusion 41 Verwirrung, Verwechslung
to **connect** 19 verbinden
connection 19 Verbindung
conscious *15T* bewusst
conservatory *44T* Wintergarten, Gewächshaus
to **consider sth** 75 etw in Erwägung ziehen
to **consider sth sth** 63 etw für etw halten
considerable 48 beträchtlich, erheblich
consideration 112 Überlegung, Erwägung

considered, to be ~ sth *57* als etw gelten
considering *74* angesichts
consignee *87* Adressat, Empfänger
consignment *25* Sendung, Lieferung
consignment note *88* Frachtbrief
consignor *87* Versender
to **consist of sth** *66T* aus etw bestehen
to **consult sb** *50* jdn fragen, jdn zu Rate ziehen
consultant *62* Berater/in
consumer *64* Verbraucher/in
to **contain** *62* enthalten, beinhalten
content(s) *79* Inhalt
context *27* Zusammenhang
continually *10* kontinuierlich, stetig
to **continue to do sth** *16* etw weiterhin tun
contract *28* Vertrag
contract of sale *32* Kaufvertrag
contractual *86* vertraglich
contrast *105* Gegensatz
to **contribute** *71* beitragen
contribution *114T* Beitrag; *to make a ~* *114T* etw beitragen
convenience, at your earliest ~ *112* sobald es Ihnen möglich ist
convention *52* Versammlung
conventional *70* herkömmlich, konventionell
to **convey** *70* vermitteln
to **convince** *27* überzeugen
copper *37* Kupfer
cordless *43* schnurlos
corporation *94* Kapitalgesellschaft, Unternehmen
corridor *11T* Flur, Korridor, Gang
Cost and Insurance Paid (CIP) *32* frachtfrei versichert
Count me in. *58T* Ich bin dabei.
counter *47* Tresen, Theke
country code *20* Ländervorwahl
country of origin *86* Ursprungsland, Herkunftsland
course *15T* Verlauf, Lauf; *43* *(Menü:)* Gang
court *75* (Tennis-)Platz
to **cover sth** *33* etw *(Kosten)* decken, für etw aufkommen; *54* *(Thema)* behandeln; *79* etw decken, abdecken
cover letter *112* Anschreiben, Begleitschreiben
cow *56T* Kuh
CPT (Carriage Paid to) *31* frachtfrei
to **crash** *35* einen Unfall haben
crash, plane ~ *94* Flugzeugabsturz
crazy *60* verrückt
creator *71* Schöpfer/in
credit, to give sb ~ for sth *71* jdm etw zutrauen, jdm etw zuschreiben
credit card *38* Kreditkarte
credit check *77T* Bonitätsprüfung, Kreditprüfung
credit controller *113* Sachbearbeiter/in Kreditcontrolling
creditworthiness *36* Kreditwürdigkeit
criterion *103* Kriterium
criticism *67* Kritik
to **cross your arms** *16* die Arme verschränken
crowded *116* übervölkert, überfüllt
crude(ly) *70* primitiv, simpel
to **crush** *16* zerquetschen
cubic metre *87* Kubikmeter
cult *62* Kult
cultural *8* kulturell, Kultur-
currency *86* Währung
current *37* Strom; high ~ *37* Starkstrom
current(ly) *14* aktuell, momentan
curriculum vitae (CV) *(BE)* *106* Lebenslauf
custody *32* Obhut
to **customize** *48* individuell anpassen
custom-made *48* maßgefertigt
customary *32* handelsüblich
customer *6* Kunde/Kundin; *end ~* *8* Endkunde/-kundin
customer base *10* Kundenstamm
customer loyalty *42* Kundentreue, Kundenbindung
customer-focused *112* kundenorientiert
customs clearance *37* (Erledigung der) Zollformalitäten
customs duty *32* Zollgebühr(en)
to **cut costs** *15T* Kosten senken
to **cut off** *21T* trennen
cycle *61* Fahrrad
cyclist *64* Radfahrer/in

D
data sheet *37* Datenblatt
database *27* Datenbank
dated … *35* vom …
deadline *95* Frist, Termin
deal *33* Geschäft
to **deal with sth** *13* etw bearbeiten, erledigen, sich um etw kümmern; *36* mit etw zurechtkommen, mit etw fertig werden
dealings *(pl)* *82* Geschäftsgebaren, Geschäfte
decent *60* anständig
to **decrease** *55* abnehmen, sinken
to **deduct** *36* abziehen
defect *79* Fehler
to **define** *32* definieren
definite(ly) *60* bestimmt
to **degenerate** *60* ausarten
degree *55* Ausmaß, Grad
delay *96* Verspätung, Verzögerung
to **delay sb** *7* jdn aufhalten
delayed *95* verspätet
delighted *45* erfreut; *to be ~ to do sth* *10* etw gern tun, sich freuen, etw zu tun
to **deliver** *25* liefern, anliefern, zustellen
delivery *29* Lieferung; *cash on ~* *78* (per) Nachnahme, zahlbar bei Lieferung; *terms of ~* *29* Lieferbedingungen
delivery period *33* Lieferfrist
demand *69* Nachfrage, Bedarf; *to meet ~* *69* die Nachfrage befriedigen, den Bedarf decken
to **demonstrate** *16* vorführen, zeigen
demonstration *27* Vorführung
to **depart** *39* abfahren, -fliegen, -reisen
department *7* Abteilung
departure *41* Abreise, Abfahrt, Abflug
to **depend on sth** *36* von etw abhängen
design *66T* Entwurf, Gestaltung
to **design** *65* gestalten, entwerfen
to **despatch** *116* verschicken, absenden
despite *25* trotz
destination *32* Bestimmungsort, Zielort; *41P* Reiseziel
to **detail** *81* (im einzelnen) aufführen
to **develop** *14* entwickeln
development *15T* Entwicklung
device *27* Gerät
to **dial** *18* *(Telefon:)* wählen
diary *30T* Terminkalender
digit *20* Ziffer
digital projector *43* Beamer
dimensions *37* Abmessungen
to **dine** *43* speisen
dip *11T* Rückgang
direction *116* Richtung
disability *58T* Behinderung
disabled toilet *31* Behindertentoilette
disadvantage *27* Nachteil
to **disagree** *55* nicht zustimmen, anderer Meinung sein
disconnector *37* Trennschalter

discount *29* Rabatt
dish *56T* Gericht, Speise
to **dismantle** *31* abbauen, demontieren
dismayed *100* bestürzt
dispatch *86* Versand, Lieferung
to **display sth** *71* etw zur Schau stellen
disruption *82* Störung, Unterbrechung
dissatisfied *97* unzufrieden
to **distinguish** *63* unterscheiden
distribution *82* Versand, Auslieferung
distribution area *11* Versandbereich
distribution centre *10* Versandzentrum
distribution channel *62* Vertriebskanal
distributor *48* Vertrieb, Händler
to **do business** *8* Geschäfte machen
doable *77T* machbar
document of title *88* Traditionspapier
documentary credit *35* Dokumentenakkreditiv
documentation *32* Dokumente, Dokumentation, Unterlagen
documents against payment (D/P) *33* Dokumente gegen Zahlung, Kasse gegen Dokumente
domestic *10* Inlands-, inländisch
dormitory *31* Schlafsaal
dot *22* Punkt
double room *43* Doppelzimmer
doubt *50* Zweifel
downside *36* Nachteil, Kehrseite
downturn *15T* Rückgang, Abschwung, Rezession
downward *55* abwärts
dozen *60* Dutzend
draft *50* Entwurf; *91T* Wechsel
dramatic *15T* dramatisch, drastisch
dramatically *55* dramatisch
to **draw** *49* zeichnen
driving licence *111* Führerschein
to **drop** *55* fallen, sinken
to **drop sth off** *44T* etw abgeben, dalassen
drum *84* Trommel
dry *89* trocken
dual system *110* duales Ausbildungssystem
due *36* fällig
due to *36* aufgrund
duty *108* Pflicht, Aufgabe
duty, customs ~ *32* Zollgebühr(en); *import ~ 32* Einfuhrzoll

E

eager, to be ~ to do sth *48* etw (unbedingt) tun wollen
earthquake *94* Erdbeben
Easter *57F* Ostern
eatery *43* Restaurant, Speiselokal
eco- *47* Öko-
economics *110* Wirtschaftswissenschaft(en)
economy *15T* Wirtschaft
edge *26* Kante
educational *60* lehrreich
effect, in ~ *62* eigentlich, tatsächlich
efficiency *111* Effizienz
effort *63* Bemühungen, Anstrengungen
electrolysis *37* Elektrolyse
elsewhere *96* anderswo
emotional *26* Gefühls-, Gemüts, gefühlsmäßig, emotional
to **employ sb** *10* jdn beschäftigen, anstellen, einstellen
employee *10* Angestellte/r, Beschäftigte/r
employment center *(AE) 106* Arbeitsamt
to **enable** *112* befähigen, (es) ermöglichen
Enc (= enclosure[s]) *29 (Brief:)* Anlage(n), Anhang
to **enclose** *29* beifügen, beilegen
to **encourage** *15T* ermutigen, motivieren
end customer *8* Endkunde/-kundin
to **engage sb** *16* jdm begegnen
to **engage in sth** *36* an etw teilnehmen, in etw aktiv sein; *63* sich mit etw beschäftigen
to **engage with sb** *71* sich mit jdm auseinandersetzen
engaged *18 (Telefon:)* besetzt
engineering *15T* Maschinenbau
enhanced *48* verbessert
enormous *62* gewaltig, enorm
to **enquire about sth** *73* sich nach etw erkundigen
enquiry *28* Anfrage
to **enrol for sth** *58T* sich für etw anmelden
en-suite bathroom *43* eigenes Badezimmer
to **ensure** *92* sich vergewissern; *108* sicherstellen, gewährleisten
to **enter sth** *37* nach/in *(ein Land)* kommen, gelangen; *42* etw *(Text etc.)* eingeben
to **entertain** *60* unterhalten
entire *29* ganze/r/s, gesamte/r/s
entry *48* Eintrag, Aufnahme
environment *82 hier:* Umfeld
environmentally conscious *64* umweltbewusst
equal (to) *16* gleich, gleichwertig
to **equip** *27* ausstatten, ausrüsten
equipment *28* Geräte, Ausrüstung, Ausstattung
equivalent *19* Entsprechung
escalator *104T* Rolltreppe
especially *58T* besonders, insbesondere
essential *26* wesentlich, unerlässlich
to **establish** *10* gründen; *48* herstellen; *63* feststellen
established *64* etabliert, herkömmlich
estimate *75* Schätzung
to **evacuate** *99* evakuieren
to **evaluate** *32* bewerten, auswerten, einschätzen
to **even out** *55* sich einpendeln
event *28* Veranstaltung; *94* Ereignis
Ex Works (EXW) *80* ab Werk
exam(ination) *57P* Prüfung; *final ~ 112* Abschlussprüfung
to **exceed** *45* überschreiten, übertreffen
except for *20* außer
exception *75* Ausnahme
to **execute** *26* ausführen
excess baggage *42* Übergepäck
excessive(ly) *26* übertrieben, übermäßig
excitement *66T* Spannung, Aufregung
excluding *32* ausgenommen
executive *71* Manager/in
exercise bike *104T* Heimtrainer
exhibition *39* Ausstellung
exhibition and conference centre *39* Ausstellungs- und Konferenzzentrum
exhibitor *48* Aussteller
expectation *115* Erwartung
expediency *103* Zweckdienlichkeit
expense *33* Kosten; *at sb's ~ 90* auf jds Kosten; *travel ~s (pl) 51* Reisekosten, Reisespesen
experienced *82* erfahren
expertise *82* Sachkenntnis
expiry *42* Ablauf
explanation *60* Erklärung, Erläuterung
to **explore** *74* erkunden, *hier:* ausführlich besprechen
to **export** *6* exportieren, ausführen
export *7* Export; *cleared for ~ 32* zur Ausfuhr freigemacht/verzollt; *to clear for ~ 32* Ausfuhrformalitäten erledigen

export licence *91T* Ausfuhrgenehmigung
exporter *10* Exporteur
to **express** *15T* ausdrücken, zum Ausdruck bringen
expression *8* Ausdruck
extension *18* Durchwahl
extent *82* Umfang, Ausmaß
external *88* Außen-
extract *60* Auszug
extreme *49* extrem
eye contact *16* Blickkontakt
eyeball, to roll ~s *60* mit den Augen rollen

F
face value *36* Nennwert
face-to-face *49* persönlich
facilities *(pl)* *10* Einrichtungen, Anlagen, Gebäude
to **fail** *68* scheitern, nicht funktionieren
fall-back position *72* Rückzugsposition
familiar *116* vertraut, bekannt
fascia panel *48* Blendentafel
fascinating *61* hochinteressant, faszinierend
fashion *23T* Mode
fashionable *64* modebewusst
fastener *79* Verschluss
fault, to be at ~ *101* Schuld sein
faulty *101* fehlerhaft, defekt, schadhaft
favour, in sb's ~ *35* zu jds Gunsten
to **fear** *26* befürchten
feature *48* Merkmal, Eigenschaft
to **feature sth** *63* etw aufweisen
fee *36* Honorar, Gebühr
fence *48* Zaun
field *111* Feld
figure *15T* Zahl; *ballpark ~* *75* ungefähre Zahl, Anhaltswert
to **finalize** *51* festlegen, beschließen, abschließen
finance department *11* Finanzabteilung
finances *11T* Finanzen
findings *(pl)* *64* Ergebnisse
finish *32* Schluss, Ende
to **fire sb** *49* jdn entlassen
fire, to catch ~ *99* in Brand geraten
firm *16* fest; *75* konkret; *76* entschlossen
first name *19* Vorname
first thing *21T* gleich, als erstes
to **fit** *27* passen
flammable *89* brennbar, leicht entzündbar
flat *57P* Wohnung
flexibility *81* Flexibilität
flexible *72* flexibel
floor plan *11* Grundriss
floor space *11T* Grundfläche
to **flow** *37* fließen
flow chart *68* Flussdiagramm
fluent *108* fließend
flyer *43* Werbezettel, Prospekt
folder *66T* Mappe
food critic *94* Restaurantkritiker/in
footprint *83* Fußabdruck
to **force** *75* zwingen, drängen
forklift *89* Gabelstapler
to **formulate** *78* formulieren, ausarbeiten
formation *56* Bildung
fortunately *26* glücklicherweise
to **forward sth** *53* etw weiterleiten
forward slash *22* Schrägstrich
forwarder's certificate of receipt *86* Spediteur-Übernahmebescheinigung
forwarding *86* Spedition, Versand
foul *88* faul
to **found** *10* gründen
fraction *15T* Bruchteil
fragile *89* zerbrechlich
frantically *16* wie verrückt
Free Carrier (FCA) *85* frei Frachtführer
free line *52* Leerzeile
free of charge *48* kostenlos
freedom *58T* Freiheit
freight *86* Fracht
freight forwarder *33* Spediteur, Spedition
frequent(ly) *23* häufig
fresh *10* neu, frisch
front, up ~ *77T* im Voraus
frustrating *27* frustrierend
fuel *45* Treibstoff, Benzin
to **fulfil (an order)** *10* (einen Auftrag) bearbeiten, abwickeln, erfüllen
full-time *7* Vollzeit-, auf Vollzeitbasis
fully-equipped *43* voll ausgestattet
function *8* Funktion, Aufgabe
functionality *27* Funktionalität

G
to **gain** *111* gewinnen, erwerben
gallery *59* Galerie
to **gang up on sb** *60* sich gegen jdn zusammenschließen
gas *84* Gas, Benzin
to **gather** *66T* sammeln
to **generate** *10* *(Gewinn, Umsatz etc.)* erzielen, erwirtschaften
generous *75* großzügig
to **get along** *60* gut miteinander auskommen, sich gut verstehen
to **get back to sb** *19* jdn zurückrufen, sich bei jdm melden
to **get on with sth** *11T* (mit etw) weitermachen
to **get down to business** *77* zur Sache kommen
to **get in touch with sb** *30T* sich bei jdm melden
to **get into full swing** *60* richtig ins Rollen kommen
to **get to the point** *53* zum Thema kommen
to **give away** *66T* verschenken
to **give up on sth** *27* etw aufgeben, auf etw verzichen
to **give sb credit for sth** *71* jdm etw zutrauen, jdm etw zuschreiben
glad *26* froh
glamorous *71* glanzvoll, glamourös
glance *71* Blick
global *11T* weltweit, global
globalized *27* globalisiert
to **glow** *60* leuchten
to **go ahead** *53* anfangen
goggles *(pl)* *60* (Schutz-)Brille
goodness, for ~' sake *16* um Himmels willen
goods *(pl)* *8* Ware(n)
gossip *60* Klatsch, Tratsch
government *60* Regierung, öffentliche Verwaltung
grade *110* Note; *final ~* *110* Abschlussnote
graph *12* Diagramm
grateful *73* dankbar
to **greet sb** *59* jdn begrüßen
greeting *26* Begrüßung, Grußformel
grid *48* Gitter
gross *87* brutto
group dynamics *(pl)* *60* Gruppendynamik
growth *11T* Wachstum
to **grumble** *33* meckern, klagen, sich beschweren
guarantee *85* Garantie
to **guarantee** *70* garantieren
guest house *58T* Pension
guide *48* Führer
guideline *26* Richtlinie
guilt *101* Schuld
guilty *101* schuldig
guy *116* Typ, Kerl
gym *39* Fitnessstudio

H
hall *12* Flur
handling *95* Handhabung, Umschlag, Beförderung
to **hand over** *91T* übergeben
hands-on *112* praxisorientiert

handshake *16* Handschlag, Händeschütteln
hard-nosed *82* abgebrüht
to **hard sell sb** *75* jdn zum Kauf drängen/zwingen
hard-working *114* fleißig
to **head (for)** *70* hinführen zu, zulaufen auf
to **head sb/sth up** *13* jdm vorgesetzt sein, etw leiten
heading *10* Überschrift
headline *16* Überschrift
headquarters *(pl)* *10* Zentrale, Firmensitz
heat *57* Hitze
hectolitre *55* Hektoliter
helper *58T* Helfer/in
helpful *23* hilfsbereit
hereafter *79* im Folgenden, nachfolgend
to **hesitate** *96* zögern
high current *37* Starkstrom
hire *46* Miete
to **hire sb** *62* jdn beauftragen
history *110* Geschichte
to **hit** *15T* treffen
hold, to put sb on ~ *18* *(Telefon:)* jdn in die Warteschleife stellen/legen
to **hold** *11T* fassen, Platz haben/bieten für; *29* *(Veranstaltung etc.)* abhalten
to **hold the line** *18* *(Telefon:)* am Apparat bleiben
Hold on. *18* Einen Moment.
homestay accommodation *57P* Unterbringung bei Gastfamilien
honest *26* ehrlich; *to be ~* *74* ehrlich gesagt
hook *89* Haken
hostile *76* feindselig
to **house sb** *28* jdn unterbringen, beherbergen
human *60* Mensch
human resources (HR) *11T* Personalabteilung
humble *94* bescheiden, einfach, klein
hurry, to be in a ~ *42* in Eile sein, es eilig haben
hyphen *22* Bindestrich

I

ID sign *47* Namensschild
ideally *81* im Idealfall
to **identify** *65* identifizieren, feststellen, herausfinden
idiomatic *103* idiomatisch
to **ignore** *60* ignorieren, nicht beachten
to **illustrate** *16* veranschaulichen, darstellen
to **imagine sth** *15T* sich etw vorstellen
immediate *36* sofortig, unmittelbar
immense(ly) *112* enorm
to **impact** *36* sich auswirken auf
impolite *57* unhöflich
to **import** *6* importieren, einführen
import duty *32* Einfuhrzoll
importance *46* Bedeutung, Wichtigkeit
importer *10* Importeur
to **impress** *15T* beeindrucken
impression *16* Eindruck
impressive *27* beeindruckend
to **improve** *15T* verbessern
improvement *104T* Verbesserung
inclined *47* schräg, geneigt
to **include** *45* einschließen, beinhalten
including *29* einschließlich
inconvenience *96* Unannehmlichkeiten
increase *35* Steigerung
to **increase** *55* zunehmen, steigen; *69* erhöhen
increasing *8* zunehmend, steigend
increasingly *15T* zunehmend, immer *(+Komparativ)*; *27* in zunehmendem Maße
incredible *27* unglaublich
to **incur** *46* *(Kosten:)* anfallen
independent *63* unabhängig
to **indicate** *55* anzeigen
industrial *6* Industrie-
industrial estate *86* Industriegebiet
inexpensive *64* preiswert
inferior *98* minderwertig, schlecht
infrastructure *27* Infrastruktur
initial *73* erste/r/s, Erst-, anfänglich, *hier:* vorläufig
initial order *76* Erstauftrag, Erstbestellung
initially *77T* anfänglich, zunächst
initiative, to take the ~ *114T* die Initiative ergreifen
inquisitive *56T* neugierig
insight *111* Einblick
to **insist on sth** *80* auf etw bestehen
inspection *86* Prüfung, Kontrolle, Inspection
to **install** *50* installieren
instance, for ~ *63* zum Beispiel
instantly *71* augenblicklich, sofort
instruction *86* Anweisung
insurance *32* Versicherung
insurance certificate *89* Versicherungsschein
insurance claim *91* Schadenmeldung; *94* Versicherungsanspruch, -forderung
insurance cover *91* Versicherungssumme
insurance police *91* Versicherungspolice/-schein
insurance premium *91* Versicherungsprämie
to **insure** *33* versichern
insurer *33* Versicherer
intercultural *8* kulturübergreifend, interkulturell
interest *36* Zins(en)
interest charge *36* Zinsgebühr, -forderung
internal *88* Innen-
internal(ly) *58T* intern
internship *(AE)* *106* Praktikum
to **interrupt** *55* unterbrechen
(job) interview *49* Vorstellungsgespräch
interviewee *64* Befragte/r
intonation *67* Tonfall, Betonung
to **introduce** *8* vorstellen, einführen
introduction *16* Bekanntmachen, Vorstellen; *68* Einleitung, Einführung
to **invent** *59* erfinden
to **invest** *15T* investieren
to **investigate** *75* sich erkundigen, untersuchen
investment *13* Geldanlage, Investitionen
to **invite sb to do sth** *19* jdn dazu auffordern, etw zu tun
invoice *13* Rechnung
to **invoice sb** *36* jdm eine Rechnung stellen
involved, to be ~ in sth *48* mit etw zu tun haben; *58T* an etw beteiligt sein, bei etw mitmachen
irrevocable *91* unwiderruflich
isolator *37* Isolator
issue *51* Frage, Thema, Problem
to **issue** *88* *(Dokument)* ausstellen
item *38* Gegenstand, Artikel, Sache

J

jacket *27* Jacke, Sakko
job centre *(BE)* *106* Arbeitsamt
job hunting *107* Stellensuche
job interview *49* Vorstellungsgespräch
job-seeker *116* Stellensuchende/r
to **join** *113* beitreten, mitmachen; *~ sb* *15T* bei jdm sein
joke *60* Witz, Scherz
to **judge** *31* urteilen, beurteilen
to **justify** *115* rechtfertigen, begründen

K

keen, to be ~ to do sth *74* etw unbedingt tun wollen

to **keep up with sb** *69* mit jdm Schritt halten

to **keep sth in mind** *39* an etw denken

know, to let sb ~ *7* Bescheid sagen

L

to **label** *49* etikettieren, beschriften, benennen

lack of sth *114* Mangel an etw

landline *20* Festnetz

largely *15T* größtenteils, weitgehend

latest *43* neueste/r/s; *at the ~* *29* spätestens

the latter *71* letztere/r/s, der/die/das Letztgenannte

to **laugh at sb/sth** *60* jdn auslachen, über etw lachen

to **launch** *61* (in den Markt) einführen

to **lay sth out** *63* etw gestalten, anlegen, niederlegen

leading *29* führend

leather portfolio *60* lederne Aktenmappe

to **leave a message** *22* eine Nachricht hinterlassen

legally binding *79* rechtsverbindlich

leisure *43* Freizeit

to **let sb know** *7* Bescheid sagen

letter of credit (L/C) *91T* Akkreditiv

letterhead *29* Briefkopf

liability *94* Haftung

life, to bring sb to ~ *116* jdn zum Leben erwecken, lebendig machen

to **lift** *11T* sich auflösen, allmählich verschwinden

lighting *48* Beleuchtung

liking, to be to sb's ~ *31* jds Vorstellungen entsprechen, Zustimmung finden

limited *44T* begrenzt, beschränkt

linguistic *112* sprachlich, Sprach-

link *114* Verbindung

to **link sth up to sth** *66T* etw mit etw verbinden

listener *26* Zuhörer/in

lit, a ~ cigarette *99* eine brennende Zigarette

literalness *71* Wörtlichkeit

litre *10* Liter

lively *68* lebendig

livestock *84* Vieh

load *33* Ladung

to **load** *33* verladen

located in ..., to be ~ *6* in ... ansässig sein, seinen/ihren Sitz in ... haben

lock *79* Schloss

logistics *(pl)* *82* Logistik

look, to take a close ~ at sth *85* sich etw genau ansehen

to **look out for sth** *66T* nach etw Ausschau halten

to **look sth up** *8* etw nachschlagen, nachschauen

lookout, to be on the ~ for sth *10* nach etw Ausschau halten

lorry *35* Lastwagen

loss *94* Verlust

lot *71* *etwa:* Haufen

lucky *11T* glücklich

luggage *42* Gepäck

lunch break *109* Mittagspause

lunchtime *25* Mittag(szeit)

M

machine tool *15T* Werkzeugmaschine

to **make sth up** *62* etw ausmachen, bilden

to **make sense** *27* sinnvoll sein

to **make sure** *13* sicherstellen, gewährleisten, sich vergewissern

mainly *6* hauptsächlich

maintenance *101* Wartung, Instandhaltung

major *8* größte/r/s, bedeutend(ste/r/s), Haupt-

managing director *11T* Geschäftsführer/in

to **manufacture** *31* herstellen, fertigen

manufacturer *10* Hersteller

marine *94* See-

marital status *111* Familienstand

marker *66T* (Filz-)Stift

to **market** *61* vermarkten

market research *62* Marktforschung

marketeer *70* Vermarkter/in, *(im Plural:)* Marketingleute

marvellous *104T* wunderbar

massive *94* massiv

matter *36* Angelegenheit, Sache

to **maximize** *103* maximieren

meaning *8* Bedeutung

means, by ~ of *63* mittels

means of transport *83* Transportmittel

meantime, in the ~ *100* in der Zwischenzeit

to **measure** *69* messen

measurement *88* Maß

meat *56T* Fleisch

mechanic *99* Mechaniker/in

to **meet demand** *69* die Nachfrage befriedigen, den Bedarf decken

to **mention** *15T* erwähnen, sagen

merchant *94* Kaufmann

merit *110* Verdienst, *(als Schulnote:)* gut

message, to leave a ~ *22* eine Nachricht hinterlassen; *to take a ~* *18* *(Telefon:)* etw ausrichten

metal *37* Metall

method *42* Art, Weise, Methode

microphone *43* Mikrofon

mile *45* Meile

mileage allowance *45* Freikilometer *(bzw.* -meilen*)*

militant *64* *jd, der entschieden für etw eintritt*

mind, to keep sth in ~ *39* an etw denken; *Never ~.* *21T* Das macht nichts.

to **mind** *23* etw dagegen haben; *Would you ~ ...* *23* Könnten Sie bitte ...

to **minimize** *82* minimieren

minor *67* unbedeutend, kleinere/r/s; *110* Neben-

minutes *50* Protokoll; *to take the ~* *58* Protokoll führen

to **mirror** *26* spiegeln, widerspiegeln

misprint *94* Druckfehler

to **miss the point** *74* nicht verstehen, worum es geht

misunderstanding *104T* Missverständnis

misuse *79* Missbrauch, Zweckentfremdung

mode *82* Modus

mode of transport *83* Transportart

to **model sth on sth** *110* etw für etw als Muster nehmen

modular building *28* Haus in Modularbauweise, Fertighaus

to **monitor** *69* kontrollieren, überwachen

moon *27* Mond

motion, to go into ~ *60* in Bewegung geraten

motor *94* Auto-

motorway *7* Autobahn

to **move on** *54* weitergehen, übergehen (zu)

multimodal transport *32* kombinierte Beförderung, multimodaler Transport

N

name, first ~ *19* Vorname

nationality *111* Staatsangehörigkeit

native speaker *57* Muttersprachler/in

neat(ly) *27* schlank, formschön, elegant

negligibly *55* vernachlässigbar

negotiable *88* *(Konnossement:)* begebbar
to **negotiate** *33* verhandeln, aushandeln
negotiation *72* Verhandlung
negotiator *82* Unterhändler/in
neighbouring *82* benachbart
nerve wracking *16* nervenaufreiben
nervous *16* nervös
net *87* netto; *101* Netz
nevertheless *70* trotzdem, dennoch, nichtsdestotrotz
no doubt *50* zweifellos, bestimmt
noisy *99* laut, lärmend
to **nominate** *32* benennen
to **note sth** *41* etw beachten
to **note down** *22* notieren, aufschreiben
notice *113* Bescheid, Ankündigung; *at a week's ~* *113* eine Woche im voraus; *at short ~* *113* kurzfristig
nought *87* null
nutshell, in a ~ *114T* kurz gesagt; *to put sth in a ~* *15T* etw kurz sagen

O

obedient *71* gehorsam, folgsam
objective *67* Ziel
obligation *32* Pflicht, Verpflichtung
to **observe** *8* beobachten
obsolete *27* veraltet, überholt
to **obtain** *37* erhalten, bekommen
obvious *16* offensichtlich
obviously *15T* natürlich, selbstverständlich
off-putting *16* abstoßend, unangemehm
offering *116* Darbietung, Angebot
official(ly) *7* offiziell
OHP *66T* Overheadprojektor
oil rig *94* Bohrinsel
old-fashioned *19* veraltet, altmodisch
once *35* sobald
opening *46* Eröffnung
opening hours *59* Öffnungszeiten
to **operate sth** *43* betreiben, *hier:* vertreten, umsetzen; *50* etw bedienen, betreiben
operation voltage *37* Betriebsspannung
operations *(pl)* *82* Geschäftstätigkeit(en)
operations director *13* Betriebs-/Produktionsleiter/in
opportunity *15T* Chance, Gelegenheit
opposed, as ~ to *64* im Gegensatz zu
to **optimize** *110* optimieren
order, cash with ~ *31* Vorauszahlung, Vorkasse, Zahlung bei Auftragserteilung
order, confirmation of ~ *35* Auftragsbestätigung
order, receipt of ~ *31* Auftragseingang
order, third party ~ *84* Streckenauftrag, -bestellung
order acknowledgement *86* Auftragsbestätigung
order situation *50* Auftragslage
order size *75* Bestellmenge, Auftragsvolumen
organization chart *13* Organigramm
organizer *28* Organisator/in
otherwise *52* ansonsten, sonst, auch
to **outline** *116* skizzieren
outset, at the ~ *64* zu Beginn
to **outsmart** *27* überlisten
to **overcome sth** *15T* etw überwinden
overdue *96* überfällig
overhead *48* von oben, obenliegend
overloaded *68* überfrachtet, überladen
overseas *10* in/aus/nach Übersee, in/aus dem/ins Ausland
overtime *109* Überstunden
overview *64* Überblick
ownership *89* Eigentumsrecht

P

package *48* Paket
to **package** *11T* verpacken
packing *32* Verpackung
packing list *86* Packliste, Versandliste
pain *27* Schmerz(en)
pallet *11T* Palette
to **panic sb** *75* jdn in Panik versetzen
paperwork *13* Formalitäten, Unterlagen, Schriftverkehr
paragraph *52* *(Text:)* Absatz
participant *43* Teilnehmer/in
particular *60* bestimmt
particularly *60* insbesondere, ganz besonders
party *79* (Vertrags-)Partei; *third ~ order* *84* Streckenauftrag, -bestellung
to **pass (from sb to sb)** *33* (von jdm auf jdn) übergehen
to **pass sth on** *54* etw weitergeben, -leiten, -reichen
passenger *42* Passagier/in
passionate(ly) *52* leidenschaftlich
passport *38* Reisepass
past, to run sth ~ sb *77T* jdm etw (zur Genehmigung) vorlegen
pattern *12* Muster
pay *108* Bezahlung, Lohn, Gehalt
payable *81* zahlbar
payload *88* Zuladung
payment *13* Zahlung, Auszahlung; *terms of ~* *29* Zahlungsbedingungen
peace and quiet *43* Ruhe und Frieden
penalty *86* Strafe
per, as ~ *86* gemäß, wie
per annum *10* pro Jahr
percentage *35* Anteil, Prozentsatz, prozentual
perception *64* Wahrnehmung
permanent *108* unbefristet
permission *114T* Genehmigung, Erlaubnis
to **persuade** *68* überzeugen, überreden
to **photocopy** *43* fotokopieren
to **pick sth (out)** *48* sich etw aussuchen
to **pick sb/sth up** *39* jdn/etw abholen
pitch *68* Tonhöhe
to **pitch** *63* anbieten
to **place** *48* platzieren
to **place an order** *35* einen Auftrag erteilen
plane crash *94* Flugzeugabsturz
plastic wrap *84* Plastikfolie
pleasant *26* angenehm
pleased, to be ~ to do sth *31* etw gern tun
Pleased to meet you. *7* Nett, Sie kennen zu lernen.
pleasure *8* Vergnügen
pocket *27* Tasche
point, to miss the ~ *74* nicht verstehen, worum es geht; *There's little ~ in …* *63* Es hat wenig Sinn, …
point of view *115* Standpunkt, Gesichtspunkt
to **point out** *31* darauf hinweisen
policy *43* Politik, Vorgehensweise, Linie
polite *8* höflich
politeness *23* Höflichkeit
politics *(pl)* *57* Politik
pollution *83* Umweltverschmutzung
poorly finished *98* schlecht verarbeitet
port *14* Hafen
portfolio, leather ~ *60* lederne Aktenmappe
portion *63* Teil, Anteil
to **possess** *94* besitzen
post *106* Stelle, Posten

to **post sb** *114T* jdn versetzen
to **postpone** *50* verschieben
potential *61* potenziell
power *26* Macht, Stärke, Kraft; *27* Strom
the powers that be *103* die da oben, die maßgeblichen Stellen
precise(ly) *112* genau
preferably *30T* am besten, am liebsten
to **prejudice** *107* beeinflussen
premises *(pl) 10* (Betriebs-)Gelände, Räumlichkeiten
prepared *72* bereit
presentation *23T* Präsentation, Vorstellung
press officer *56* Pressereferent/in
pressure *108* Druck
to **pressure sb into sth** *76* jdn zu etw drängen
pretty *16* ziemlich
to **prevent** *79* verhindern
prevention *101* Schutz
previous *52* vorherig/r/s, frühere/r/s
previously *8* zuvor, vorher
price, unit ~ *35* Einzelpreis, Preis pro Stück
price tag *111* Preisschild
primary *65* Haupt-, hauptsächlich
principle *68* Prinzip
prior to *86* vor
prison *92* Gefängnis
prize *110* Preis, Auszeichnung
procedure *111* Verfahren, Ablauf
process *37* Verfahren
product launch *15T* Produkteinführung
production facilities *(pl) 84* Produktionsanlagen, Werk
production line *18* Fertigungsstraße
proficient, to be ~ in sth *112 (Sprache etc.)* beherrschen
profile *10* Porträt, Profil
to **profit** *15T* profitieren
to **progress** *82* weitergehen, fortschreiten
progress *62* Fortschritt(e)
progress report *61* Zwischenbericht
to **promote sth** *71* etw bewerben, für etw Werbung machen
promotion *62* Werbung
prompt *96* prompt, unverzüglich
prompt card *68* Moderationskarte
proof *71* Beweis(e), Nachweis(e)
proper(ly) *13* richtig, korrekt, ordentlich
proportion *94* Anteil, Teil
protection *37* Schutz
to **prove sth** *48* sich als etw erweisen
provided *76* vorausgesetzt
providing *70* vorausgesetzt
publicity *21T* Werbung, Werbe-
to **publish** *92* veröffentlichen
punctual *51* pünktlich
punctuality *105* Pünktlichkeit
punishment *85* Strafe
purchase *64* Kauf
purchase order *84* Bestellung
purchasing assistant *13* Einkaufsassistent/in
purchasing department *32* Einkaufs-, Beschaffungsabteilung
purchasing director *28* Einkaufsleiter/in, Leiter/in Beschaffung
purchasing manager *13* Einkaufsleiter/in, Leiter/in Beschaffung
purpose *67* Zweck
to **put sb off sth** *82* jdn von etw abschrecken
to **put sb through** *18 (Telefon:)* jdn durchstellen, verbinden
to **put sth into action** *24* etw in die Tat umsetzen
to **put sb on hold** *18 (Telefon:)* jdn in die Warteschleife stellen/legen

Q

qualification *110* Abschluss, Qualifikation
qualified *114T* qualifiziert
to **qualify for sth** *36* für etw in Frage kommen
quantity *25P* Menge
query *13* Frage, Anfrage
question, in ~ *64* fraglich
quotation *31* Angebot, Preisangebot, Kostenvoranschlag
to **quote** *31 (Preis)* angeben, nennen; *~ sb 33* jdm ein Angebot machen

R

to **radiate** *50* sternförmig ausgehen
to **raise sth** *74 (Thema etc.)* ansprechen; *80* etw anheben, erhöhen
range *10* (Produkt-)Palette, Sortiment, Auswahl, Angebot
to **rank** *49* einstufen
rapid(ly) *48* rasch, schnell
rapport *108* gutes Verhältnis, gute Beziehung(en)
rate *33* Gebühr, Satz; *hourly ~ 109* Stundenlohn
rated current *37* Nennstrom
raw material *84* Rohstoff
to **reach** *18* erreichen
realistic *15T* realistisch
reality *27* Wirklichkeit
realization *71* Erkenntnis
to **realize sth** *71* etw erkennen
to **reassure** *96* beruhigen
receipt *86* Erhalt, Empfang
receipt, forwarder's certificate of ~ *86* Spediteur-Übernahmebescheinigung
receipt of order *31* Auftragseingang
received, to be well ~ *53* gut *(beim Publikum etc.)* ankommen
reception *11* Empfang
receptionist *7* Empfangsmitarbeiter/in
recession *11T* Rezession, Konjunkturrückgang
to **recharge** *27 (Akku)* aufladen
recipient *52* Empfänger/in
to **recognize** *66T* erkennen, wiedererkennen
recommendation *62* Empfehlung
record *51* Aufzeichnung, Unterlage
to **record** *23* aufnehmen, aufzeichnen
to **recruit sb** *13* jdn einstellen, anwerben
recruitment agency *106* Personalagentur, Arbeitsvermittlung
recruitment manager *112* Leiter/in Personalbeschaffung
to **refer to sth** *29* in etw nachschauen; *52* auf etw verweisen, etw erwähnen
reference *25P* Bezug, Referenz; *52* Erwähnung
reference initials *29* Zeichen, Referenz
to **refill** *45* auffüllen
to **reflect** *76* (sich) widerspiegeln
refreshment *8* Erfrischung
to **refuse** *94* sich weigern
regard, Best ~s *45* Mit freundlichen Grüßen
to **regard sb/sth as sth** *65* jdn/etw für etw halten
regard, as ~s *31* bezüglich, was … anbelangt
regarding *62* betreffend, bezüglich
to **register** *66T* anmelden, registrieren
regret *101* Bedauern
to **regret** *101* bedauern
regulations *(pl) 83* Bestimmungen, Vorschriften
to **reject** *76* ablehnen
relationship *13* Verhältnis, Beziehung
to **relax** *43* sich ausruhen, sich entspannen

signatory *29* Unterzeichner/in
signature *29* Unterschrift
significant(ly) *55* erheblich
silence *60* Schweigen
similar *8* ähnlich
sincere *26* aufrichtig
sincerity *26* Aufrichtigkeit
single room *43* Einzelzimmer
single speed (bicycle) *62* Eingangrad
to **sit back** *70* sich zurücklehnen
site *10* Gelände
site of use *37* Einsatzort
situated *10* gelegen
skiing *111* Skifahren
slash, forward ~ *22* Schrägstrich
slight *11T* leicht, klein
slightly *55* geringfügig
to **slouch** *60* sich lümmeln
to **slow down** *24* langsamer werden/sprechen
to **smoke** *39* rauchen
smoker *39* Raucher/in
snack *43* Imbiss
social(ly) *8* sozial, gesellschaftlich
sociology *60* Soziologie
socket *47* Steckdose
to **soften** *23* abmildern, mildern
softly spoken, to be ~ *66T* leise sprechen
solution *15T* Lösung
to **solve** *105* lösen
sophisticated *15T* hoch entwickelt, raffiniert, fortschrittlich
sort *15T* Art
source *28* Quelle
to **source** *10* beschaffen, beziehen
spare part *104T* Ersatzteil
to **speak up** *24* lauter sprechen
to **specialize in sth** *6* sich auf etw spezialisieren
specialty *94* Spezialgebiet, Spezial-
specific *8* bestimmt, speziell; *15T* genau
to **specify** *25P* (genau) angeben, bestimmen
speech *67* Sprechweise
speed *62* Gang
speed, to get up to ~ *70* sich auf den neuesten Stand bringen
speedy *42* schnell
to **spell** *21* buchstabieren
to **spell sth out** *71* etw einfach darlegen
to **split** *52* teilen, aufteilen
spoilt, to be ~ for choice *43* die Qual der Wahl haben
sporty *64* sportlich
spotlight *47* Scheinwerfer
spring *35* Frühling, Frühjahr
square metre *11T* Quadratmeter
stable *55* stabil
to **stack** *89* stapeln
staff *6* Mitarbeiter, Belegschaft, Personal
staff café *11* Cafeteria
staff member *13* Mitarbeiter/in
stage *16* Phase, Stadium, Etappe
to **stampede sb into doing sth** *75* jdn dazu drängen, etw zu tun
to **stand in for sb** *87* jdn vertreten
to **stand out** *116* herausragen
to **stand up** *16* aufstehen
standardized *48* genormt
state *26* Zustand
statistics *(pl)* *10* Statistik(en)
to **steal** *68* stehlen
steel *84* Stahl
steel mill *84* Stahlwerk, Walzwerk
to **step** *18* treten, gehen
sticker *64* Aufkleber
to **stink** *60* stinken
to **stipulate** *91* festlegen
stipulation *91T* Festlegung
stock *77* Lager(bestand)
to **stock sth** *18* etw *(Ware)* führen, ins Sortiment nehmen
stool *47* Hocker
store *10* Laden, Geschäft
to **store** *11T* lagern
straight *47* gerade
straight (away) *21T* sofort, gleich
straight on/ahead *12* geradeaus
straightforward *70* einfach, unkompliziert
strategy *62* Strategie
strength *114* Stärke
stress *67* Betonung
stressed (out) *107* gestresst, fix und fertig
stressful *108* anstrengend, stressig
to **stretch to sth** *66T* *(Geld:)* für etw reichen
string *94* Reihe
structure *13* Struktur
to **structure** *56* strukturieren
stupid *71* dumm, doof
to **submit** *31* einreichen
sub-standard *98* minderwertig
subject line *29* Betreffzeile
sudden *97* plötzlich
to **suggest** *51* vorschlagen
suggestion *50* Vorschlag
to **suit** *30T* passen
suitability *113* Eignung
suitable *28* geeignet
(suit)case *56T* Koffer
suite *11T* (Büro-)Räume; *43* Suite
sum *79* Summe, Betrag
to **sum up** *58T* zusammenfassen
to **summarize** *16* zusammenfassen
summary report *64* zusammenfassender Bericht
supplier *28* Lieferant/in, Zulieferer, Anbieter
to **supply** *10* liefern, versorgen, (an)bieten
supply voltage *37* Betriebsspannung, Netzspannung
support *77T* Unterstützung
to **support** *52* unterstützen
to **suppose** *56T* annehmen, glauben; *I ~ so.* *58T* Mag sein. Kann schon sein.
surname *42* Nachname
surprised *70* erstaunt, überrascht
survey *64* Umfrage, Studie
survey report *92* Schadensbericht, Gutachten
to **sway sb** *71* jdn beeinflussen
swing, to get into full ~ *60* richtig ins Rollen kommen
switch *37* Schalter
to **switch to** *27* wechseln zu
to **switch sth on** *37* etw einschalten
syndicate *94* Konsortium

T

tab *10* *(Karteikarte etc.:)* Reiter
to **tailor sth to sth** *107* etw auf etw zuschneiden
to **take sb on** *7* jdn einstellen, anstellen
to **take action** *95* Maßnahmen ergreifen
to **take care of sth** *39* sich um etw kümmern
to **take place** *23T* stattfinden
to **take a message** *18* *(Telefon:)* etw ausrichten
tank *45* Tank
tare weight *87* Leergewicht, Tara
to **target sth at sb/sth** *65* etw an jdn/etw richten
target group *48* Zielgruppe
taste bud *94* Geschmacksknospen
tax *32* Steuer
taxation *13* Steuern, Besteuerung
technique *70* Methode, Technik
technological *15T* technologisch, technisch
temporary *28* vorübergehend, provisorisch; *111* befristet
to **tend to do sth** *26* dazu neigen, etw zu tun
tense *60* angespannt
term *15T* Begriff; *in ~s of* *15T* was … angeht
terminology *91* Terminologie
terms *29* Konditionen, Bedingungen

Alphabetical word list

terms and conditions *42* Konditionen, (Allgemeine) Geschäftsbedingungen
terms of delivery *29* Lieferbedingungen
terms of payment *29* Zahlungsbedingungen
terrific *15T* fantastisch, toll
theft *79* Diebstahl
theme *52* Motto, Thema
then, back ~ *71* damals
thereafter *90* danach
thief, thieves *92* Dieb, Diebe
thin *50* dünn
thing, first ~ *21T* gleich, als erstes
third party order *84* Streckenauftrag, -bestellung
this way *7* hier entlang
This way up *89* Hier oben
thoroughly *54* völlig; *68* gründlich
to **threaten** *96* drohen
throughout ... *31* in ganz ...
to **throw sth up** *116* etw zutage fördern
tight *112* engere Auswahl
time, at a ~ *27* auf einmal, jeweils; *on ~* *25* pünktlich
time difference *58T* Zeitverschiebung
time frame *112* Zeitrahmen
time off *109* Freizeit
to **tolerate** *73* tolerieren
tone *23* Ton, Tonfall
to **toast sth** *71* auf etw anstoßen
tool *27* Werkeug, Hilfsmittel
total, in ~ *64* insgesamt
touch, to get in ~ with sb *30T* sich bei jdm melden
tour *11* Rundgang, Führung
toxic *89* giftig
trade *32* Handel, Handelsverkehr; *48* Branche
trade fair *38* Handelsmesse, Fachmesse
traffic jam *7* Stau
to **train sb** *13* jdn ausbilden, schulen
to **train as** *115* eine Ausbildung zum/zur ... machen
trainee *56* Auszubildende/r
traineeship *8* Ausbildung, Lehre
training officer *56* Ausbildungsleiter/in
to **transfer** *21* weiterleiten, weitergeben; *36* *(Geld)* überweisen
transferable *89* übertragbar
to **transform** *116* (grundlegend) verändern
to **transport** *8* befördern, transportieren
transport, means of ~ *83* Transportmittel; *mode of ~* *83* Transportart; *multimodal ~* *32* kombinierte Beförderung, multimodaler Transport
travel arrangements *(pl)* *38* Reisevorbereitungen
travel expenses *(pl)* *51* Reisekosten, Reisespesen
trial order *98* Probebestellung, Probeauftrag
to **trust** *96* vertrauen, hoffen
to **turn to sth** *61* sich einer Sache zuwenden
to **turn up** *48* auftauchen, ankommen
to **turn right/left** *11T* rechts/links abbiegen
turnover *10* Umsatz
twin room *45* Zweibettzimmer

U

unclear(ly) *24* undeutlich, unklar
unconventional *70* unkonventionell
to **uncover** *62* enthüllen, aufdecken, *hier: (Daten)* erheben
undamaged *13* unbeschädigt, unbeschadet
to **undergo** *15T* durchmachen, sich unterziehen
underscore *22* Unterstrich
to **underwrite** *94* versichern
undoubtedly *71* zweifellos
to **unfold** *66T* sich entwickeln
unfortunate *101* unglücklich, bedauerlich
unfortunately *7* leider, unglücklicherweise
unique selling point *63* Alleinstellungsmerkmal
unique(ly) *94* einzigartig
unit *31* Einheit, Gebäude
unit price *35* Einzelpreis, Preis pro Stück
unknown *73* unbekannt
unlimited *94* unbegrenzt, unbeschränkt
to **unload** *32* entladen
to **unpack** *104T* auspacken
unsatisfactory *98* unzulänglich, nicht zufriedenstellend
unsuitable *44* ungeeignet
unsurprisingly *64* erwartungsgemäß
to **unwind** *43* sich entspannen, abschalten
up front *77T* im Voraus
up to, to be ~ sb *75* an jdm liegen; *to be ~ sth* *62* etw vorhaben, etw machen; *98* einer Sache entsprechen, genügen
up-to-date *43* auf dem neuesten Stand
up to now *33* bislang, bis jetzt
up to speed, to get ~ *70* sich auf den neuesten Stand bringen
to **upset sb** *76* jdn verärgern
upward *53* aufwärts
to **urge sb to do sth** *66T* jdm dringend empfehlen, etw zu tun
urgent *18* dringend, eilig
use, to make ~ of sth *43* etw nutzen, benutzen

V

vacancy *112* offene Stelle, Stellenangebot, -ausschreibung
vacant *116* frei
to **vacate** *44T* räumen
vacation *(AE)* *112* Ferien
value *31* Wert; *re-sale ~* *31* Wiederverkaufswert
various *7* verschieden
to **vary** *8* schwanken, unterschiedlich sein; *67* variieren
VAT (value added tax) *45* Mehrwertsteuer
vehicle *45* Fahrzeug
vessel *94* Schiff
vibes *60* Schwingungen, Atmosphäre
to **view** *71* betrachten, sehen
village *28* Dorf
virtual *116* virtuell
visual aids *(pl)* *67* visuelle Hilfsmittel
visuals *67* visuelle Hilfsmittel
vocational college *58T* Berufsfachschule
voltage *37* Spannung; *supply ~* *37* Betriebsspannung, Netzspannung
volume *68* Lautstärke; *87* Volumen

W

walking distance, within ~ *43* in Laufweite
wall *47* Wand
warehouse *6* Lager
warranty *79* Garantie, Gewährleistung
to **waste** *26* verschwenden, vergeuden
to **wave sth about** *16* mit etw herumfuchteln
way, this ~ *7* hier entlang; *This ~ up* *89* Hier oben
weakness *114* Schwäche
wealth *94* Vermögen
wear *18* Bekleidung, Kleidung
wear and tear *79* Verschleiß, Abnutzung

weekly *49* wöchentlich
to **weigh** *27* wiegen
weight *37* Gewicht
welcome, You're ~. *7* Bitte (sehr). Gern geschehen.
well received, to be ~ *53* gut *(beim Publikum etc.)* ankommen
whereas *109* während, dagegen
while, in a little ~ *11T* gleich
to **whip sth out** *60* etw zücken
whole, on the ~ *67* im Großen und Ganzen
wholesale *7* Großhandel
wholesaler *7* Großhändler, Händler
widely *8* *hier:* stark
width *87* Breite
willingness *70* Bereitschaft
windy *33* windig
wireless *43* drahtlos
word spider *84* Wortnetz
work experience *111* Berufserfahrung
work placement *106* Praktikum
working environment *112* Arbeitsumfeld
working hours *(pl)* *109* Arbeitszeit(en)
working principle *37* Funktionsweise, Funktionsprizip
workmanship *79* Verarbeitung(squalität)
workmate *57P* Arbeitskollege/-in
worried *44T* besorgt
worth, to be ~ *41* sich lohnen
wrap, plastic ~ *84* Plastikfolie
to **wrap sth up** *54* etw abschließen
writing, in ~ *87* schriftlich, in Schriftform

Y

Yours sincerely *29* Hochachtungsvoll, Mit freundlichen Grüßen

Z

zinc *37* Zink

Basic trade vocabulary (German–English)

Firmenorganisation – *Company organization*

Aktiengesellschaft (AG)	Public Limited Company (plc) *BE;* open corporation *AE*
Aktie	share
Aktionär/in, Teilhaber/in	shareholder
Einzelunternehmen	sole proprietor
Gesellschaft mit beschränkter Haftung (GmbH)	Limited Company (Ltd) *BE;* closed corporation *AE*
Kommanditgesellschaft (KG)	limited partnership
Personengesellschaft, offene Handelsgesellschaft (OHG)	(general) partnership

Firmenabteilungen – *Company departments*

Buchhaltung	accounts (department)
Einkauf(sabteilung)	purchasing (department)
Forschung(s-) und Entwicklung (sabteilung)	research and development (department, R&D)
Geschäftsführung, Vorstand	board (of directors)
Lager(halle)	warehouse
Marktforschung (sabteilung)	market research (department)
Personal(abteilung)	human resources (department, HR)
Rechnungswesen	finance (department)
Rechtswesen	legal department
Rezeption, Empfang	reception
Verkauf(sabteilung), Vertrieb	sales (department)
Vertrieb	distribution (department)
Verwaltung	administration
Zentrale	head office, headquarters

Mitarbeiter/innen – *Members of staff*

Abteilungsleiter/in	head of department
Arbeitgeber/in, Unternehmer/in	employer
Arbeitnehmer/in, Beschäftigte/r	employee
Arbeitsplatz	workplace
Ausbildung	training
Buchhalter/in	accountant
Groß- und Außenhandelskaufmann/-frau	Trainee management assistant in Wholesale and Foreign Trade
Empfangsmitarbeiter/in	receptionist
Gehalt	salary
Geschäftsführer/in	managing director (MD), chief executive officer (CEO)
Handelsvertreter/in	sales representative
Kollege, Kollegin	colleague
Lehre	apprenticeship
Manager/in	manager
Personal	staff
Persönliche/r Assistent/in	personal assistant (PA)
Qualifikation, Abschluss	qualification
Sekretär/in	secretary

Bürotätigkeiten – *Office activities*

etw ausrichten	to take a message
Berichte schreiben	to write reports
Briefe beantworten	to reply to letters
etw faxen	to fax sth
Mitteilungen, Vermerke, Notizen	to write memos
ein Telefongespräch annehmen	to answer the telephone
Textverarbeitung	word processing
Überstunden machen	to work overtime
Unterlagen, Schriftstücke	paperwork
etw weiterleiten	to forward sth

Geschäftsbriefe – *Commercial correspondence*

Absatz	paragraph
Absender	sender
Adresse	address
anhängen (E-Mail)	to attach sth
Anhang	attachment
Anlage(n)	enclosure (enc)
Anrede	salutation
Antwort	reply
beifügen (Brief)	to enclose
Betreff(zeile)	subject (line)
Briefkopf	letter head
Datum	date
Einschreiben	registered mail/post
Empfänger/in	addressee
Entschuldigungsschreiben	letter of apology
Mit den besten Wünschen	Best wishes
Mit freundlichen Grüßen (Hochachtungsvoll)	Yours faithfully
Mit freundlichen Grüßen	Yours sincerely
Mit freundlichen Grüßen, Viele Grüße	Best wishes, Regards
Mit herzlichen Grüßen	Best wishes, Cordially *AE*
Schlussformel	complimentary close
Unterschrift	signature
Zeichen	reference (ref)
zu Händen	attention (attn)

Basic trade vocabulary (German–English)

Besprechungen/Präsentationen – *Meetings/presentations*

Abwesenheit	absence
Bericht	report
Einladung	invitation
Liniendiagramm	line chart
Protokoll	minutes *pl*
eine Rede halten	to make a speech
Säulendiagramm	bar chart
die Sitzung leiten	to take the chair / to be in the chair
stattfinden	take place
Tagesordnung	agenda
Tagesordnungspunkt	item on the agenda
teilnehmen	to participate
Teilnehmer/in	participant
Termin	date
Tortendiagramm	pie chart
Verschiedenes	any other business (AOB)
Vortrag	talk; lecture
vortragen	to report; to state
X-Achse	x-axis

Dienstreisen – *Business trips*

absagen	to cancel
Anforderung	requirement
Anschlussflug	connecting flight
Ausstellung	exhibition
etw besuchen, an etw teilnehmen	to attend sth
Bitte, Anfrage	request
einfacher Flug	one-way flight
Hin- und Rückflug	return flight
Messe	(trade) fair
Passagier	passenger
Reservierung, Buchung	reservation
stornieren	to cancel
Termin	appointment
Unterkunft	accommodation
verschieben	to postpone

Geschäftspartner und Händler – *Business partners and traders*

Einzelhändler/in	retailer
Exporteur	exporter
Großhändler	wholesaler
Importeur	importer
Käufer/in	buyer
Klient/in	client
Konkurrent/in, Konkurrenz	competitor
Konkurrenz	competition
Kunde, Kundin	customer, client
Lieferant	supplier
Spediteur	carrier; forwarding agent; freight forwarder
Verkäufer/in	seller

Geschäftsvorgänge – *Business transactions*

Anfrage	enquiry
Angebot, Kostenvoranschlag	quotation
Auftrag, Bestellung	order
einen Auftrag erteilen	to place an order
einen Auftrag erledigen	to fill an order
Auftragsbestätigung	acknowledgement/ confirmation (of an order)
einen Auftrag bestätigen	to acknowledge an order
Bestellformular	order form
Bestellnummer	order number
Erhalt, (Waren-)Eingang	receipt (of goods)
Folgeauftrag	repeat order
Lieferbedingungen	terms of delivery *pl*
liefern	to deliver
Lieferung	delivery
Muster	sample
Probeauftrag	trial order
Reklamation, Beschwerde	complaint
eine Reklamation bearbeiten/regulieren	to adjust a complaint
Sendung	consignment
Umsatz	turnover
Verkäufe, Umsatz	sales *pl*
Versandanzeige, Versandmitteilung	advice of dispatch
Versandpapiere	shipping documents *pl*
versenden	to ship
versenden, absenden	to dispatch
Vertrag	contract
Ware(n), (Lager-)Bestand	stock
Zahlungsanzeige	advice of payment
Zahlungsbedingungen	terms of payment *pl*

Zahlung – *Payment*

Dokumente gegen Akzept	documents against acceptance
Dokumente gegen Zahlung	documents against payment
Dokumentenakkreditiv	documentary letter of credit
fällig, ausstehend	overdue
Konto, Kreditkonto	account
letzte Mahnung	final demand
Mahnung	reminder
MwSt = Mehrwertsteuer	VAT = value added tax
Nicht(be)zahlung	non-payment

Rabatt, Nachlass	discount
Rate	instalment
Rechnung	bill, invoice
Skonto, Barzahlungsrabatt	cash discount
überweisen	to remit, to transfer
Überweisung, Zahlung	bank transfer, remittance
Vorauszahlung, Vorkasse	cash in advance
Wechsel	bill of exchange
zahlbar bei Lieferung, per Nachnahme	cash on delivery (COD)

Irregular verbs

be – was/were – been	*sein*
beat – beat – beaten	*schlagen, besiegen*
become – became – become	*werden*
begin – began – begun	*anfangen, beginnen*
bleed – bled – bled	*bluten*
break – broke – broken	*brechen*
bring – brought – brought	*bringen*
build – built – built	*bauen*
burn – burnt – burnt	*(ver)brennen*
buy – bought – bought	*kaufen*
catch – caught – caught	*fangen*
choose – chose – chosen	*wählen*
come – came – come	*kommen*
cost – cost – cost	*kosten*
cut – cut – cut	*schneiden*
do – did – done	*tun, machen*
draw – drew – drawn	*zeichnen*
dream – dreamt/dreamed – dreamt/dreamed	*träumen*
drink – drank – drunk	*trinken*
drive – drove – driven	*fahren*
eat – ate – eaten	*essen*
fall – fell – fallen	*fallen*
feed – fed – fed	*füttern, ernähren*
feel – felt – felt	*(sich) fühlen, empfinden*
fight – fought – fought	*kämpfen*
find – found – found	*finden*
fit – fit/fitted – fit/fitted	*passen*
fly – flew – flown	*fliegen*
forget – forgot – forgotten	*vergessen*
freeze – froze – frozen	*frieren*
get – got – got (*AE* gotten)	*bekommen*
give – gave – given	*geben*
go – went – gone	*gehen, fahren*
grow – grew – grown	*wachsen*
hang – hung – hung	*hängen*
have – had – had	*haben*
hear – heard – heard	*hören*
hide – hid – hidden	*(sich) verstecken*
hit – hit – hit	*schlagen*
hold – held – held	*halten, festhalten*
keep – kept – kept	*behalten*
know – knew – known	*kennen, wissen*
lay – laid – laid	*legen*
lean – leant/leaned – leant/leaned	*(sich) lehnen, neigen*
learn – learnt/learned – learnt/learned	*lernen*
leave – left – left	*abfahren, verlassen, weggehen*

let – let – let	*lassen*
lie – lay – lain	*liegen*
light – lit – lit	*anzünden, beleuchten, anmachen*
lose – lost – lost	*verlieren*
make – made – made	*machen*
mean – meant – meant	*meinen, bedeuten*
meet – met – met	*treffen*
pay – paid – paid	*bezahlen*
put – put – put	*setzen, stellen, legen*
quit – quit/quitted – quit/quitted	*verlassen, aufhören*
read – read – read	*lesen*
ride – rode – ridden	*reiten, fahren*
rise – rose – risen	*(an)steigen*
run – ran – run	*laufen, rennen*
say – said – said	*sagen*
see – saw – seen	*sehen*
sell – sold – sold	*verkaufen*
send – sent – sent	*senden, schicken*
set – set – set	*setzen, stellen*
show – showed – shown	*zeigen*
shut – shut – shut	*schließen*
sing – sang – sung	*singen*
sit – sat – sat	*sitzen*
sleep – slept – slept	*schlafen*
smell – smelt/smelled – smelt/smelled	*riechen*
speak – spoke – spoken	*sprechen*
spell – spelt/spelled – spelt/spelled	*buchstabieren*
spend – spent – spent	*ausgeben, verbringen*
stand – stood – stood	*stehen*
steal – stole – stolen	*stehlen*
swim – swam – swum	*schwimmen*
take – took – taken	*nehmen*
teach – taught – taught	*unterrichten, beibringen*
tear – tore – torn	*zerreißen*
tell – told – told	*sagen, erzählen*
think – thought – thought	*denken*
throw – threw – thrown	*werfen*
understand – understood – understood	*verstehen*
wake – woke – woken	*aufwachen/aufwecken*
wear – wore – worn	*tragen (Kleidung)*
win – won – won	*gewinnen*
write – wrote – written	*schreiben*

Quellen

Bildquellen

S. 6/1/Shutterstock/Andresr, S. 6/2/Picture-Alliance/euroluftbild.de/Grahn, S. 6/3/Shutterstock/06photo, S. 6/4/Shutterstock/Sebastian Duda, S. 6/5/Shutterstock/Yuri Arcurs, S. 7/Shutterstock/prodakszyn, S. 8/ Shutterstock/IKO, S. 10(Hintergrund)Shutterstock, S. 10/2/Shutterstock/dean bertoncelj, S. 14/Shutterstock/ Worldpics, S. 18/Shutterstock/auremar, S. 19/Shutterstock/gnohz, S. 20/Shutterstock/Mihai Simonia, S. 21/ Istockphoto/diego_cervo, S. 22/Shutterstock/Nikolay Mikhalchenko, S. 23/Shutterstock/Pablo Eder, S. 24/1/ Shutterstock/iconspro, S. 25/1/Shutterstock, S. 25/2/Shutterstock, S. 27/1/Shutterstock/Anna Chelnokova, S. 27/2/Shutterstock/Oleksiy Mark, S. 28/a/Picture-Alliance/Hubert Link, S. 28/b/Shutterstock/EDHAR, S. 28/c/Shutterstock/Ricardo Alday, S. 28/d/Shutterstock, S. 28/unten/Shutterstock/benicce, S. 30/123RF/ Hannu Viitanen, S. 31/Shutterstock/grekoff, S. 32/Shutterstock/Alexander Raths, S. 33/Shutterstock/ micro10x, S. 34/Shutterstock/CHRISTOPHE ROLLAND, S. 35/Shutterstock/Pakhnyushcha, S. 36/Shutterstock/Raphael Daniaud, S. 37/Ritter Starkstromtechnik GmbH & Co. KG, S. 38/1/Shutterstock/pjcross, S. 38/2/ Shutterstock/Jaroslaw Kubak, S. 38/3/Shutterstock/Shots Studio, S. 38/4/Shutterstock/ARENA Creative, S. 38/unten/Shutterstock, S. 39/1/Shutterstock/Geanina Bechea, S. 41/Shutterstock/Darrin Henry, S. 43/ oben/Shutterstock/Sam Strickler, S. 43/1/Shutterstock/John Lock, S. 43/2/Shutterstock/John Lock, S. 43/3/ Shutterstock/John Lock, S. 43/4/Shutterstock/John Lock, S. 44/Shutterstock/Dmitriy Shironosov, S. 45/Shutterstock/Andresr, S. 47/Shutterstock/Adriano Castelli, S. 48/Shutterstock/bayberry, S. 49/a/Alamy/Image Source/IS457, S. 49/b/Shutterstock/Monkey Business Images, S. 49/c/Corbis RF, S. 49/d/Alamy/F1online digitale Bildagentur GmbH, S. 50/Shutterstock/bluecrayola, S. 52/IstockPhotos, S. 53/Alamy/OJO Images Ltd/Tom Merton, S. 56/Picture-Alliance, S. 60/1/Shutterstock, S. 61/a/Alamy/ersoy emin, S. 61/b/Shutterstock/Sergej Khakimullin, S. 61/c/ Shutterstock/Adriano Castello, S. 61/d/Shutterstock/Jorge Salcedo, S. 61/unten/CIAO/ MathiasMaier, S. 63/a/Alamy/Blue Tulip, S. 63/b/Alamy/STOCKFOLIO®, S. 63/c/CIAO/Mathias Maier, S. 63/d/ Shutterstock/wavebreakmedia ltd, S. 66/1-6 Shutterstock, S. 68/1/Shutterstock/nulinukas, S. 68/2/Shutterstock/sofist, S. 70/1/Fotofinder/KEYSTONE/Keystone, S. 70/2/Advertising Archive/KitKat Advert, S. 71/ Alamy/A.Babii, S. 73/Shutterstock/HadK, S. 74/Shutterstock/StockLite, S. 75/Shutterstock/Imagenfx, S. 78/1/ Shutterstock/Ariwasabi, S. 78/2/Shutterstock/Kurhan, S. 79/Shutterstock/luckyraccoon, S. 82/Alamy/Radius Images, S. 83/a/Shutterstock/E.G.Pors, S. 83/b/Shutterstock/Oleksiy Mark, S. 83/c/Picture-Alliance/KEYSTONE/MARTIN RUETSCHI, S. 83/d/Shutterstock, S. 83/e/Shutterstock/Picsfive, S. 83/f/Picture-Alliance/PhotoXpress/Mikhail Voskresensky, S. 84/Cornelsen-Archiv, S. 85/Shutterstock/Reda, S. 89/a/Shutterstock/MADDRAT, S. 89/b/Shutterstock/MADDRAT, S. 89/c/Shutterstock/andrzej80, S. 89/d/Shutterstock/oblong1, S. 89/e/Shutterstock/MADDRAT, S. 89/f/Shutterstock/MADDRAT, S. 89/g/Shutterstock/Fotokon, S. 90/ Shutterstock/Michael Klenetsky, S. 91/Shutterstock/Evgeny Murtola, S. 94/1/Alamy/Elena Elisseeva, S. 94/2/ Picture-Alliance/Landov Robert Pitts 2252928, S. 95/2/Shutterstock/StockLite, S. 97/Shutterstock/vgstudio, S. 102/Shutterstock/wavebreakmedia ltd, S. 104/1/Shutterstock/Yuri Arcurs, S. 104/2/Shutterstock/sevenke, S. 105/Yang Liu Design, Berlin, S. 106/a/Fotofinder/VISUM/Marion Losse, S. 106/b/Picture-Alliance/ dpa/Fotoreport monster.de, S. 106/c/Alamy/vario images/Christoph Papsch, S. 107/Picture-Alliance/dpa/Julian Stratenschulte, S. 114/Shutterstock/Ingrid W., S. 115/Shutterstock/ARENA Creative, S. 116/Alamy/i love images/teenagers, S. 121–123/Lloyd's of London, S. 126/Hans Turck GmbH & Co. KG, Mühlheim an der Ruhr, S. 132/Shutterstock/Edw, S. 136/Picture-Alliance/Deutsche Messe AG

Gabi Heinisch: S. 17, S. 24/2, S. 60/2
Oxford Designers Illustrators: S. 26, S. 68, S. 72, S. 95/1, S. 128

Textquellen

- Unit 1, S. 16, Body language: adapted from: http://www.businessknowhow.com/growth/meet.htm
- Unit 2, S. 26, Telephone greetings that customers – and employees – will love: http://www.proedgeskills.com/Customer_Service_Articles/telephone_greetings_that_custome.htm
- Unit 5, S. 60, I hate meetings and they stink: http://www.govloop.com/profiles/blogs/i-hate-meetings-and-they-stink
- Unit 9, S. 103: Factors which can cause communication problems for you in English at work: Communicating Internationally in English, Bob Dignen and Ian McMaster, York Associates in Association with Business Spotlight, Unit 4 Native and non-native speakers, S. 53
- Unit 10, S. 116, Virtual job-hunting: Technology fills situations vacant: abridged from: www.bbc.co.uk/news/business-12194581
- KMK mock exam, S. 132–133, adapted from http://www.bbc.co.uk/news/world-south-asia-15180831

Danksagung
Wir bedanken uns bei folgenden Firmen, die uns freundlicherweise Material für dieses Lehrwerk zur Verfügung gestellt haben.

Hans Turck GmbH & Co. KG, Mülheim an der Ruhr
Ritter Starkstromtechnik GmbH & Co. KG, Wilnsdorf